DIVERSITY ISSUES IN AMERICAN COLLEGES AND UNIVERSITIES

ABOUT THE EDITOR

Lamont A. Flowers is an Assistant Professor in the College of Education at the University of Florida. He received a Bachelor of Arts in Accounting from Virginia Commonwealth University, a Master of Arts in Social Studies Education, and a Doctorate in Higher Education from the University of Iowa.

Dr. Flowers has published numerous articles in the areas of business management, social studies education, higher education, and student development. His research interests include investigating the effects of the college experience on student learning and examining the impact of ethnic and racial diversity on cognitive and affective outcomes in college.

His research has appeared in the *College Student Affairs Journal, College Student Journal, Educational Research Quarterly, Journal of College Student Development, Journal of Compensation and Benefits, Journal of Higher Education, National Association of Student Affairs Professionals Journal, NASPA Journal, Planning and Changing, The Professional Educator,* and *Research in Higher Education.*

He has conducted sponsored research for the American College Personnel Association (ACPA), Association of College and University Housing Officers–International (ACUHO–I), Association for Institutional Research (AIR), and the American Educational Research Association (AERA). Dr. Flowers has received a number of academic honors and accolades including the Melvene D. Hardee Dissertation of the Year Award (runner-up) sponsored by the National Association of Student Personnel Administrators (NASPA) and the ACPA's Annuit Coeptis Award (Emerging Professional).

DIVERSITY ISSUES IN AMERICAN COLLEGES AND UNIVERSITIES

Case Studies for Higher Education and Student Affairs Professionals

Edited by

LAMONT A. FLOWERS, PH.D.

Foreword by

Nancy J. Evans, PH.D.

CHARLES C THOMAS • PUBLISHER, LTD.
Springfield • Illinois • U.S.A.

Published and Distributed Throughout the World by

CHARLES C THOMAS • PUBLISHER, LTD.
2600 South First Street
Springfield, Illinois 62794-9265

© 2004 by CHARLES C THOMAS • PUBLISHER, LTD.

ISBN 0-398-07450-X (hard)
ISBN 0-398-07451-8 (paper)

Library of Congress Catalog Card Number: 2003059660

With THOMAS BOOKS *careful attention is given to all details of manufacturing and design. It is the Publisher's desire to present books that are satisfactory as to their physical qualities and artistic possibilities and appropriate for their particular use.* THOMAS BOOKS *will be true to those laws of quality that assure a good name and good will.*

Printed in the United States of America
MM-R-3

Library of Congress Cataloging in Publication Data

Diversity issues in American colleges and universities : case studies for higher
    education and student affairs profesionals / edited by Lamont A. Flowers ;
    forword by Nancy J. Evans.
        p. cm.
    Includes bibliographical references and index.
    ISBN 0-398-07450-X (hard) − ISBN 0-398-07451-8 (pbk.)
    1. Minorities−Education (Higher)−United States. 2. Multicultural
education−United States. 3. Student affairs services−United States−
Administration. I. Flowers, Lamont A.

LC3727.D5775 2003
378.1'9829'073−dc22

                                                                                2003059660

CONTRIBUTORS

This valuable resource includes the perspectives, insights, and experiences of many faculty, student affairs practitioners, and higher education researchers working in and studying two-year and four-year institutions in the United States. The contributors present an enormous amount of challenging dilemmas, thought-provoking scenarios, and even disturbing realities that provide readers the opportunity to practice their skills solving diversity issues in higher education, responding to the needs of diverse populations on campus, and communicating with unique cultural groups.

I am extremely grateful to these individuals because it was through their help, patience, and dedication that this book was developed. In many ways, the quality of this book is a testament to their devotion, willingness, and commitment to improving multicultural competence among student personnel in higher education, and facilitating understanding between diverse cultural groups that constitute the higher education community (e.g., faculty, students, and administration). Each contributor is listed below in alphabetical order.

Emmanuel (Sonny) Ago was raised in New York City. He received his B.A. in Anthropology from Amherst College, his M.A. in Sociology from New York University, and his Doctorate of Education in Higher Education from the University of Pennsylvania. Dr. Ago has worked both at Swarthmore College and at the University of Pennsylvania's Intercultural Centers, serving as the primary advisor to minority students. He has also worked with at-risk youth in New York City's Chinatown, Harlem, and Washington Heights. Dr. Ago is the Director for Multicultural Affairs at Barnard College, Columbia University.

Schevaletta M. Alford, an Associate Professor, is the Acting Director and Chairperson of the SEEK Program at John Jay College of the City University of New York; she was previously the counseling coordinator. She received her doctorate in Higher and Adult Education from Teachers College, Columbia University. Her publications have been primarily in the area of student development and racial/ethnic relations.

Maricela Alvarado received two B.A. degrees (English and Spanish) from

Washington State University, M.Ed. from University of Florida, and is currently an Academic Support Coordinator at the University of Florida in the College of Engineering. Maricela also has experience working in other academic institutions such as Embry Riddle Aeronautical University and Ohio University. Maricela plans to pursue a Ph.D. in Education.

Alvin Alvarez is an Assistant Professor and Coordinator of the College Counseling Program at San Francisco State University. He received his Ph.D. in counseling psychology from the University of Maryland at College Park and completed his undergraduate work at the University of California at Irvine. His professional interests focus on Asian Americans, racial identity, and the psychological impact of racism. He is a coeditor of the New Directions for Student Services monograph entitled, *Working with Asian American College Students.*

Cheryl M. Anderson is the Dean of Students at Wichita State University. She received two Bachelors of Arts (Sociology and Pan African Studies) from California State University, Northridge; her Master of Science (Counselor Education) from Mississippi State University and the Doctor of Education (Higher Education Administration) degree from The University of Alabama.

Sharon K. Anderson is an Associate Professor at Colorado State University and teaches courses in counseling and the student affairs higher education program. Dr. Anderson has a successful publishing record. She has authored and coauthored several articles and book chapters. She researches and writes in the area of professional ethics and multicultural issues in education.

Sheri Atkinson is the coordinator for Gay, Lesbian, Bisexual, and Transgender (GLBT) Services at St. Cloud State University in St. Cloud, Minnesota. She does trainings on homophobia and diversity issues including Safe Space training for the campus and surrounding communities. Interacting with students on a daily basis, Sheri also advises two GLBT student organizations and Jugglers Against Oppression (JAO). JAO is a group that uses juggling to get peoples' attention in order to educate about all issues of oppression. She received her Master of Arts in Higher Education and Student Affairs from The Ohio State University.

Joseph Baggot is the Associate Dean of Students at the University of Wisconsin–Oshkosh. He is also an advanced doctoral student at the University of Wisconsin–Madison. His academic emphasis is in the administration of colleges and universities with a personal interest in student affairs administration.

Dennis M. Baskin is a Ph.D. student in the Department of Educational Administration at the University of Wisconsin. He earned a masters degree in business management and a bachelors in finance, both from the University of Wisconsin–Whitewater. He is a native of Beloit, Wisconsin.

Doris Bitler serves as Associate Professor of Psychology and Associate Dean for Undergraduate Academic Affairs in the College of Arts and Sciences at George Mason University. She was selected as the first recipient of the Staff Senate's "Supervisor of the Year Award" in 2002, and named "Faculty Member of the Year" by the GMU Alumni Association in 2003. Her current research interests include the prediction of academic success, disability issues in higher education, and the development of effective assessment programs. In addition to teaching and administrative duties, Dr. Bitler advises two academic honor societies, Golden Key and Alpha Lambda Delta.

J. Bradley Blankenship received a B.A. in Psychology from George Mason University. He currently works at American University as an Admissions Counselor where he has developed a Gay, Lesbian, Bisexual, and Transgender (GLBT) prospective student outreach program. He continues to research the experiences of GLBT students within the college selection and application process and develop college-counseling programs with GLBT youth centers across the country.

Ellen M. Broido is Assistant Professor in the College Student Personnel (masters) and Higher Education Administration (doctoral) programs at Bowling Green State University. Her research and teaching interests focus on issues of diversity and social justice on college student campus, particularly on how students come to be advocates for diversity issues, and on lesbian, bisexual, gay, and transgender student issues.

Deborah Casey, M.S., C.A.G.S., PHR, is the Dean of Student Affairs/504 Compliance Officer at South University in West Palm Beach, Florida. Prior to becoming Dean, she was Assistant Dean for Disability Services/504 Compliance Officer at the University of Florida. She has presented nationally at ACPA, NASPA, and Association on Higher Education and Disability (AHEAD) on professional development of faculty in providing accommodations to students. She is the author and editor of *College and University Apartment Housing.* Presently she is completing her doctoral degree in Educational Leadership at Florida Atlantic University. Deborah received the NASPA Region III Mid-Level Student Affairs Professional Award for 2002.

Linda G. Castillo is an Assistant Professor in the counseling psychology program at Texas A&M University. She received her Ph.D. from the University of Utah in 1999. She is a licensed psychologist and diversity trainer. Her professional interests included feminist therapy, Chicanos in higher education, racial identity, and multicultural training.

Tony W. Cawthon is an Associate Professor at Clemson University in the Counselor Education program. His primary teaching responsibilities are in the Student Affairs track of the Counselor Education program. Dr. Cawthon has over 20 years of experiences in higher education, serving both as a practitioner and faculty member.

Marcia L. Childs is a Ph.D. student in the Counselor Education Program in the College of Education at The Ohio State University. She received her B.S. in Business Management from Central State University and a Master of Arts in Counselor Education from The Ohio State University. Her research interests are the following: career counseling, cross-cultural counseling, substance abuse counseling, and interventions for success of at-risk students in grades six thru 12.

Catherine Choi-Pearson received her Ph.D. in Counseling Psychology from the University of Utah in 1998. She has been licensed as a psychologist in the state of Nevada since 2001. Her first experience working in Student Affairs was as a graduate student at a university counseling center. Currently, she is the Director of Student Life and Grant Development at the University of Nevada, Reno. In this position, she assists students who have extenuating circumstances with university withdrawals. Outside of work, Catherine enjoys spending time with her family and dog, reading books, and running with friends.

Carl Chung is an Assistant Professor of Humanities in the General College at the University of Minnesota–Twin Cities. He teaches Introduction to Logic and Introduction to Film. His research interests include the role and significance of post-secondary access programs in American higher education, the theoretical structure of developmental education, and the importance of confidence and academic self-concept to the success of at-risk, first-year students.

Robert Coffey is the LGBT Program Coordinator for the Office of Multicultural Student Affairs at the University of New Hampshire. This marks his second year in this position and his seventh as a student affairs practitioner. Robert earned his B.A. in Canadian Studies and History from the University of Vermont, and a M.A. in Canadian History from the University of Maine. He is currently completing course-work towards a Masters in Public Administration at UNH. Robert enjoys active membership in several student affairs professional organizations in the United States and Canada and frequently presents on issues of equity and diversity.

Vanessa Cooke is a doctoral candidate at Virginia Polytechnic Institute and State University. She is the Director of the Alcohol, Tobacco, and Other Drug Prevention Center at Bowie State University. She has five years of experience teaching psychology and substance abuse courses at Bowie State University, Morgan State University, and the University of Baltimore. Ms. Cooke is a member of the National Historically Black Colleges and Universities Substance Abuse Consortium; a member of the Governor's Office on Crime Control and Prevention for the state of Maryland; and a member of the Prince George's County Highway Task Force.

Jay Corwin is a Ph.D. candidate in Adult and Higher Education at the University of Oklahoma. He currently works on the OU campus in University College where he is in charge of developing retention programs and educational activities for freshman success. Previously, he has worked in student affairs and has received both of his degrees at OU.

Angela M. Cottrell is currently a second year master's student in the Higher Education program at Iowa State University in Ames, Iowa. Currently working in the Office of Admissions, Angela's professional focus is on orientation and first-year experience programs. Angela received her bachelor's degrees from the University of Northern Iowa in May 2001, having double majored in political science and public administration. Angela is an active member in the Iowa Student Personnel Association (ISPA) as well as the American College Personnel Association (ACPA).

Michael Dannells is Professor in the College Student Personnel (masters) and Higher Education Administration (doctoral) programs at Bowling Green State University, as well as serving as director of the latter program. His research interests focus on policy and practice of student discipline and judicial affairs.

Donna S. Davenport is a licensed psychologist and has worked on college campuses, both teaching and counseling, for over 25 years. She has written numerous articles, book chapters, and papers related to the understanding and counseling of diverse clients. Dr. Davenport is currently Associate Professor in the doctoral training program of Counseling Psychology at Texas A&M University, where she teaches and conducts research related to diversity issues; she also has an independent practice in psychotherapy. Additionally, she has a mild hearing loss, so has "inside" knowledge about the effects of this disability.

J. Shay Davis has nine years of professional experience in housing and residence life and has been employed in the Department of University Housing at the University of Georgia for five and a half years. She recently completed her doctoral degree in Student Affairs Administration at UGA. Dr. Davis has also worked in housing at UNC–Wilmington. She earned her Master's degree in Counseling and Student Personnel Services at Oklahoma State University and a Bachelor of Arts degree at Baylor University. She also has experience working in a program similar to the one described in her case study.

Gypsy M. Denzine is an Associate Professor of Educational Psychology at Northern Arizona University. She is currently the Interim Associate Dean in the College of Education. She coordinates the student affairs graduate program and has also served as the doctoral coordinator of the Ed.D. in Educational Psychology: Learning and Instruction at NAU. She earned a Ph.D. in Educational Psychology: Learning and Cognition emphasis from the University of Northern Colorado. Her research interests are in the area of achievement motivation, self-efficacy theory, implicit learning, and academic help-seeking among college students.

Norbert W. Dunkel is currently the Director of Housing at the University of Florida. He has authored or edited six books and over 35 articles concerning housing-related topics. He has served as Editor for *The Journal of College and University Student Housing* and Associate Editor of *The College Student Affairs Journal.* Mr. Dunkel served on the Association of College and University Housing Officers International Executive Board from 1997–2000 as the Publications Coordinator.

Judith C. Durham is an Assistant Professor, Department of Counselor Education, Saint Joseph College, West Hartford, Connecticut. She is a Licensed and Nationally Certified Counselor, an Approved Clinical Supervisor, and also an APRN Clinical Specialist and has worked in a number of hospital and community-based settings with a variety of client populations. Prior to joining the faculty at Saint Joseph College, she taught and supervised students at Antioch New England Graduate School, Keene, New Hampshire, in their Masters Program in Mental Health Counseling. Her research is in the area of Multicultural Counseling and she currently teaches the Diversity and Multicultural Counseling Course at Saint Joseph College.

Corey Ellis is the Assistant Director of Student Involvement and Leadership at Rollins College. He has responsibility for campus programming, student organization coordination, and cocurricular leadership programs. He is a 2002 graduate of the Student Personnel in Higher Education (SPHE) program at the University of Florida and has a B.A. in Political Science from the University of Oklahoma. In 2002, the SPHE program awarded Corey the J. Ed and Betty B. Price Scholarship. This award is given to two SPHE students, annually, in recognition of potential to make significant contributions to the personal and academic development of college youth through counseling and teaching.

Mike Esposito is the Student Organization Coordinator at Boise State University, in Idaho. A Kentucky native, Mike graduated from Morehead State University in 1995, and then earned his masters degree in 1997 from Western Kentucky University. He worked at The University of Montana for three years as Greek Advisor prior to coming to Boise State University. He is starting his sixth year in student affairs. A gay and lesbian rights activist, Mike helped found the Montana Gay & Lesbian Center and is a board member of Boise's Gay & Lesbian Community Center. His regular opinion column, "Singular Wit" appears in Idaho's Diversity Newsmagazine.

Donna M. Fox is an Assistant Dean in the Undergraduate Academic Affairs Office of the College of Arts and Sciences at George Mason University. Her career in higher education began in GMU's Biology Department in 1993 where she was principle instructor and course coordinator for the introductory biology course for majors. She authored *Cell Structure and Function: A Laboratory Manual* and taught upper division cell biology before moving to the CAS Dean's Office in 2000. She has been recognized by her university for excellence in teaching and is listed in *Who's Who of America's Teachers.*

Joy L. Gaston is an assistant professor in the higher education program at Florida State University. She is a former student athlete and completed a Bachelor of Science degree at Shaw University. After receiving a postgraduate scholarship from the National Collegiate Athletic Association (NCAA), she completed a Master of Science degree at Auburn University. She received a Ph.D. from The Ohio State University, where she also worked as an academic counselor and coordinator of student athlete advising in the office of Undergraduate Student Academic Services. Her research interests include the achievement of student athletes and African Americans in higher education.

Lynne Guillot-Miller earned a B.A. from Nicholls State University and a M.S. from the University of Louisiana-Monroe. Previously, she worked as a secondary school counselor educator. She is currently pursuing a Ph.D. in Counselor Education at the University of New Orleans.

Lisa A. Guion received the Doctor of Education and Master of Public Administration degrees from North Carolina State University in May 1997 and 1993 respectively. She specialized in adult and higher education administration in both degree programs. Dr. Guion is currently an Assistant Professor in the Department of Family, Youth and Community Sciences, Institute of Food and Agricultural Sciences (IFAS), at the University of Florida. She teaches a four credit hour undergraduate course in research methods, as well as advises graduate and undergraduate students. Prior to joining UF in 2000, Dr. Guion served as an Extension Specialist with the North Carolina Cooperative Extension Service, North Carolina State University, for six years.

Pamela A. Havice is an Assistant Professor at Clemson University in the Counselor Education program. Her primary teaching responsibilities lie in the Student Affairs track of the Counselor Education program. Dr. Havice has over 23 years of experience in higher education at various institutions.

Willie J. Heggins, III is an Assistant Professor in the Educational Leadership and Counseling Psychology Department at Washington State University. Dr. Heggins conducts research in higher education related to governance, faculty development, and international education reform. His teaching responsibilities include courses related to Governance in Higher Education, Multicultural Leadership, and Student Affairs Administration. In addition to his duties at the university, Dr. Heggins has served as an editorial reviewer with the *Journal of College Student Development* and currently reviews manuscripts for the *American Educational Research Journal.*

Wilma J. Henry is Associate Vice President for Student Affairs and Associate Professor in the College of Education where she teaches in the College Student Affairs Masters degree program at the University of South Florida in Tampa. Prior to her appointment at USF, she served as Assistant Dean and Associate Professor in the College of Education at Wright State University in Dayton, Ohio. She received a Masters degree in Student personnel in Higher Education from the University of Georgia and a Doctorate of Education degree with emphasis in Counseling Psychology from East Texas State University, Commerce, Texas.

Michael K. Herndon, who is an alumnus of Howard University, earned his Ph.D. in Higher Education and Student Affairs at Virginia Polytechnic Institute and State University (Virginia Tech). Currently, he is an assistant professor and director of the Interdisciplinary Studies degree program in the College of Arts at Sciences at Virginia Tech. His research interests include the participation of African American families in higher education, the civil rights movement, and issues surrounding masculinity.

Sharon L. Holmes is an Assistant Professor in the Department of Counseling, Adult and Higher Education in the College of Education at Northern Illinois University. She received a Bachelor of Business Administration (Management) degree from Detroit College, and both the Master of Science (Student Personnel) and Doctor of Philosophy (Higher Education Administration) degrees from Iowa State University.

John Wesley Lowery is Assistant Professor in the Higher Education and Student Affairs program in the University of South Carolina's College of Education. He earned his doctorate at Bowling Green State University in Higher Education Administration. He previously held administrative positions at Adrian College and Washington University. John has a Masters degree in student personnel services from the University of South Carolina and an undergraduate degree in religious studies from the University of Virginia. He is a frequent speaker and author on topics related to student affairs and higher education, particularly legislative issues and judicial affairs.

Jerlando F. L. Jackson is interested in the study of administrative diversity, executive behavior, and the nexus between administrative work and student outcomes in higher and postsecondary education. He is an Assistant Professor of Higher and Postsecondary Education in the Department of Educational Administration and Faculty Associate for the Wisconsin Center for the Advancement of Postsecondary Education at the University of Wisconsin–Madison. In addition, he serves as a Research Associate for the Center for the Study of Academic Leadership, which is developing and publishing a new generation of research on academic administrators. Dr. Jackson's central interest has been to contribute to administrative science, with a focus on the impact of administrators on higher and postsecondary education.

Barbara J. Johnson an assistant professor in the Department of Educational Leadership at the University of New Orleans earned a B.S. at Winston-Salem State University, a M.B.A. at Ohio State University, and a Ph.D. at Vanderbilt University. Her research interests include the recruitment and retention of students across a variety of postsecondary institutions.

Adam J. Kantrovich received his Ph.D. in Vocational and Technical Education from Virginia Tech in May of 2000 and has done extensive research and work in program evaluation, needs assessment, and qualitative research. Experiences include the commodity futures market, small business management, cooperative extension, federal government work, and eight years of teaching. Dr. Kantrovich is presently a faculty member at Morehead State University.

Octavia Madison-Colmore is an Assistant Professor in Counselor Education at Virginia Polytechnic Institute and State University. She has more than 15 years experience in the field of counseling, specializing in the treatment of substance abusers and working with diverse populations. Dr. Madison-Colmore has presented numerous papers at state, regional, and national conferences. She was recently invited by the People's Republic of China to teach a course on substance abuse and HIV/AIDS. Dr. Madison-Colmore has published both articles and book chapters on topics related to substance abuse and diversity.

Linda McCarthy is a doctoral candidate in the Social Justice Education Program at the University of Massachusetts, Amherst. She teaches social diversity and sociology at UMass and Holyoke Community College. She is an Editorial Assistant at the School of Education's journal, *Equity & Excellence in Education.* Linda's dissertation work is on female-bodied transgender identity.

Patricia McKenna has worked in student affairs for six years and has special interest in working with students with physical and mental disabilities, as well as with women's issues and eating disorders. McKenna is also a graduate student in the Counseling Program at Saint Joseph College, West Hartford, Connecticut.

Robert E. Meeks, Jr. is a second-year graduate student studying, Sports Administration in higher education; with aspirations of someday becoming an Athletic Director. He completed his undergraduate work at Auburn University, where he was also a four-year letter in football. After ending his career with the Denver Broncos, he returned to school and currently pursues one of his passions, which is working with athletes.

Lauren Miller is Assistant Dean of Students and Director of the Student Disability Resource Center at Florida State University. She has a B.A. in Psychology and an M.A. in Counseling from East Carolina University, and an Ed.D. in Educational Leadership/Higher Education from Florida State University.

H. Richard Milner is an Assistant Professor in the department of Teaching and Learning at Peabody College of Vanderbilt University. Dr. Milner earned his Ph.D. from The Ohio State University in Curriculum and Teaching. His research interests concern teacher thinking, teacher reflection, and teacher self-efficacy beliefs in cultural contexts. Dr. Milner's work has appeared in: *Teaching and Teacher Education, Race, Ethnicity and Education, the Journal of Curriculum and Supervision, Action in Teacher Education, Teachers and Teaching: Theory and Practice, The High School Journal, Journal of Critical Inquiry into Curriculum and Instruction, Teacher Education and Practice, Teaching Education,* and *Theory into Practice.*

James L. Moore III is an Assistant Professor in Counselor Education at The Ohio State University. He received his B.A. in English Education from Delaware State University and earned both his M.A.Ed. and Ph.D. in Counselor Education at Virginia Polytechnic Institute and State University. Dr. Moore's research interests are the following: Black male issues; academic persistence and achievement; cross-cultural counseling issues in schools; counseling student-athletes; and using innovative approaches to technology in counselor education.

John Moore is currently enrolled in the College Student Affairs program at the University of South Florida. He has previously worked as a Resident Director and as Assistant Director for Academic Support Services and Director of the Preparation, Retention, and Enrichment Program at University of the Sciences in Philadelphia.

Randy Moore is a professor of biology in General College at the University of Minnesota–Twin Cities. Moore studies how to teach science effectively to at-risk students. Moore edits *The American Biology Teacher,* has received numerous grants and awards, and has published more than 150 papers, monographs, and books. Moore's most recent book is *Evolution in the Courtroom: A Reference Guide.*

Quincy L. Moore is the Dean of Undergraduate Studies and Student Support Services at West Chester University. Prior to moving to West Chester University, he was the Executive Director of the Academic Success Center at Virginia Commonwealth University.

Adrienne M. Mustiful earned a B.A. from Dillard University and a M.S. from Mississippi State University. Previously, she worked at the Holmes Cultural Diversity Center at Mississippi State University. She is currently pursuing a Ph.D. in Higher Education at the University of New Orleans.

Kelly A. Norton is the Director of the Academic Services Center at High Point University. She coordinates accommodations for students with disabilities. She instructs the Foundations for Academic Success course and coordinates the Summer Advantage program, a program aimed at transitioning students into college in an academically structured environment. Ms. Norton is a doctoral candidate in Higher Education Administration at the University of Florida. Current research includes intent to turnover among disability services staff, factors affecting students' transition to college, and death and grieving in college athletics.

Myron L. Pope is an assistant professor in the Adult and Higher Education Program at the University of Oklahoma. His research interests include minority student recruitment and retention issues, faculty and student governance, and community college student affairs. Previously, he served as the Director of Minority Recruitment for the College of Education at the University of Alabama and also at Alabama Southern Community College as a Talent Search Counselor.

Melanie Rago is currently the Coordinator for Student Affairs and an Instructor in the University Experience Program at the University of South Florida. She has previously worked as the Assistant Director for Student Life and as an Adjunct Professor for Leadership Studies at University of the Sciences in Philadelphia.

Walter Rankin earned his doctorate at Georgetown University with a focus on comparative cultures and literatures. He has published articles and presented papers on a variety of topics in higher education, including disability issues and technology in higher education, and he was awarded the 2003 "Excellence in the Profession Award" by the ACPA Commission for Academic Support in Higher Education. He is Affiliate Associate Professor of English at George Mason University, where he serves as Deputy Associate Dean for Undergraduate Academic Affairs in the College of Arts and Sciences. His teaching experience includes all levels of English and German at the university level.

Lee Covington Rush is an Assistant Professor of Counselor Education at North Dakota State University. He received his Ph. D. in Counselor Education at The Ohio State University with focus on Multicultural Counseling and Life Span Career Development. While at The Ohio State University Dr. Rush taught Career Development Seminars and was an Adjunct Lecturer in the Department of African and African American Studies. His current research activities are in the areas of African-American and American Indian Career Development along with Multi-Racial/Multi-Cultural Identity Development.

Ronni Sanlo is the director of the UCLA LGBT Campus Center. Her research focuses on sexual orientation issues in higher education. Before joining the staff at UCLA, Dr. Sanlo was the LGBT Center director at Michigan. Her three books– *Working with LGBT College Students: A Handbook for Faculty and Administrators* (1998), *Unheard Voices: The Effects of Silence on Lesbian and Gay Educations* (1999), and *Our Place on Campus* (2002)–are published by Greenwood Press. Her undergraduate work was at the University of Florida. Her doctoral degree is from the University of North Florida. Dr. Sanlo is a faculty in residence at UCLA.

Arthur Sandeen is Professor of Educational Leadership at the University of Florida. He served for six years as Dean of Students at Iowa State University, and for 26 years as Vice President for Student Affairs at the University of Florida. He is the author of five books and served as President of NASPA in 1977–78. He is the recipient of the Scott Goodnight award, the Fred Turner award, and the Outstanding Contribution to Literature and Research award from NASPA. He chaired the committee that wrote *A Perspective on Student Affairs* in 1987, commemorating the 50th anniversary of the *Student Personnel Point of View*.

John Schuh is professor and chair of the department of educational leadership and policy studies at Iowa State University. Previously he held administrative and faculty assignments at Wichita State University, Indiana University (Bloomington), and Arizona State University. Schuh is the author, coauthor, or editor of over 180 publications, including 17 books and monographs, 45 book chapters, and 90 articles. Schuh received the Contribution to Knowledge Award from the American College Personnel Association, and the Contribution to Research or Literature Award from the National Association of Student Personnel Administrators. He also received a Fulbright award to study higher education in Germany in 1994.

Dionne M. Smith received her B.A. degree in Sociology from the University of

Virginia and her M.A.Ed. in Counselor Education from Wake Forest University. She is currently a Ph.D. Candidate in Counseling Psychology at The University of Tennessee, Knoxville. Her research interests focus on multicultural issues, in general, and issues related to African American females, in particular. Ms. Smith also serves as the Coordinator for the African American Achiever Scholar Program at The University of Tennessee, Knoxville. She plans to pursue a career in academe upon completion of her degree, thereby allowing her to further pursue interests related to research, teaching, consultation, and practice.

Ralphel Smith is an employee in the Department of University Housing at the University of Georgia. He has been employed there for five years. Prior to working at the University of Georgia, he was employed at the University of Tennessee. Mr. Smith is currently a doctoral candidate in the Student Affairs Administration Program at the University of Georgia. He has a Master's degree in College Student Personnel Services in Higher Education from the University of Georgia. He also has an undergraduate degree from Lander University in Greenwood, South Carolina.

Alfred Souma, M.A., is the Disability Support Services Coordinator and a tenured faculty member at Seattle Central Community College in Seattle, Washington. His experience includes 12 years inpatient work as a rehabilitation counselor in a psychiatric setting in Madison, Wisconsin and two years counseling in an outpatient psychiatric day treatment program in Santa Barbara, California. In the past several years, he has been conducting national presentations at colleges and professional organizations across the country on the topic of accommodating psychiatric disabilities on campuses. Alfred was the recipient of the 2002 Association on Higher Education and Disability (AHEAD) Professional Award.

Dafina Lazarus Stewart is an Assistant Professor of College Student Personnel and Higher Education at Ohio University. She has practiced student affairs in several functional areas including, multicultural affairs, judicial affairs, and residence life. Her scholarship covers identity development, students of color, and university-community interaction.

Mary Taylor serves as Coordinator of the President's Commissions for Equity and Diversity at the University of New Hampshire. These Commissions include the Commission on the Status of Women, the Commission on the Status of People of Color, and the Commission on the Status of Gay, Lesbian, Bisexual and Transgender Issues. Mary holds a B.A. in English Literature from the University of Arizona and an M.A. in Educational Leadership and Counseling from Eastern Michigan University.

LaRonta M. Upson, M.S., Ed.S., is a Ph.D. student in School Psychology at the University of Tennessee, Knoxville. Her research and professional interests include cognitive assessment of culturally and linguistically diverse students, education reform and policy issues, disproportionate representation of minorities in special education, and academic and behavioral intervention. She is currently the Editorial Assistant for the *Journal of Psychoeducational Assessment,* Graduate Instructor in the department of Educational Psychology, and a Holmes Scholar.

Mary Lee Vance (first name said together) earned her doctorate in Higher Education Administration at Michigan State University. She has been a full-time professional in higher education institutions since 1984. Over the years, she has direct-ed a variety of student services, including but not limited to: Disability Student Services, Career Services, Academic Advising, McNair Post-Baccalaureate Achieve-ment Program, Asian Pacific American Student Outreach, New Student Orientation, Registrar, and Field Experiences in public higher education institutions ranging from 2,700 to over 45,000 student enrollment. She is currently the Director of Undergraduate Academic Advisement at the University of Wisconsin–Superior, and was recently selected to be one of the editors on the *NACADA Journal.* In addition, Dr. Vance has made over 100 presentations internationally, serving as a keynoter or major presenter at several national conferences. She has published numerous arti-cles, chapters and stories in several professional books and journals, and over 36 book reviews in the *National Academic Advising Association Journal, Journal of Organizational Change Management,* and the *Korean Quarterly.*

Susan Weir is a Senior Academic Counselor in the Oklahoma State University Department of Psychology in Stillwater, Oklahoma. She has seven years of academ-ic advising experience. Her educational background includes a bachelor's degree in journalism from the University of Oregon, a master's degree in Counseling Psychology from the University of Missouri-Columbia, and a Ph.D. (anticipated, May 2003) in Educational Psychology from Oklahoma State University.

Cyrus Williams has been the Assistant Dean and Director for Student Judicial Affairs at the University of Florida since 2000. He has also worked in Residential Life as a Residence Director, and served as Associate Director for the Ronald E. McNair Scholars Program at the University of Florida. In addition, he was a Counselor for the Student Support Services at the University of Connecticut for five years. He has 12 years of experience counseling, mentoring, and advising students in various university student affairs departments.

Sarah L. Williamson is a graduate student in the Higher Education Administration program in the Department of Educational Leadership, Policy and Technology Studies at The University of Alabama, Tuscaloosa. Ms. Williamson earned her Bachelor of Arts degree in Psychology from Mississippi University for Women 2002.

Sheila Witherspoon is a doctoral student in Counselor Education at the University of South Carolina. Ms. Witherspoon received a Bachelor of Arts in Political Science and a Master of Education in Counselor Education from South Carolina State University. A former school counselor, Ms. Witherspoon has served as an employment counselor and college admissions counselor and recruiter. Ms. Witherspoon is a member of the American Counseling Association, Association of Counselor Educators and Supervisor, Southern Association of Counselor Educators and Supervisor, South Carolina Counseling Association, Chi Sigma Iota Counseling Professional Academic Counseling Honor Society, and Alpha Kappa Alpha Sorority, Inc.

Yanmei Zhang is a doctoral student in the Department of Educational Leadership, Policy and Foundations at the University of Florida. She majors in the Higher Education Administration Program. She received both her Bachelors degree and Masters degree in English Language and Literature in China. Before she came to America, she was a professor, teaching English. Her research interests include organizational leadership in higher education, comparative higher education policy and administration, student affairs administration, and student development. As an international student, she is especially interested in issues and concerns of international students, particularly of Chinese international students in American higher education.

FOREWORD

This book of case studies, so carefully edited by Lamont Flowers, fills a void in the student affairs literature in a number of ways. First, it addresses issues related to diversity in higher education in a comprehensive and meaningful manner. Second, it is a helpful tool for teaching and staff development that will enable students, student affairs staff, and faculty to engage with the issues in concrete and practical ways. Third, it provides useful suggestions for conducting research about the issues that each case study raises. This book is much needed by those of us in student affairs education and practice who are given the responsibility to prepare students to work with a diverse student population in a wide range of higher education settings.

That this country is becoming more diverse is not news to anyone who reads the newspaper, watches television, or looks at the names in their local phone book. Carlos Cortez, in a keynote speech for the American College Personnel Association in 2000, pointed out that in many phone books in this country the listings for Patel (a common Indian name) and Gonzalez (a common Latino name) exceed those for common "American" names, such as Smith. The recent 2000 census revealed migration trends indicating that great numbers of Latino/as are moving into traditionally white parts of the country, such as the upper Midwest and plains states. Racial and ethnic diversity is a fact of life in the United States and we need to embrace the varied cultures and traditions that a multicultural nation has to offer.

At the same time that the United States is becoming more diverse, the world is developing a global consciousness. We are greatly affected by political and economic situations in other countries. Clearly, the recent wars in Afghanistan and Iraq are examples of the significance that situations half way around the globe can have in our lives. Less visible, but no less important, is the impact of a depressed economy in Japan or a drought in Argentina. Increasingly, our ability to understand and interact with individuals from other countries is of critical importance to our own well-being as a country and as individuals who live in a global society.

Religious differences, too, have become more salient in recent years. The attacks on the World Trade Center and the war with Iraq sent us scurrying to find out more about Islam. In our own country, religious beliefs often are the basis for differing positions on social issues such as abortion, euthanasia, prayer in school, and a host of other value-laden concerns. In a country founded on the concept of religious freedom, acceptance of religiously based differences is still a contentious issue.

Other types of diversity also are gaining recognition. Women have made the most evident gains. Most women are now employed outside the home and many hold leadership positions in business, government, health care, and education. They play an active role in policy making and economic development in this country. Individuals with disabilities are taking a much more active role in the workplace and educational system. The Americans with Disabilities Act, technological advances that allow individuals with disabilities to more easily carry out daily activities, and mainstreaming of students with disabilities in our public schools has led to greater visibility and activism. Similarly, gay, lesbian, bisexual, and transgender individuals have fought their way into the public eye and are receiving greater recognition as an important part of society. While this population always has made important contributions in all aspects of life in the U.S., they now are doing so as openly gay, lesbian, bisexual, and transgender people.

Higher education institutions are a microcosm of society. The diversity that is found in the U.S. also is found on our college and university campuses. This diversity will continue to increase as the demographics of our country change. Population projections indicate that in the near future, the college-age population will be "majority minority;" that is, students of color will outnumber white students. While it is encouraging that many colleges and universities are now requiring diversity courses, the lack of information that college graduates have about diversity and their inability to effectively communicate with individuals from other cultures is apparent. This is true of students entering student affairs preparation programs, a group that one expects to be somewhat knowledgeable and accepting of diversity based on their career choice, as well as of graduates in general. I offer the statements of my own master's students as evidence.

I teach a class entitled Student Development Theory II in which we examine identity development of students who are members of diverse populations. As part of this class, I ask students to email their reactions to me after each class. Students frequently comment that they lack knowledge of diverse populations and that they are uncomfortable interacting with students who are different from them. For example,

Growing up in a small, rural community and attending a fairly small undergraduate institution, I have never really been exposed to the Latino culture in any way, much less learned about it in depth.

Discussions about sexual orientation [do] not regularly occur. The past two weeks were the first formal discussions I have experienced about LGBT issues.

I feel that the entire discussion that we had in class on students with disabilities was useful and interesting. I feel that this is an issue on campuses that is sometimes overlooked and I am very interested in learning more.

Being white I find that it is sometimes difficult to discuss the issue of race with individuals who do not identify themselves as white . . . because of a lack of knowledge or the ever so present feeling of awkwardness that the subject creates.

Unfortunately, graduate preparation programs in student affairs do little to address the deficits in students' knowledge and sensitivity related to diversity. As Flowers points out in his opening chapter, multicultural competencies rarely are addressed. Indeed, the newly revised CAS standards for professional preparation in student affairs at the master's level make no mention of these important skills. While course content related to student characteristics and identity development is required, the development of skills and attitudes necessary to work effectively with a diverse student population is not mentioned.

How then should faculty and supervisors go about preparing graduate students and student affairs professionals to respond appropriately to a complex multicultural student body? I believe that we need to do more than share information about various populations. While knowledge is important, awareness, sensitivity, and skills are equally–if not more–important. As we prepare lesson plans for our classes and our staff development sessions, we need to include goals that are affective and behavioral as well as cognitive. Being aware of ways in which oppression is manifested in higher education, being sensitive to the difficulties of international students trying to learn in a second language, or having some appreciation for the importance of family in the lives of Latino/a students are examples of affective outcomes that will enable student affairs professionals to interact more effectively with diverse student populations. Being able to analyze the causes of a misunderstanding between roommates from different cultures, design an intervention to defuse a volatile racial incident on campus, share one's feelings openly in a discussion of religious positions on homosexuality, or advocate on behalf of a student with a learning disability who is having trouble getting the accommodations she needs from a professor are samples of behavioral outcomes that can be used immediately in practice.

Case study is a powerful method for achieving affective and behavioral goals. It requires students to think critically about the information provided and to apply learning to real-life situations. When used in group settings, case study enables students to interact with each other, sharing different viewpoints and perceptions, and bringing their own values, beliefs, and cultural understandings to the discussion. Active engagement with the material and with other students who hold differing views is as important as the resolution of the case. Students learn to listen, to respectfully disagree, and to compromise. Students develop skills in analysis, in seeking out information to inform their opinions, and in teamwork. Presentation skills are developed as students explain their analyses of the cases. At the same time, students become much more familiar with the issues being discussed and the knowledge they gain stays with them since they have been actively engaged.

In her dissertation research, Dea Forney found that the majority of student affairs master's students she surveyed were accommodators, one of the four learning styles identified by David Kolb. Accommodators grasp information best through concrete experience and process it most effectively through active experimentation. Accommodators are doers; they prefer to learn by active involvement in real-life situations. Case study provides the next best thing to real life: written scenarios that present situations that commonly occur in practice and characters who resemble the students and their colleagues. Students are presented with questions that demand careful thought, research, analysis, and a well-developed response—questions that a supervisor might ask in real life.

Returning to my students' emails from Student Development Theory II provides evidence of the positive responses students have to case study and active engagement:

While I was doing the reading I thought that I understood it fine, but then when we discussed it in class, I think that it just confused me even more. I definitely think that my small group discussion helped me to understand the difference better.

I enjoy hearing what others are thinking, and it seemed like other individuals could really bring a different view and perspective to the group discussion.

I think that the case studies helped me as a student affairs practitioner to look directly at sexual identity and see how I can provide services to students that are dealing with these issues.

While it is clearly evident that case study is an effective method of enhancing student learning, finding appropriate case studies, particularly that focus on diversity, is difficult. Many faculty and supervisors, including me, resort to the time-consuming task of developing our own. Lamont Flowers and the individuals who contributed to this book have done us all a huge favor by providing well-crafted and challenging scenarios that will enable all of us to dig deeply into the implications for student affairs practice of our increasingly diverse campus populations. I, for one, am very grateful.

NANCY J. EVANS, PH.D.
Iowa State University
April 2003

PREFACE

Recent research evidence suggests that students in higher education and student affairs preparation programs are not receiving the necessary training to effectively serve all students attending the nation's institutions (McEwen & Roper, 1994; Pope & Reynolds, 1997; Talbot, 1996; Talbot & Kocarek, 1997). In order to assist current and future student affairs professionals in gaining the above-mentioned multicultural skills, this book was developed with the assistance of many writers, researchers, and current higher education and student affairs professionals. The primary objective of this book is to help higher education and student affairs graduate students as well as current higher education and student affairs professionals practice and refine thinking skills needed to resolve diversity-related issues and problems on college and university campuses in the United States.

The intended audience for this book includes a number of constituent groups. First, the general audiences for this book are individuals interested in working (or currently working) in institutions of higher education such as student affairs professionals and higher education administrators. Second, since this book contains a number of interesting case studies written by a nationally representative group of scholars and researchers from public as well as private institutions, administrators, faculty, and students will find this book very useful and informative. Third, since this book contains a research agenda on diversity issues, educational and institutional researchers also will find this book a helpful adjunct to their research efforts. Taken as a whole, this book will assist faculty, students, and current higher education and student affairs professionals by exposing them to the types of difficult diversity-related issues and problems on today's college and university campuses.

The primary benefactors of this book, in my view, will be the many diverse and underrepresented students on U.S. college and university campuses (e.g., African Americans, American Indians/Alaska Natives, Asians, biracial-interracial students, Hispanics or Latinos, and Native Hawaiians/Pacific Islanders; gay, lesbian, bisexual, and/or transgender students; international students; and persons with disabilities). It is my belief that diverse and underrepresented students will benefit the most from this book by having the opportunity to interact with multiculturally competent higher education and student affairs professionals who have read, critically analyzed, and learned from the examples, ideas, and activities presented in the case studies.

LAMONT A. FLOWERS, PH.D.
University of Florida
May 2003

References

McEwen, M., & Roper, L. (1994). Interracial experiences, knowledge, and skills of Master's degree students in graduate programs in student affairs. *Journal of College Student Development, 35,* 81–87.

Pope, R., & Reynolds, A. (1997). Student affairs core competencies: Integrating multicultural awareness, knowledge, and skills. *Journal of College Student Development, 38,* 266–277.

Talbot, D. (1996). Master's students' perspectives on their graduate education regarding issues of diversity. *NASPA Journal, 33,* 163–178.

Talbot, D., & Kocarek, C. (1997). Student affairs graduate faculty members' knowledge, comfort, and behaviors regarding issues of diversity. *Journal of College Student Development, 38,* 278–287.

CONTENTS

CASE STUDIES

DIVERSITY ISSUES IN AMERICAN COLLEGES AND UNIVERSITIES

Chapter 1

INTRODUCTION

Why Assemble a Book of Case Studies on Diversity Issues?

Reason #1

While we have all heard claims about the growing numbers of diverse and underrepresented persons attending colleges and universities, it is now a fact of life on many campuses that persons from diverse backgrounds are attending college in larger numbers than ever before (Bennett, 2001; Carter & Wilson, 1996; National Center for Education Statistics, 1993, 2002; Talbot, 1996a). Thus, in light of the reality that colleges and universities are becoming more racially, ethnically, and culturally diverse, extensive knowledge of diversity issues and topics related to multiculturalism are vital for higher education and student affairs professionals (Ebbers & Henry, 1990; Flowers, in press; Flowers & Howard-Hamilton, 2002; McEwen & Roper, 1994a, 1994b; Pope, Reynolds, & Cheatham, 1997; Talbot, 1996b; Talbot & Kocarek, 1997). Thus, this book was produced to help graduate students as well as current higher education and student affairs professionals learn how to critically evaluate diversity-related issues and problems and support the cognitive and psychosocial development of all students on campus.

Reason #2

As a professor in a higher education and student affairs professional preparation program who has taught a course entitled *Diversity Issues in Higher Education*, I know through firsthand experience, the importance of a book that encourages students to connect theory to practice to solve authentic problems related to diversity and multiculturalism. The initial thoughts that would later be transformed into this book materialized during the first semester I taught *Diversity Issues in Higher Education* as I passed out the final examination at the end of semester. It was then, at that moment, that I began to reflect on the entire teaching experience and my perceptions of how well the class met its primary objectives, which were (a) to help students to become familiar with salient issues in multiculturalism in higher education; (b) to encourage students to examine their feelings, attitudes, and beliefs concerning the culturally different; (c) to motivate students to challenge misconceptions they held about culturally different individuals and groups; and (d) to demonstrate through course readings and other assignments how to communicate and solve problems across racial and cultural lines. While examining these goals, I began to realize that unless students were given the opportunity to engage in thoughtful discussions about critical incidents and real-life circumstances on college campuses, students (even students who had successfully passed the diversity course) might be ill-equipped to resolve issues or problems involving multiculturalism. Toward that end, this book was developed to meet this important need and provide a representative sample of realistic snapshots of some of the most critical issues on today's college campuses.

Reason #3

This book was also developed to assist higher education and student affairs professionals in being outstanding professionals who have the ability to promote student development for all students. To accomplish this goal, I examined the *Principles of Good Practice in Student Affairs,* a document developed by the American College Personnel Association and the National Association of Student Personnel Administrators (1997). The document elucidated seven tenets of acceptable practice for higher education and student affairs professionals:

1. Engage students in active learning.
2. Help students develop coherent values and ethical standards.
3. Set and communicate high expectations for student learning.
4. Use systematic inquiry to improve student and institutional performance
5. Use resources effectively to achieve institutional missions and goals.
6. Forge educational partnerships that advance student learning.
7. Build supportive and inclusive communities.

What I found most interesting about these practices is an implicit reliance on knowledge, skills, and abilities that requires a meaningful understanding of students. Stated differently, I discovered that in order to implement the recommended practices, all higher education and student affairs professionals must have a firm understanding and knowledge of how to respond to student problems regardless of race, socioeconomic class, gender, and sexual orientation. Thus, since the *Principles of Good Practice in Student Affairs* documented essential and necessary skill domains needed by all professionals working in postsecondary settings and since the practices rely heavily on professionals' abilities to understand and incorporate cultural knowledge, values, and related skills, I assembled this collection of case studies to help graduate students and professionals alike to better serve our diverse and multicultural students on the nation's college campuses.

Conceptual Framework of the Book

Since this book consists of a series of case studies that focus on issues related to diversity and multiculturalism in higher education and student affairs, the conceptual framework is based on insights derived from various academic literature written about the nature and potential uses of case studies for pedagogical and research purposes. While it should be noted that case studies used in qualitative research designs may differ from case studies used for instructional purposes (Merriam, 1998), the intent of all case studies is to provide rich, detailed descriptions of an event, incident, or activity in a way that fosters discussion and debate while centering on the facts of the case and drawing on relevant knowledge bases and skills sets. Case studies are a detailed description of events, situations, and circumstances that involve people, programs, and institutions. Johnson (1990) espoused the view that "a case is a scaled-down replication of a real experience or series of events, with ample problems or issues to generate a good discussion" (p. 43). Creswell (1998) defined a case study as an "exploration of a 'bounded system' or a case over time through detailed, in-depth data collection involving multiple sources of information rich in context" (p. 61). Other scholars have noted that case studies are useful in educational settings because they enable students to: (a) discuss the facts of an incident or program, (b) debate the potential outcomes of various courses of action, and (c) connect relevant theoretical models that may provide a lens through which the problem or issue may be understood (Johnson, 1990; Merriam, 1998; Yin, 2003).

This case study book also was informed by Miller and Kantrov's (1998) helpful book entitled *A Guide to Facilitating Cases in Education* in which they noted five important goals that should be achieved by those who facilitate case studies. While their book was written primarily for case study facilitators, I believe that the five goals of case study facilitation they outlined have relevance for readers as well as facilitators of case studies:

• Focus on analysis over evaluation.
• Promote inquiry into different perspectives.
• Refrain from problem solving too quickly.

• Build common understanding.
• Adopt a learning stance. (p. 7)

According to Miller and Kantrov, case studies are best utilized if readers attempt first to comprehend the facts in the case and differentiate between the stated assumptions in the case and accurate observations based on the data presented in the case. In other words, *a focus on analysis over evaluation* emphasizes a critical examination of the case while paying attention to the multifaceted issues being presented and addressed.

One way to *promote inquiry into different perspectives* is to avoid trying to reduce the ideas presented in the case or the case as whole to one problem or issue; instead, readers should seek to think about the complexity of the case and the multiple perspectives embedded in each case in order to gain a more meaningful appreciation of diversity-related problems and the solutions they require. Also, this goal involves recognizing that we are all different and that even members of similar cultural groups may view the world through completely different lenses. Thus, as you read the case studies in this book, you should be open to discussing and critically examining the diverse responses to the discussion questions and approaches to research activities that may emerge from other participants who are examining the same case study.

Miller and Kantrov also advised that readers of case studies should *refrain from problem solving too quickly.* Simply stated, this goal involves resisting the natural inclination to generate solutions or holding back from moving to the solution phase of the process until you have thoroughly explored the theoretical, political, and practical issues of the case study.

Building common understanding, the fourth goal, involves working together with other members of your class or group to seek to determine some of the universal ideas embedded in each case. Thus, while each person may have his or her own personal experience that may result in different interpretations, readers also are encouraged to identify those common or similar perspectives, experiences, and values that are shared by the entire group, the university community, and society. This goal may be difficult to achieve and may seem to be in conflict with promoting inquiry into different perspectives; however, I believe that if readers first acknowledge that multiple perspectives on these issues exist then they are more likely to be able to recognize that though multiple perspectives exist, there are agreed-upon values that cut across cultural lines that need to be identified and discussed in a group setting.

Finally, *adopt a learning stance,* the fifth goal, encourages case study readers to be curious in their reading and evaluation of the case. In other words, as a case study reader, you should always challenge yourself to go further and develop and ask other questions that may stimulate additional discussion. If you consider these five goals as you read the case studies in this book, I am confident that you will find the case study experience more rewarding because you will discover that each case study contains challenges as well as opportunities and has the potential to stimulate new ideas for addressing diversity issues on college campuses.

Organization of the Book

The organization of this book is based on current thinking regarding what constitutes the major sources of diversity at colleges and universities in the United States. Since research and other writings suggest that diversity is a complex, multidimensional term (Bennett, 2001; El-Khawas, 1996; McEwen & Roper, 1994a; Pope & Reynolds, 1997; Pope, Reynolds, & Cheatham, 1997; Talbot & Kocarek, 1997; Takaki, 1993), diversity was defined for this book as the complex interaction of constructs, issues, and experiences related to race/ethnicity (e.g., African Americans, American Indians/Alaska Natives, Asians, biracial/interracial, Hispanics or Latinos, and Native Hawaiians/Pacific Islanders, international); religious differences; regional differences, social class differences, sexual orientation (e.g., gay, lesbian, bisexual, and/or transgender); gender differences; and disabilities. The organization of this book is based in part on the notion that one way to gain a better understanding of the complex interaction of the multidimensional issues incorporated into the term diversity is to analyze a series of cases studies, followed by critical questions and research activities to assist students and professionals in becoming familiar and comfortable with solving diversity-related problems in a multicultural institutional setting.

The separation of case studies by broad categories was done merely for the purposes of organizing the many case studies in this book. However, as you examine the case studies you will discover that issues and problems of diversity and multiculturalism are intertwined. You also will discover that even if you are examining cases that focus on religious differences, for example, other issues such as racial and gender diversity also may be relevant to your analysis of the case. In fact, in most cases, failure to consider the multiple dimensions of diversity when analyzing case studies or actual problems may result in a less-than-adequate resolution of the problem or issue. Therefore, within each chapter, I have included case studies that address (either directly or indirectly) all of the different aspects of diversity and the following functional areas within higher education and student affairs: academic advising, administration, admissions, career services, counseling and psychological services, financial aid, Greek affairs, international education, institutional research, judicial affairs, multicultural affairs, orientation services, residence life, student activities, student development in the two-year college, teaching, and wellness and student health (American College Personnel Association, 2003). This organization is designed to maximize four important aims of the book: (a) to encourage students and higher education and student affairs professionals to discuss diversity-related issues in classes or in groups, (b) to help students and professionals increase their multicultural competency, (c) to sensitize students and professionals to the diverse needs and perspectives of students on campus, and (d) to encourage students and professionals to analyze diversity-related issues and problems using student development theory and related research.

As stated earlier, all of the case studies in this book are intended to encourage discussion and thoughtful consideration regarding a multitude of diversity-related issues and concerns on college campuses. While some of the case studies are based on actual events, keep in mind that the case studies are not intended to represent any one specific event. In addition, the primary persons involved in the case are based on fictitious characters and thus are not intended to offend anyone. In addition, the case studies are not intended to stereotype individuals or groups or reduce the totality of anyone's personality or culture. In contrast, the case studies are designed to serve as a useful starting point to enable students and professionals to practice examining and thoughtfully articulating appropriate plans of action in response to the issues presented in the case studies. Specifically, each case study is designed to help readers recognize and develop multicultural awareness and become competent users of multicultural knowledge and related skills.

To further support the learning process, I have obtained permission to reprint a useful framework developed by Pope and Reynolds (1997), in which they described the various types of values and abilities that are needed to work on a diverse college campus. The information contained in Table 1 should be used as a self-assessment checklist or rubric to chart your personal development of important attributes and skills that you need in order to effectively serve, support, and protect all students in institutions of higher education. For example, if, after you read Table 1, you noticed that you do not believe that differences are valuable and that learning about others who are culturally different is necessary and rewarding (multicultural awareness), perhaps it may be worthwhile for you to seek to understand why you disagree with this statement and how your disagreement might affect how you work with members of culturally diverse groups. This is but one example of how the information contained in Table 1 can assist you in better understanding yourself, changing your attitudes and behaviors, and increasing your capacity to effectively plan programs and support the development of students from diverse backgrounds. Furthermore, each case study contributor also focused on at least one aspect of the information shown in Table 1

Table 1
CHARACTERISTICS OF A MULTICULTURALLY
COMPETENT STUDENT AFFAIRS PRACTITIONER

Multicultural Awareness	*Multicultural Knowledge*	*Multicultural Skills*
A belief that differences are valuable and that learning about others who are culturally different is necessary and rewarding.	Knowledge of diverse cultures and oppressed groups (i.e., history, traditions, values, customs, resources, issues).	Ability to identify and openly discuss cultural differences and issues.
A willingness to take risks and see them as necessary and important for personal and professional growth.	Information about how change occurs for individual values and behaviors.	Ability to assess the impact of cultural differences on communication and effectively communicate across those differences.
A personal commitment to justice, social change, and combating depression.	Knowledge about the ways that cultural differences affect verbal and nonverbal communication.	Capability to empathize and genuinely connect with individuals who are culturally different from themselves.
A belief in the value and significance of their own cultural heritage and world view as a starting place for understanding others who are culturally different from them.	Knowledge about how gender, class, race and ethnicity, language, nationality, sexual orientation, age, religion or spirituality, disability, and ability affect individuals and their experiences.	Ability to incorporate new learning and prior learning in new situations.
A willingness to self-examine and, when necessary, challenge and change their own values, world view, assumptions, and biases.	Information about culturally appropriate resources and how to make referrals.	Ability to gain the trust and respect of individuals who are culturally different from themselves.
An openness to change and belief that change is necessary and positive.	Information about the nature of institutional oppression and power.	Capability to accurately assess their own multicultural skills, comfort level, growth, and development.
An acceptance of other world views and perspectives and a willingness to acknowledge that they, as individuals, do not have all the answers.	Knowledge about identity development models and the acculturation process for members of oppression groups and its impact on individuals, groups, intergroup relations, and society.	Ability to differentiate between individual differences, cultural differences, and universal similarities.

Continued

Table 1–*Continued*

Multicultural Awareness	Multicultural Knowledge	Multicultural Skills
A belief that cultural differences do not have to interfere with effective communication or meaningful relationships.	Knowledge about within-group differences and understanding of multiple identities and multiple oppressions.	Ability to challenge and support individuals and systems around oppression issues in a manner that optimizes multicultural interventions.
Awareness of their own cultural heritage and how it affects their world view, values, and assumptions.	Information and understanding of internalized oppression and its impact on identity and self-esteem.	Ability to make individual, group, and institutional multicultural interventions.
Awareness of their own behavior and its impact on others.	Knowledge about institutional barriers which limit access to and success in higher education for members of oppressed groups.	Ability to use cultural knowledge and sensitivity to make more culturally sensitive and appropriate interventions.
Awareness of the interpersonal process which occurs within a multicultural dyad.	Knowledge about systems theories and how systems change.	

Source: Pope, R., & Reynolds, A. (1977). Student affairs core competencies: Integrating multicultural awareness, knowledge, and skills. *Journal of College Student Development, 38,* 266–277. Reprinted by permission of the publisher.

(i.e., multicultural awareness, multicultural knowledge, and multicultural skills) to develop his or her case study, discussion questions, and research activities for further exploration.

How to Use This Book

This case study book may be used as a supplementary textbook or as a stand-alone textbook in undergraduate or graduate-level courses, training modules, workshops, and seminars designed to provide students or professionals with opportunities to learn how to communicate with persons from different cultural backgrounds, work with and plan programs and services for students from diverse backgrounds, and work within a postsecondary institution to make the college or university environment a safe and welcoming place for all students, staff, faculty, and administrators. This book also may be used in conjunction with a college student development textbook to further explore issues of culture and race while focusing on the theoretical dimensions of college student development, most of which were developed based on research studies with majority populations (Evans, Forney, & Guido-DiBrito, 1998). Moreover, this case study book contains a number of research projects that students and researchers will find interesting and challenging. Some of the research activities in this book also may be expanded to serve as dissertation projects and/or research publications. The aforementioned strategies are only a few ways that this book can be utilized for instructional purposes. I encourage you to find additional uses of this text in other instructional and research-based contexts.

To be sure, there are multiple strategies and techniques for reviewing case studies (Johnson, 1990; Merriam, 1998; Miller & Kantrov, 1998; Yin, 2003). However, after considering the dynamic nature of diversity issues in higher education, I developed the PEER approach to examine the case studies presented in this book. The PEER approach consists of the following stages: *preparation, examination, evaluation,* and *reflection.* Each stage in the process is described below.

Preparation

The preparation stage is the time to obtain all of the necessary resources that you may need to thoroughly explore the case study. The necessary resources may include a history book with a multicultural focus such as Takaki's *A Different Mirror: A History of Multicultural America* (1993), a book designed to assist you in understanding conceptual and practical definitions of diversity issues in the United Statues, such as *The Convergence of Race, Ethnicity, and Gender: Multiple Identities Counseling* (Robinson & Howard-Hamilton, 2000), as well as a college student development theory textbook such as *Student Development in College: Theory, Research, and Practice* (Evans, Forney, & Guido-Dibrito, 1998). Furthermore, it is important to have a writing instrument and notepad nearby to take notes on what you are reading or record your reactions to the case study.

Also, in the preparation stage, before you read each case study, think about your initial assumptions of the group of people that make up the broad category of case studies in the chapter. For example, before you read the case studies in Chapter 3, think about (and record in a journal or on separate sheets of paper) all of the stereotypes of the different cultural and ethnic groups you have been taught or heard about in your lifetime. Also, think about and record how you personally feel about specific cultural groups. This particular technique in the preparation stage is paramount because it is well known that we have all been taught various lessons about different cultural groups from our parents, relatives, friends, and/or teachers. It is also well known that previously learned information sometimes is used to learn additional information (Cole, John-Steiner, Scribner, & Souberman, 1978) and that the sum total of our knowledge base guides and directs the way that we behave and interact with members of other groups (Dewey, 1910).

Examination

This stage begins with a careful reading of the case study. Then, before you read the discussion questions, take a moment to list as many of the case's larger issues as you can. Then list all of the stakeholder groups that may be affected by the issues or problems in the case study. Brainstorm and record how each issue may be resolved for each stakeholder group and/or individual in the case study. Following this preliminary examination, read and answer the discussion questions. You will notice that your ability to address the salient issues involved in the case study will increase every time you thoroughly examine another case study in this book. The examination stage could potentially end with a group discussion or presentation in which you discuss the larger issues introduced by the case study, results from your stakeholder analysis, and answers to the discussion questions.

Evaluation

Whether you are in an individual, small-group, or large-group setting, the evaluation stage should commence with a description of several strategies or approaches for resolving the issues and problems presented in the case study. You could accomplish this task in a number of ways. For example, after you have read a case study, identified the central issues, and answered the discussion questions, you and/or your group could try to develop policy or mission statements that could help to clarify your university's position on the matters presented in the case study. Or you and/or your group could generate new ideas for innovative programs and campus services to support persons from diverse cultural groups. Once you and/or your group members have had a chance to produce a list of possible strategies to mitigate the effects of the problem or eliminate the problem altogether, you and/or your group should select the most viable strategy for solving the problem and then focus on developing an assessment plan that will enable higher education and student affairs professionals from various functional areas to determine if your strategy for solving the problem or issue is effective.

Reflection

In this last phase, you are encouraged to engage in deep reflection about your initial and concluding perspectives, assumptions, and teachings related to the issues raised in this case. While it is not important how long the reflection period takes place, it is important that you reflect about each aspect of the case study experience. During this process, be sure to consider how your ideas about the particular cultural group have been altered and how this modification of your assumptions and perspectives may inform your practice as a higher education and student affairs professional when working with members of that group. Also, remember that each member of a particular group may not respond or react in the same way and your reflection must also incorporate a degree of flexibility so that you do not make the mistake of overgeneralizing your assumptions, world views, and perceptions about individual members of diverse groups to all members of that group.

Conclusion

All over the country, postsecondary institutions are beginning to provide courses, workshops, lectures, training opportunities, and services for students, staff, faculty, and administrators regarding issues of diversity and multiculturalism on campus (Association of American Colleges and Universities, 2000; Brazzell & Reisser, 1999). Though programs and services vary by institution, the overall goal of these courses, programs, and/or services is to provide opportunities for students, staff, faculty, as well as higher education and student affairs professionals to learn more about the multicultural world in which they live and work to better serve the needs of all students on U.S. college campuses (McCauley, Wright, & Harris, 2000). Overall, the intended result of these efforts is to reduce misunderstanding and discrimination, and make the campus environment a welcoming place for all students, staff, faculty, and administrators. Toward that end, *Diversity Issues in American Colleges and Universities: Case Studies for Higher Education and Student Affairs Professionals* was produced to serve as a resource that can help higher education and student affairs professionals develop important skills that are required to work effectively with all students attending postsecondary institutions in the United States.

References

American College Personnel Association. (2003). *ACPA Special Interest Commissions.* Retrieved May 5, 2001, from http://www.acpa.nche.edu/comms/comm.htm

American College Personnel Association & National Association of Student Personnel Administrators. (1997). *Principles of good practice for student affairs.* Washington, DC: Author.

Association of American Colleges and Universities. (2000). *National survey on diversity in the undergraduate curriculum.* Washington, DC: Author.

Bennett, C. I. (2001). Research on racial issues in American higher education. In J. A. Banks & C. A. McGee Banks (Eds.), *Handbook of research on multicultural education* (2nd ed., pp. 663–682). San Francisco: Jossey-Bass.

Brazzell, J. C., & Reisser, L. (1999). Creating inclusive communities. In G. S. Blimling & E. J. Whitt (Eds.), *Good practices in student affairs: Principles to foster student learning* (pp. 157–177). San Francisco: Jossey-Bass.

Carter, D., & Wilson, R. (1996). *Minorities in higher education. 1995–96 Fourteenth annual status report.* Washington, DC: American Council on Education, Office of Minorities in Higher Education.

Cole, M., John-Steiner, V., Scribner, S., & Souberman, E. (Eds.). (1978). *Mind in society: The development of higher psychological processes.* Cambridge, MA: Harvard University Press.

Creswell, J. (1998). *Qualitative inquiry and research designs: Choosing among five traditions.* Thousand Oaks, CA: Sage.

Dewey, J. (1910). *How we think.* Boston: D. C. Heath.

Ebbers, L., & Henry, S. (1990). Cultural competence: A new challenge to student affairs professionals. *NASPA Journal, 27,* 319–323.

El-Khawas, E. (1996). Student diversity on today's campuses. In S. R. Komives & D. B. Woodard (Eds.), *Student services: A handbook for the profession* (pp. 64–80). San Francisco: Jossey-Bass.

Evans, N. J., Forney, D. S., & Guido-DiBrito, F. (1998). *Student development in college: Theory, research, and practice.* San Francisco: Jossey-Bass.

Flowers, L. A. (in press). National study of diversity requirements in student affairs graduate programs. *NASPA Journal.*

Flowers, L. A., & Howard-Hamilton, M. F. (2002). A qualitative study of graduate students' perceptions of diversity issues in student affairs preparation programs. *Journal of College Student Development, 43,* 119–123.

Johnson, G. R. (1990). *First steps to excellence in college teaching* (2nd ed.). Madison, WI: Magna Publications.

McCauley, C., Wright, M., & Harris, M. (2000). Diversity workshops on campus: A survey of current practice at U.S. colleges and universities. *College Student Journal, 34,* 100–114.

McEwen, M., & Roper, L. (1994a). Incorporating multiculturalism into student affairs preparation programs: Suggestions from the literature. *Journal of College Student Development, 35,* 46–53.

McEwen, M., & Roper, L. (1994b). Interracial experiences, knowledge, and skills of Master's degree students in graduate programs in student affairs. *Journal of College Student Development, 35,* 81–87.

Merriam, S. (1998). *Qualitative research and case study applications in education.* San Francisco: Jossey-Bass.

Miller, B., & Kantrov, I. (1998). *A guide to facilitating cases in education.* Portsmouth, NH: Heinemann.

National Center for Education Statistics. (1993). *Profile of undergraduate students in U.S. postsecondary institutions: 1989–1990.* Washington, DC: U.S. Department of Education.

National Center for Education Statistics. (2002). *Profile of undergraduate students in*

U.S. postsecondary institutions: 1999–2000. Washington, DC: U.S. Department of Education.

Pope, R., & Reynolds, A. (1997). Student affairs core competencies: Integrating multicultural awareness, knowledge, and skills. *Journal of College Student Development, 38,* 266–277.

Pope, R., Reynolds, A., & Cheatham, H. (1997). American College Personnel Association strategic initiative on multiculturalism: A report and proposal. *Journal of College Student Development, 38,* 62–67.

Robinson, T. L., & Howard-Hamilton, M. F. (2000). *The convergence of race, ethnicity, and gender: Multiple identities counseling.* Columbus, OH: Prentice Hall.

Takaki, R. (1993). *A different mirror: A history of multicultural America.* Boston: Little Brown.

Talbot, D. (1996a). Multiculturalism. In S. R. Komives & D. B. Woodard (Eds.), *Student services: A handbook for the profession* (pp. 380–396). San Francisco: Jossey-Bass.

Talbot, D. (1996b). Master's students' perspectives on their graduate education regarding issues of diversity. *NASPA Journal, 33,* 163–178.

Talbot, D., & Kocarek, C. (1997). Student affairs graduate faculty members' knowledge, comfort, and behaviors regarding issues of diversity. *Journal of College Student Development, 38,* 278–287.

Yin, R. K. (2003). *Applications of case study research.* Thousand Oaks, CA: Sage.

Chapter 2

LESBIAN, GAY, BISEXUAL, AND TRANSGENDER CASE STUDIES

TWO-SPIRIT OR NOT TWO-SPIRIT

SHERI ATKINSON

Description of the Institutional Environment

White Cloud State University (WCSU) is a public institution with approximately 14,500 students, 700 faculty, and 2,100 full- and part-time staff. WCSU is the second largest school in the state, with a student body that represents 48 U.S. states and more than 50 countries. About 14 percent of WCSU's student population consists of international students, primarily at the graduate level. Approximately 10 percent of the total student body consists of students of color and approximately 5 percent are lesbian, gay, bisexual, and transgender (LGBT) students.

Description of the Surrounding Community

The city of White Cloud is located in the middle of a Midwestern state and has a population of approximately 50,000 people, 95 percent of whom are of European American descent. Most people who live in White Cloud are members of either the Roman Catholic or Lutheran churches. The White Cloud community is less supportive of people of color and LGBT people than is the WCSU campus community.

Primary Persons Involved in the Case

- Steve Johnson is an American Indian student. Steve is well known throughout the WCSU community for his activism and willingness to speak out on behalf of students.

- OutLoud! is the LGBT student organization that is in charge of organizing OutProud Week.
- Melissa Hunt is the coordinator of the WCSU Office for LGBT Services and the advisor to OutLoud!

Information Germane to the Case

- Over the past three years, issues related to sexual orientation have been brought to the forefront of campus awareness at WCSU. OutLoud! has been visible and active in a number of different capacities on campus.
- There are 65 American Indian students, seven American Indian faculty, and an American Indian Center on campus.
- "Two-Spirit" is an American Indian concept that means an individual's spirit differs from his or her biological sex. Once called "berdashe" by some Native Americans, Two-Spirit has been used more recently to describe people who take up the traditional roles of the opposite sex and share certain features, such as cross-dressing and homosexuality. In some American Indian nations, a Two-Spirit person is seen as having great spiritual power, bridging the gap between the earthly and spirit worlds. However, not all American Indian tribes have the same definition of Two-Spirit.

The Case

The members of OutLoud! recently planned and executed a regional LGBT conference. It was a great success with over 900 people in attendance. One of the main issues the students took from the conference was the importance of creating an LGBT movement that included the voices of people of color. Several of the conference's keynote speakers, including an American Indian man, were people of color speaking about their experiences within the LGBT community. Throughout the conference, American Indian people used the term "Two-Spirit" to describe their sexual orientation and gender identity.

After the conference, members of OutLoud! began planning OutProud Week, an annual week of events centered around LGBT awareness. The program announcement read: "OutProud Week: A Celebration of Gay, Lesbian, Bisexual, Transgender, Intersex, Two-Spirit, Queer, and Ally Pride!" One of the presentations scheduled for the week was entitled "Two-Spirit: American Indian Concepts of Gender and Sexual Orientation." At a rally prior to OutProud Week's events, Steve Johnson remarked that the inclusion of the term Two-Spirit in OutProud Week's publicity was offensive to American

Indians and was a form of cultural appropriation. Steve demanded that the term Two-Spirit be removed immediately from OutProud Week's events and publicity. Melissa Hunt met with Steve to discuss his concern. During their conversation, Melissa attempted to explain that many WCSU students learned about the term Two-Spirit from an American Indian speaker at the LGBT regional conference. Melissa commented that the speaker said Two-Spirit was used by some American Indians to define themselves. By including this term in OutProud Week's publicity, OutLoud! hoped to demonstrate their commitment to creating a welcoming space for all people.

At the conclusion of their meeting, Steve emphasized that he still believed Two-Spirit was a term placed on American Indians by European Americans. He continued to insist that the name be removed and that this language never be used again. Melissa invited him to attend some of the OutProud Week programs to share information from his perspective. Several days after the meeting with Steve, Melissa began to hear reports that Steve was telling other activists within his circle that LGBT services and OutLoud! were racist organizations.

Discussion Questions

1. What are the main issues in this case from OutLoud!'s perspective? From Steve Johnson's perspective?
2. Was Melissa's response to Steve appropriate? Why or why not?
3. Given the current situation, what should Melissa do to resolve this issue?
4. What roles should other student affairs practitioners or administrators play to create a welcoming atmosphere for LGBT students on campus?
5. Should LGBT student organizations and organizations designed for students of color work together? Why or why not? How?
6. How can student affairs professionals evaluate relationships between LGBT organizations and other student organizations on campus?

Research Activities for Further Exploration

1. Interview an American Indian student and ask about his or her experiences on campus (and also about his or her perceptions of the concept of "Two Spirit").
2. Research the history of LGBT activism on your campus and/or in your local community.
3. Compare the coverage of recent LGBT issues and events by student-run media on your campus with local community coverage. What is conveyed about the climate on campus and in the community for the LGBT students, faculty, and staff?

READING BETWEEN THE LINES

J. Bradley Blankenship

Description of the Institutional Environment

Capital College is a private four-year liberal arts institution with approximately 5,000 undergraduate students. The average incoming first-year student had a 3.4 GPA in high school and scored 1240 on the SAT and/or 27 on the ACT. With respect to ethnicity, 49 percent of the students identify themselves as white or Caucasian, 10 percent identify as African American or black, 6 percent as Hispanic or Latina/Latino, 5 percent as Asian or Pacific Islander, 2 percent as Native American, and 28 percent are international students from more than 150 countries.

Description of the Surrounding Community

Capital College is located in a suburb of Capital City. It is one of eight four-year institutions in the Capital City metropolitan area and is known throughout the area as having the most diverse campus population. Myriad government agencies, corporations, and nonprofit organizations benefit from student interns from the local schools.

Primary Persons Involved in the Case

- Peter Sacks is a high school senior looking at prospective colleges. Though he identifies himself as a gay student, he has not come out to his parents and is not an active member of his high school's Gay-Straight Alliance for fear of rejection and physical harm.
- Lisa Grundy is an admissions representative at Capital College who works with prospective applicants.
- Roger Hamilton is a senior at Capital College and gives tours for the Office of Admissions.

Information Germane to the Case

- Four years ago, a Lesbian, Gay, Bisexual, Transgender, and Ally (LGBTA) Resource Center was established on campus with a full-time staff member to help educate the Capital College campus and community and to provide resources for the LGBT student population.
- Student volunteers serve as tour guides on campus. Selection is based on

a brief interview with the tour guide advisor and the student's enthusiasm for Capital College. Tour guides are required to go through sensitivity training for students with disabilities, students of color, and international students; LGBT issues are not addressed.

The Case

During a recent visit to Capital College, his first-choice school, Peter Sacks attended an information session given by Lisa Grundy. She asked the group of prospective students what was important in a campus community. Peter replied that diversity was a key factor in his decision about which college he would attend and asked about the diversity at Capital College. Lisa gave several examples of how diverse Capital College was with its 150 countries represented and students from all 50 states and U.S. territories. She mentioned the Office of Multicultural Affairs where students of color can go for guidance and listed several cultural and ethnic student groups on campus. Peter wanted to ask questions to better understand how LGBT students were treated on campus but was uncomfortable bringing up the subject with his parents sitting next to him.

Roger Hamilton led Peter's tour of the campus. While on the tour, Peter asked about social activities. Roger spoke about the active nightlife in Capital City and the various coffee shops where Capital students hang out but made a point of telling the group to "stay away from the southwest quadrant of the city. That's where all the gays hang out."

When Peter went home, he searched the admissions literature he had picked up that day to see if there were any references to sexual orientation. He saw photos of students from several ethnic and racial backgrounds as well as a few photos of students who were in wheelchairs, but there was nothing that indicated a gay and lesbian presence on campus. Peter looked for a statement of the college's antiharassment and antidiscrimination policy but could not find it in any of the literature. Feeling isolated and afraid that college would not be any different from high school, Peter got ready for bed. When Peter's mother came in to say goodnight, she noticed that the application to Capital College was in the wastebasket.

Discussion Questions

1. What are some of the issues that Peter Sacks is dealing with in his college search?
2. How well did Lisa Grundy answer Peter's diversity question?
3. What was your reaction to Roger Hamilton's comment about nightlife in Capital City? Do you believe it is important for Roger and other tour

guides to know about LGBT life on campus? If so, discuss how Capital College could educate their tour guides on LGBT issues.

4. What was Peter using to form his assessment of the climate for LGBT students on campus? How else could a student assess the campus climate for LGBT students when looking at colleges?

5. Based on the criteria that Peter used in his assessment and any extra criteria that you may have discussed, how would you personally assess the campus climate for LGBT students at Capital College? At your own college or university?

6. Discuss how Capital College could be more proactive in portraying a LGBT presence on campus. Using your knowledge of identity-development theories, discuss how such proactive visibility can affect a LGBT student's overall development.

Research Activities for Further Exploration

1. Research the terms "heterosexism" and "heterosexual privilege." Discuss situations in the college search and admissions process in which heterosexism may make a prospective student feel isolated.

2. Research the campus climate for LGBT students at your institution. What services are available and how is information about those services disseminated? Interview support staff about the service they provide, the challenges they face, and unmet needs.

3. Research recent trends in college admissions counseling dealing with prospective LGBT students. In addition to a literature search, contact the College Board, the National Association of College Admissions Counselors, and the Gay, Lesbian, Straight Educators Network (GLSEN).

CHARLES HALL

MIKE ESPOSITO

Description of the Institutional Environment

Bellview State University (BSU) is a metropolitan commuter campus of 14,000 students, located in the Northwest. Of those enrolled, 45 percent are male and 55 percent are female; 57 percent are full-time students and 43 percent are part-time students; 57 percent are 24 years old or younger, 32 percent are 25 to 40 years old, and 11 percent are 41 years old and older. At BSU, 3 percent of the students identify themselves as black (non-Hispanic),

1 percent as Native American, 2 percent as Asian/Pacific Islander, 5 percent as Hispanic, and 84 percent as white (non-Hispanic); 5 percent of the students did not specify ethnicity. In-state students comprise 91 percent of the campus population; 2 percent are classified as nonresident aliens.

Description of the Surrounding Community

BSU is located in the city of Bellview, which is the state's population center (190,000) and capital city, a hub of government, business, the arts, health care, industry, and technology. Located along the Bellview River and nestled near the foothills of the Rocky Mountains, the city offers many outdoor activities to local residents.

Primary Persons Involved in the Case

- Terry Pearson is a self-described "full-time drag queen," in that he dresses as a woman at all times. A 20-year-old sophomore, undeclared major, Terry is biologically male and considers himself transgendered but has no plans to undergo gender reassignment surgery.
- Maureen Holt, a friend of Terry's, is an out, activist lesbian sophomore majoring in English. Maureen is the vice president of the Queers and Allies (Q & A) student group. She has lived in Charles Hall throughout her tenure at Bellview State.
- Anna Running Bear is a Native American. Since graduating from BSU two years ago, she has been the Residence Hall Director at Charles Hall.
- Thomas Brooks, Director of Housing, has been at BSU for 17 years in a variety of director-level capacities. He is responsible for the text of many policies at BSU and was instrumental in adding "sexual orientation" to the university's nondiscrimination policy.
- Dr. Diana Nelson, Vice President for Student Affairs, has been at BSU for two years. This is her first vice presidency. Her previous positions have been in auxiliary services, with limited direct interaction with students.

Information Germane to the Case

- BSU has 1,000 on-campus residents living in traditional-age residence halls and family housing. The Charles Complex accommodates 430 residents, most of whom are first- and second-year students. Charles is the newest—and one of the most popular—living spaces on campus. Each suite is divided into two bedrooms with a shared bathroom located between them. Two students are assigned to each bedroom. These suites have modular furniture and are the largest on campus.

- BSU has a nondiscrimination policy inclusive of sexual orientation, but not gender identity or perceived gender.

The Case

Terry Pearson came to BSU as a traditional-age first-year student and was assigned to Charles Residence Hall. Through his first year, Terry faced constant harassment and threats of physical violence from his suitemates. On occasion, one of his suitemates would bang on the bathroom door leading from the bathroom to Terry's room, demanding to be let in to see "the freak." Terry's roommate, had no problems with Terry and the two were friends.

Terry filed official complaints with Anna Running Bear, who immediately commenced judicial proceedings, but the penalties dispensed were minor and did little to end the situation. In the spring, when it came time to reapply for housing, Terry and his friend, Maureen Holt, agreed that Terry should move to Maureen's room. They listed each other as preferred roommates on their housing applications. Knowing the stress Terry had endured and how little judicial proceedings had helped, Anna was very much in favor of this move.

Thomas Brooks was open to the proposal. However, on the application for housing, Terry indicated that his gender was male. Anna informed Thomas that Terry was not planning to undergo gender reassignment, which left Thomas in a quandary. Under BSU policy, a male cannot live in a female student's suite in a traditional-age hall. Thomas discussed the issue with Diana Nelson, who denied the request on these grounds:

- Though appearing as a woman, Terry was a man and had declared himself a man on his application.
- There were no medical procedures underway to reassign Terry's gender.
- The needs of the suitemates also must be taken into consideration. What would the ramifications be to BSU if parents discovered that their daughter was living with a man?
- The political realities of living in the capital of a conservative state also must be considered. With the state capitol building less than a mile away, what would be the ramifications for the entire university if the state legislature became aware of the situation?

With the vice president's support, Thomas denied Terry's request and met with Terry to explain the decision. He offered Terry his choice of single rooms in another residence hall on campus, but Terry was unable to pay extra for a single room. Terry's grades, though passing, prevented him from moving into the residence hall for honors students. As a result, Terry was forced to stay in his current room in Charles Hall. Before the end of the fall semester, Terry left BSU.

Discussion Questions

1. How should gender reassignment factor into Diana Nelson's decision?
2. Should the surrounding community's conservative nature have factored into the decision not to place Terry with Maureen? Explain your answer in detail.
3. How are transgender issues similar to and different from racial issues?
4. What developmental theories could be helpful to Anna Running Bear and Thomas Brooks in this case? Explain how Anna and Thomas could apply those theories.
5. What steps could the administrators (e.g., Director of Housing, Vice President of Student Affairs) have taken once the clerical error was discovered?
6. What responsibility, if any, does the university have to retain transgender students?

Research Activities for Further Exploration

1. Research the policies other colleges and universities have instituted regarding transgender individuals.
2. What policies and procedures could an institution develop to make its environment more welcoming to transgender individuals? Draft a proposal outlining how various areas of a campus community (academic, housing, health center, student union, etc.) can demonstrate support.
3. Develop an educational presentation, lecture, or workshop that can be used to train prospective and current Resident Assistants to work with transgender students.

IS IT LOVE OR IS IT HATE?

ANGELA M. COTTRELL

Description of the Institutional Environment

Ella University (EU) is a four-year public research institution. Approximately 28,000 students attend this predominantly white institution in the Midwest. Lesbian, gay, bisexual, and transgender (LGBT) students account for a very small minority on the campus but are supported through the Dean of Students Office and several student organizations.

Description of the Surrounding Community

Ella University accounts for over half of the population of Brodhead, a midsize city with approximately 50,000 residents. Brodhead is known for being an educated community that is very supportive of Ella University and its athletic program. In fact, many Brodhead residents are EU alumni and provide generous financial donations.

Primary Persons Involved in the Case

- Christopher Jamison is the staff advisor for the Lesbian, Gay, Bisexual, and Transgender Ally Alliance (LGBTAA). Christopher also works as coordinator of the Academic Success Center on campus.
- Brandon Daniels is a senior accounting major and student president of LGBTAA.
- Peter Westfall is the current Dean of Students and is Christopher's supervisor.
- Mary Boston is a political science major and the student president of the Conservative Coalition on campus.

Information Germane to the Case

- LGBT programs are supported through Lesbian, Gay, Bisexual, and Transgender Student Services (LGBTSS), one office under the Dean of Students. Although LGBT programs are continuing to increase in numbers, many students know very little about the LGBT population on campus.
- The LGBTAA is supported by the LGBTSS. As a student-run organization, the LGBTAA has been active in speaker programs, educating the EU community for the past five years. Overall, there is a core group of 50 students that actively participate in LGBTAA functions, and Christopher Jamison and Brandon Daniels work together to advise the organization. The LGBTAA has been a victim of hate email and letters, and their student office workspace has been vandalized in the past.

The Case

Along with approximately 20 student members of the LGBTAA, Christopher Jamison and Brandon Daniels are coordinating various activities during National Coming Out Week on campus. Activities include an open house of the Dean of Students Offices, guest speakers, a fundraiser dance for the local Red Cross, and a massive poster campaign to show support for all students, regardless of sexual orientation.

Three different posters have been designed: The first has two males kissing, the second has two females kissing, and the third has a male and a female kissing. Students from other universities were photographed in order to protect EU students from being outed. All posters include the statement, "Everyone has the right to love." Posters are to be circulated in every classroom building on public bulletin boards. Poster locations are written down so that they may be removed by the LGBTAA after the week is over.

On Sunday evening, after distributing 1,000 posters on campus, Brandon began to receive numerous disturbing phone calls demanding that the posters be taken down or that they would be torn down. The anonymous callers also threatened to harm him. Scared and angry, Brandon called Christopher on Monday morning to explain the harassing phone calls. Christopher asked if Brandon had called the Department of Public Safety. Brandon had not because he did not know what they could do since the caller identification was blocked. Christopher asked if Brandon had responded to any of the callers, but Brandon said he always hung up on them. After talking with Brandon, Christopher concluded that this was beyond his reach as the LGBTAA advisor, and decided to involve Peter Westfall.

Christopher and Peter met on Tuesday morning to discuss the phone calls Brandon had been receiving as well as the overall concern for the LGBTAA. Peter contacted the Department of Public Safety to notify them of the calls Brandon has been receiving and to alert them to watch for arguments or vandalism on campus. Peter then contacted EU's president to inform her of the campus hostility. After conversing with the president, Peter decided that the best course of action is to let the situation die down on its own.

By Wednesday morning, members of the LGBTAA assessed that approximately half of the 1,000 posters have been torn down, ripped up, burned, or vandalized. Openly gay students were being ridiculed and harassed by other students for desecrating their campus with the posters.

In the Ella Daily, there has been massive outpouring in the opinion column concerning the LGBTAA posters. Some opinions are in support of the LGBTAA, stating that they are saddened by such intolerance. On the other hand, Mary Boston wrote, "Who wants to see such filth on our public bulletin boards? I'm glad that those posters are being torn down. I don't flaunt my heterosexuality at you!" On Thursday evening, Christopher and Brandon met with other LGBTAA students and decided to take down all of the vandalized posters and place them in a display case at the student union. They created a background stating, "This is what hate looks like." The LGBTAA students are threatening to file each act of vandalism as a hate crime. Peter is commanded by the president to ease the tension on campus before things get out of hand.

Discussion Questions

1. What are the main issues in this case?
2. What are Peter Westfall's responsibilities in this case?
3. Do you think these events presented in this case would be similar if the LGBTAA posters had displayed only the statement, "Everyone has the right to love" without any of the photographs?
4. How could Christopher Jamison respond to Mary Boston's statements?
5. How can the university prevent future acts of vandalism and hate?
6. What other kinds of programming can the LGBTAA provide to educate students about differences in sexual orientation and gender?

Research Activities for Further Exploration

1. Research your institution's position on hate speech and hate crimes. Include First Amendment rights in your analysis.
2. Investigate one recent report of hate speech and/or other hate crimes on your campus (or at institutions in your state) and report your findings.
3. Interview a representative of the public safety department on your campus regarding hate crime statistics, the department's investigative process, and recommendations for students who are victims of such crimes. How is this information disseminated?

WHAT'S HE DOING IN HERE?

Linda McCarthy

Description of the Institutional Environment

State University (SU) is the flagship campus of a statewide university system in a northeastern state. SU is a land-grant school that serves approximately 18,000 undergraduate and 5,200 graduate students. First- and second-year students, with a few exceptions, are required to live on campus. Transfer students enroll in sizable numbers.

Description of the Surrounding Community

SU is located in a small town, and there are several other colleges in the surrounding towns. Since it is overwhelmingly a college area, the region is known as a bastion of liberal and progressive thinking. A local transgender activist network formed two years ago. Almost every year, at one college or another, a transgender conference brings a nationally known transgender speaker to campus.

Primary Persons Involved in the Case

- Max Perry is a 19-year-old student who has just transferred to SU from a local community college. Max was born female-bodied, but currently appears and passes as a young man. At age 15, he began asking people to call him Max instead of his given feminine name, and he "came out" as transgender to his family and to a few friends at age 18. Although Max identifies as male, he has not made any physical changes to his body and therefore was placed on the women's floor of Norman Hall.
- Sarah Moheban is a first-year student majoring in chemistry. She lives in Norman Hall.
- Terry Jones is a second-year male student on the floor above Max's.
- Brittany Walker is the floor's Resident Assistant (RA). This is Brittany's second year as an RA.
- Michael Blau, an SU graduate, has been the Resident Director of Norman Hall for three years.
- Susan Means has been SU's Director of Housing for six years. Susan began working in housing as an RA when she was an undergraduate.
- Shannon Dunn has just arrived at SU as the new Vice President for Student Affairs.

Information Germane to the Case

- "Transgender" is an umbrella term encompassing those who transgress gender categories or otherwise feel that the category of male or female does not fit them. Transgender people have gained increasing recognition and visibility in the last ten years. As of 2002, six colleges and universities have proactively adopted transgender-inclusive nondiscrimination policies, and several others are bound by existing nondiscrimination laws covering transgender in that state. Two states have added gender identity to existing students' rights laws.
- Norman Hall houses 148 first- and second-year students on alternating gendered floors.

The Case

Prior to Max Perry's arrival in September, Michael Blau, the Norman Hall RD, met with Director of Housing Susan Means to discuss Max's situation. Susan expressed her view that since Max has a female body, he should use the women's bathroom. Michael disagreed, and maintained that Max should be able to use whatever bathroom felt comfortable for him. In the end, Michael agreed to support Susan's decision that Max use the women's bathroom. As an RA, Brittany was apprised of Max's situation and told to encourage him to use the women's bathroom.

For the first few weeks of school, Max used the women's bathroom on his floor. However, he became increasingly uncomfortable with the women's reactions when he entered the bathroom. It became especially clear that he was making the other women uncomfortable when Sarah refused to use the same bathroom as Max, even when he was not there. Instead, Sarah made a point of using the next nearest women's bathroom, which was two floors up. Sarah also requested a room change, although she wanted to stay in the hall to be near her friends.

Max decided to use the men's bathroom on the floor above his. At first no one seemed to notice his comings and goings, but one day Terry confronted Max and started a physical altercation, calling him a "freak." Since then, Max no longer feels safe in his residence hall, and uses the single-stall bathroom in the dining commons whenever he can. He showers late at night or very early in the morning in the women's bathroom, so as to reduce the other students' discomfort. Brittany feels that although she does not understand—and is slightly uncomfortable with—Max's identity, she wants to be an ally to him.

Max encountered similar problems when he attempted to use the locker room at the campus gym. After working out, he typically heads back to his room rather than shower in the women's locker room. Occasionally, if he works out early in the morning, he showers at the gym, but feels very uncomfortable doing so. Max would prefer to use the men's locker room, but is somewhat fearful for his safety. In the buildings where Max attends classes, there are no single-stall bathrooms. Max sometimes walks ten minutes back to the dining commons between classes in order to use the bathroom there. On Tuesdays and Thursdays, Max does not have time between classes to get back to the dining commons, so he often skips his last class in order to get back to use the bathroom.

About midsemester, Brittany talked with Max about his experiences on campus. Max expressed that he felt uncomfortable on a women's floor and that he would rather live on a mixed-gender floor. Max also shared that he was considering dropping out of SU because of the stress associated with living on campus. Brittany encouraged Max to explore other options, such as moving off campus, to another residence hall, or to the "Pride" floor.

Out of concern for Max, Brittany met with Michael, and together they requested a meeting with Susan Means and Shannon Dunn. Dr. Dunn expressed the view that since gender identity is not covered under the campus discrimination policy, Max's situation is a housing concern, which must be dealt with by Michael and Susan. Susan feels that since Max is encountering problems at the gym and during classes, as well as within the residence hall, the issue should be addressed as a campus-wide concern. The meeting concluded without any resolution.

Discussion Questions

1. Taking the perspective of each person, describe the issues involved in this situation.
2. Using identity and/or developmental theories, explain what developmental issues may be affecting the reactions of Sarah and Terry.
3. If you were Michael Blau, how would you advise Brittany to educate herself as well as the residents of her floor about transgender issues?
4. As the RD, in what ways could you advocate for Max?
5. What do you think could be done campus-wide in order to respond better to this situation?
6. How might everyone benefit from campus-wide changes that might occur as a result of this dilemma?

Research Activities for Further Exploration

1. Research the different identities that fall under the transgender "umbrella."
2. Research the discrimination policies in your local community and in your state. To what extent is gender identity or gender presentation among the protected identities?
3. Go to an admissions information session on your campus and take a prospective student tour. Assess to what extent LGBT students are included as part of your admissions office's definition of diversity.

THE COMIC BOOK

JOHN WESLEY LOWERY

Description of the Institutional Environment

Jefferson University (JU) is a private four-year research university. The undergraduate student enrollment is approximately 6,000, with a graduate student enrollment of almost equal size. Almost 90 percent of JU's undergraduate students come from outside the state in which the university is located and more than 50 percent live more than 500 miles away from the campus. Approximately 25 percent of the student body is identified as multicultural or international students. JU is consistently ranked as one of the top 25 universities in the country.

Description of the Surrounding Community

JU is located in one of the largest urban centers in the Midwest. The university's main campus is located on the edge of the city and the medical school is located several miles away in the city.

Primary Persons Involved in the Case

- James Miller is a senior art major at Jefferson University.
- Luke Dunn is a sophomore student and is an active member of the Lesbian, Gay, Bisexual, and Transgender (LGBT) Students and Allies, a recognized student group at Jefferson University. Luke also is a student worker in the Student Life suite.
- Michelle Reeve is a senior and president of the LGBT Students and Allies.
- Ted Thomas has been the Director of Judicial Programs at JU for two years.

Information Germane to the Case

- The LGBT Students and Allies student group has been active at JU for more than 10 years.
- The university began to develop a Safe Zone program for LGBT students during the spring semester of the previous academic year and the program has expanded quickly.
- The LGBT Students and Allies student group and others on campus also have lobbied to expand JU's nondiscrimination policy to include sexual orientation.

The Case

In September of each year, the Office of Student Activities sponsors a Student Activities Fair in the main lobby area of the student union. As in past years, the LGBT Students and Allies student group participated in the Student Activities Fair. Approximately halfway through the fair, Michelle Reeve and Luke Dunn were sitting at the LGBT Students and Allies' table when a student walked through the lobby and tossed several copies of a comic book entitled *Righteous Fury* onto the table without comment. Michelle and Luke became very upset when they began to look at the comic book in which the main character attacks and kills scores of people—many of whom are killed because they are gay or lesbian. Gays and lesbians were not the only target of the "righteous fury"; members of other groups including African Americans also were attacked and killed.

The following day a cover story appeared in JU's student newspaper about the incident. The article indicated that James Miller had prepared *Righteous Fury* for an independent study art course the previous semester. James was quoted as saying that he had thrown the comic book onto the group's table because "those homosexuals keep throwing away the copies of *Righteous Fury*" that he has left around campus at various locations. Quotes attributed to James in the student newspaper also indicate that he believes that homosexuality is clearly prohibited by the Bible and is a sin against God and nature.

The day after the Student Activities Fair, Luke Dunn came into the Student Life suite for work and stopped by Ted Thomas' office to talk about the previous evening's incident. Luke is concerned for his safety after reading *Righteous Fury,* but is unsure what action he wants to take at this time.

Michelle Reeve also left a message for Ted that day indicating that she wished to meet with him to file a complaint under the student judicial system against James Miller for his homophobic threat against her and the entire LGBT community at JU. The judicial code prohibits "physical abuse of any person, or other conduct which harasses, or threatens or endangers the safety or health of, any member of the University community or visitor to the University." Michelle also was quoted in the student newspaper observing, "This incident is just more proof that JU is a hostile environment for LGBT persons. JU must include sexual orientation in its nondiscrimination policy." In the article, Michelle also admitted that she and several other members of the LGBT Students and Allies group had been throwing away the copies of *Righteous Fury* that had been left around campus at various locations.

After reading the paper, James Miller also contacted Ted Thomas indicating that he wished to file charges under the student judicial code against Michelle Reeve and the other students for the theft and destruction of copies of *Righteous Fury.* The judicial code prohibits "theft, attempted theft, unauthorized taking or use of any public or private property." The code also prohibits "deliberate destruction of, damage to, malicious use of, or abuse of any public or private property."

Discussion Questions

1. Identify the issues or problems presented in this case from the perspective of (a) James Miller, (b) Luke Dunn and/or Michelle Reeve, and (c) Ted Thomas.
2. Was Michelle Reeve's comment about this incident to the student newspaper appropriate? Does there appear to be a connection between this incident and the effort to have sexual orientation added to Jefferson University's nondiscrimination policy?
3. How could you design interventions to address concerns about homophobia and increase understanding about LGBT persons on campus?
4. What are JU's legal obligations to protect James Miller's freedom of speech? What are the legal obligations to Luke Dunn and Michelle Reeve in response to their fears for their safety?
5. Luke Dunn has decided to speak with Ted Thomas about the incident the previous evening because they know each other through Luke's work-study job in the Student Life suite where Ted's office is located. Ted also is participating in the university's new Safe Zone program. Create a mock dialogue between Luke and Ted based upon your understanding of the case.
6. Given your knowledge of student development theory, how would you evaluate the development of the students involved in this case? What student development theories help you understand these students better?

Research Activities for Further Exploration

1. If your institution has a LGBT Students and Allies student group, and if the meetings generally are open, attend a meeting and write a reflection paper about the experience.
2. Is there a history of homophobic incidents at your institution? How has the community responded?
3. Does your institution include sexual orientation in its nondiscrimination policy? If so, what led to this change in the policy? If not, are there calls for the policy to be expanded? Is this a common position at institutions in your state?

LESBIAN, GAY, BISEXUAL, AND TRANSGENDER ISSUES ON CAMPUS

RONNI SANLO

Description of the Institutional Environment

Harvey University is a Research I institution with 37,000 students, 7,500 of whom live in the residence halls. Harvey prohibits discrimination based on sexual orientation and gender identity. In addition to all of the usual student affairs departments, Harvey has a large professionally staffed Lesbian, Gay, Bisexual, and Transgender (LGBT) Center and 12 LGBT student organizations are registered with student government. In general, students at Harvey have a 3.4 GPA in high school with an average score of 1386 on the SAT. The student body is 34 percent white, 37 percent Asian/Pacific Islander, and the remaining 29 percent is everyone else; more than half of the students (52%) are female.

Description of the Surrounding Community

Harvey is situated in a village environment within a large major metropolitan area. The adjacent community is upscale and urban in nature. In fact, the poshest zip codes in the state surround the institution. The village also is trendy and expensive. Few students are able to afford to live very close to campus, so most students are commuters. Parking is one of Harvey's biggest problems for students, faculty, and staff alike. While much of the major metropolitan area is extremely diverse, the area surrounding the institution is primarily white.

Primary Persons Involved in the Case

• Peg Maly is a second-year Latina student.
• Dr. Berit Sauls-Muncy is the Vice President for Student Services.
• Dr. Erik Laurens is the Director of Residential Life.
• Dr. Sara Gato is the Director of Counseling and Psychological Services.
• Dr. Elizabeth Calista is the Director of the LGBT Center.

Information Germane to the Case

• It was October 11th, National Coming Out Day. The campus LGBT organizations held a rally and resource fair on campus, brought a nationally known transgender speaker to campus, and posted a full-page ad in the school's newspaper, *The Daily Student*. The LGBT community at

Harvey was highly visible throughout the campus. The following situation occurred on October 12th.

The Case

Peg Maly, an openly lesbian student, lives in the residence hall. While walking to class the day after National Coming Out Day, she and her friends noticed a chalking on the sidewalk on campus that read "Peg is a dyke." Peg shrugged it off and went to class. Her friends, however, were furious and called Vice President Berit Sauls-Muncy to complain. Dr. Sauls-Muncy told the students that she was surprised that something like this could happen on their campus. She called Dr. Erik Laurens, the director of Residential Life, and Dr. Sara Gato, the director of the Counseling Center, both of whom personally visited Peg when she returned to her room. Peg was surprised to see these administrators. She said, "It's really no big deal. This stuff doesn't bother me anymore. I get called names on campus pretty regularly. It hurts every time, but you get used to it." She said she was more annoyed and embarrassed with the attention of the student affairs staff.

Peg figured that nothing would be done so why bother reporting it? It's happened so often since she's been on campus, and she's heard the same complaint from other LGBT students. Even though Peg is a frequent visitor to the campus LGBT Center, she simply never mentioned the incidents to the director, Elizabeth Calista. The student affairs professionals felt frustrated in their desire to do the right thing, but they understood that Peg did not want their assistance. Rather than drop the issue, however, they decide that they must appropriately deal with it. The Vice President, the director of Residential Life, and the Counseling Center director met to determine their course of action. They asked Dr. Calista of the LGBT Center to meet with them. Collectively, they agreed to have the chalking—and any future detrimental chalking directed toward any individual or group—immediately removed. Next, they created an ad to publish in the school newspaper saying that harassment and acts of hate are not part of the institution's culture and will not be tolerated. The ad stated that all are welcome at this institution regardless of the personal characteristics with which each person comes to campus. The ad indicated that whatever one's opinion might be, one may not take away the freedom of anyone else on campus.

The discussion then turned to the effects of intimidation. While they knew that the chalking was directed personally at Peg, it served to intimidate other LGBT students. Dr. Calista informed them that the LGBT population was less likely than any other to report acts of harassment. The group also discussed the following questions: Were there other incidents with which they were not familiar? Had other students experienced similar targeting? Was that targeting limited to the LGBT population? What could be done from a broader perspective beyond just issuing an admonishment in the school paper?

The administrators asked Dr. Calista about backlash. She explained that backlash nearly always occurs in a stealth manner, such as chalking, while open harassment and violence have their own sets of characteristics.

Dr. Calista also explained that most anti-LGBT behavior is more directly related to gender identity than to sexual orientation. The effeminate-appearing male or masculine-appearing female is far more often the target of anti-gay behaviors than is the lesbian or gay person who may be more androgynous or gender "normal" in appearance. In addition, on most campuses, the words "that's so gay," "faggot," and "dyke" are the most powerful negative terms one can use. The difference is in the reception of these words. If a straight male is called a faggot, he understands that this is the worst term he could be called, is angry that he was the recipient, and gets over it. A gay or lesbian person like Peg internalizes the epithet, stacks it up along side all the others he or she has heard over time, and allows the word to fester within an already deep and painful place.

Dr. Sauls-Muncy, Dr. Laurens, Dr. Gato, and Dr. Calista agreed that there was a larger institutional issue at hand. They agreed that a campus climate study must be done to determine the comfort level of LGBT students as well as LGBT faculty and staff, even though nearly all seem to be invisible. In addition, they wondered if the campus was as uncomfortable for people of color and others as well. The plan of action on which they decided was:

- The student affairs research office would collaborate with the school of education to conduct a climate study.
- The LGBT Center and other student affairs staff would host a mandatory educational presentation to all staff regarding sexual orientation and gender identity.
- Student affairs staff would collaborate with the LGBT Center and campus police to create an anonymous reporting website at which hate incidents as well as hate crimes could easily be reported and documented, and would create a publicity campaign campus-wide to advertise the website.
- All documents from any student affairs department would use inclusive language regarding sexual orientation and gender identity.
- Anyone found responsible for anti-LGBT behavior on campus would be adjudicated to the director of the LGBT Center for 40 hours of community service.

The results of their publicized plan of action were twofold. First, it gave them a broad range of data with which to define and create necessary opportunities for growth both for staff as well as for students. Second, it provided an immediate message to the LGBT student population and others that each student mattered at this institution, and that regardless of whether or not there is an identified victim or an identified event, student affairs professionals work as advocates for every student on campus.

Discussion Questions

1. When did you first hear antigay epithets? From whom? What were they? How do you think such words affect LGBT people? Think about a time when someone made fun of or bullied you, or perhaps when you made fun of someone who was different from yourself? What was that like for you?
2. Why should college and university campuses welcome LGBT people? How are LGBT students welcomed on your campus? How does your student affairs division accept or silence people who are not of the dominant culture? How could your student affairs division and your campus be more welcoming and inclusive of LGBT people?
3. What are the qualities of an ally? Why would being an ally both for colleagues and students be important on your campus? How might you become an ally for those colleagues and students who are different from yourself?
4. How would you address alumni, parents, or on-campus entities that do not want LGBT issues addressed in student affairs or on your campus?
5. How might student affairs become a profession where LGBT people are valued as staff? What changes would need to occur on your campus?
6. How might your Student Affairs administrators ensure that LGBT issues are taken seriously on your campus?

Research Activities for Further Exploration

1. Conduct research on your campus to determine how students and student affairs staff experience the climate of the campus for welcome and inclusion of LGBT students.
2. Research ways in which your campus could develop a website for reporting hate crimes and hate incidents.
3. Explore what your institution might do to create an education program for your student affairs staff so that they have a better understanding of sexual orientation and gender identity issues on campus.

THE WEB PAGE

Tony W. Cawthon & Pamela A. Havice

Description of the Institutional Environment

Discover University is a four-year public land-grant institution. Approximately 10,000 students attend this rural school. The composition of the student body is 85 percent white, 10 percent African American, 5 percent other (Latino, Asian, and American Indian). Despite the appearance of a homogeneous population at this institution, the university is committed to creating a multicultural campus. The majority of students at Discover University are first-generation college students from blue-collar families in the region. For most of these students, their religious heritage has played an important part in their development.

Description of the Surrounding Community

Discover University is located in a rural setting in the Southeast. The university is central to the economic development of the area, since many community residents work there. This community of 20,000 has a long history of supporting multicultural and diversity initiatives in the arts, education, and industry. The university and the community have excellent Town-Gown relationships as evident by their collaboration in creating a technologically advanced community and university environment.

Primary Persons Involved in the Case

- Alice Brown is the president of the Students for a Conservative Campus (SCC). She also is actively involved in several conservative political and religious organizations.
- Tim Lewis, a 21-year old gay male, is the president of the Coalition of Lesbian, Gay, Bisexual, and Transgender Students (CLGBT). Tim is a senior who is very comfortable with his homosexuality and serves as a role model for other students.
- Karen Jones is a Resident Hall Director of Hastings Hall, a coeducational facility that houses mostly upper-division students.
- Mark Peyton is the Chief Judicial Officer at Discover University. He oversees the entire judicial process for the campus, including individual and organizational violations. Mark reports directly to Denise Warren.
- Denise Warren has been the Dean of Students at Discover University for the past year. She was hired with the charge to increase diversity enrollment and to maintain the university's commitment to multicultural issues.

Information Germane to the Case

- The campus has been open to diversity issues of race, ethnicity, gender, but not to LGBT issues. While the SCC has no difficulty finding a faculty adviser, the CLGBT organization has struggled as the university has only two openly gay and lesbian faculty. The CLGBT officers are highly visible on campus, but most of the general members of the CLGBT are not "out" or open about their sexual orientation.
- The university has created a wireless environment and the student population is highly knowledgeable about the use of computer technology. The university has struggled with developing a campus computer-use policy. Currently, they follow their university code of conduct for behavioral violations. A review of judicial violations in the past three years reveals that most of these violations involve harassment issues.
- The membership in the SCC and CLGBT organizations is quite small compared to other organizations on campus.
- All enrolled students are required to live on campus. For graduation, students must participate in a certain number of campus activities emphasizing multicultural issues.

The Case

Karen Jones is proud of the atmosphere she has created in Hastings Hall. She has worked hard to create a living environment where all students feel supported and comfortable sharing their views. However, over the weekend an incident occurred between two residents who are in leadership positions. This conflict has her questioning how effective she has been in creating this atmosphere. On Monday morning, Karen called Mark Peyton to notify him that he would be receiving an incident report regarding an altercation between Tim Lewis and Alice Brown.

For the past year and a half Tim has served as president of the CLGBT organization. He is proud of the fact that this organization has created a supportive environment for LGBT students and their allies. Equally proud of her work, Alice Brown has served the SCC in different capacities for the last three years.

Approximately two weeks ago, while researching an advanced social psychology paper, Tim discovered some disturbing information. On the SCC website was a link to a web page of photographs identifying CLGBT members. Of equal concern was a list of students on campus who were suspected of being LGBT. Additionally, the following day, students, faculty, and staff arrived on campus to find numerous messages written on campus sidewalks. On many of these sidewalks, phrases such as "homosexuality equals AIDS" have suddenly appeared.

Tim and other CLGBT executive board members decided to attend the next SCC meeting to confront the members about the links on the SCC web page. At the meeting, emotions escalated and Tim and Alice got into an altercation. Specifically, Alice shared that she felt verbally and physically threatened as Tim came toward her, yelled at her, towered over her, stuck his finger in her face and berated her, and bumped up against her. Tim, on the other hand, indicated he was simply disagreeing and debating with Alice over the issues.

Dean Warren has called you to express her concern about this incident. All morning the advisors of these organizations as well as the parents of several students have been calling her office. She would like this situation to be resolved quickly by asking you to shut down the website immediately. She believes that shutting down the website will send a message to the campus community that this type of behavior is not acceptable at Discover University.

Discussion Questions

1. What are the judicial issues in this case? What actions would need to be taken to immediately assist the students involved?
2. Was it appropriate for Tim and the other executive board members of CLGBT to confront the SCC? Justify your response.
3. What challenges does the increased use of technology pose for the campus as it maintains its commitment to multiculturalism? For example, do students have the right to post what they want on a university website? Does the university have responsibility for this site? As part of your answer, discuss how the university would proceed with creating a computer-use policy.
4. As Discover University is committed to creating a multicultural campus, does the university have a responsibility to allow all groups to express their thoughts, opinions, and viewpoints? Set up a debate demonstrating your knowledge of the implications of allowing all parties to express their viewpoints.
5. Based on your knowledge of student development theory, what interventions and strategies would you recommend in working with Alice Brown, Tim Lewis, the SCC, the CLGBT, and those students who were identified on the web page as "suspected" LGBT students? Provide an outline of the appropriate response or approach for each of the following people: Karen Jones (the RD), Mark Peyton (the Chief Judicial Officer), and Denise Warren (the Dean of Students). In your answer, discuss what action each person needs to take immediately to handle the crises and what long-term

actions they need to take in working with these students and organizations.

6. How would you involve other entities on campus (e.g., the office of Multicultural Affairs, organizational advisors, housing, and the informational technology staff) to evaluate and address the issues raised in this case study? Take into consideration current campus policies, culture, and constituent groups.

Research Activities for Further Exploration

1. Conduct focus groups with the various constituents to explore the campus environment as related to LGBT students. Utilize the qualitative data collected from the focus groups to develop a questionnaire to identify the student population's perception and knowledge of LGBT issues. Compile data from the focus groups and from the questionnaire into a report that will be shared and discussed with various campus leaders (e.g., various student organizations, the student affairs staff, the faculty senate, the president's cabinet).

2. Conduct interviews with the leadership of the eight largest student organizations on your campus. Have these campus leaders describe their organization and ways they can create a more supportive environment for LGBT students, thus meeting the university's commitment to a multicultural campus. Report these findings and discuss their significance.

3. Research the identity development models pertaining to LGBT individuals. Write a paper focused on how the models identified in the research literature assist student affairs professionals in working with LGBT students.

THE NEW VICE PRESIDENT'S CHALLENGE

Arthur Sandeen

Description of the Institutional Environment

Oaktree University is a large public institution offering a wide array of undergraduate, graduate, and professional degree programs. The enrollment is 36,000, and the institution is one of the most selective public universities in the country. While the majority of students are white, almost 35 percent of the students are African American, Asian American, or Hispanic American.

Description of the Surrounding Community

Oaktree University is located in a southwestern city of about 500,000 residents. The campus is primarily residential, and most of the students are enrolled on a full-time basis. The city is supportive of the university, but it is a vibrant industrial, medical, and cultural center on its own. Its population is well educated, and the city is viewed as quite liberal within a state known for its political conservatism.

Primary Persons Involved in the Case

- Mary Doe has been the Vice President for Student Affairs at Oaktree for six months.
- Frank Smith is the President of Oaktree University.
- Bill Jones is the Chair of the Oaktree University Board of Trustees.
- Joe Johnson is the student Chair of the Lesbian, Gay, Bisexual, and Transgender (LGBT) organization at Oaktree University.

Information Germane to the Case

- Students and faculty at Oaktree are tolerant but not openly supportive of LGBT students. The LGBT student organization is registered with Student Government, but has had difficulty acquiring funding to support its activities. Most of the LGBT students at Oaktree feel isolated, rejected, and insecure.
- Oaktree's official antidiscrimination policy does not include sexual orientation, and efforts to change this have been consistently rebuffed in the state legislature.

The Case

The LGBT student organization, led by its student Chair, Joe Johnson, is seeking more support on the Oaktree campus. Specifically, the LGBT student group is demanding that the university establish an office within the student affairs division that is staffed with professionals who can meet their academic, personal, and social needs. The LGBT student organization has presented a comprehensive report to Mary Doe and Frank Smith, describing their student experiences at Oaktree. The organization reminded them that similar professional offices exist at comparable universities, and that there have been three professionally staffed offices at Oaktree for several years dedicated to the needs of African American, Asian American, and Hispanic American students.

Vice President Doe has had extensive experience at three other universities where substantial financial, policy, and staffing commitments were made to LGBT students, faculty, and staff. She is determined to support the LGBT students at Oaktree but knows there is a climate and a history at the institution that is sometimes hostile, and most often silent on this issue. President Smith has been in his position at Oaktree for seven years. He is a distinguished chemist, and is widely respected on campus and in the state for his commitment to academic excellence, fairness, and civility. While President Smith is privately supportive of LGBT students, faculty, and staff, he has not spoken publicly on this issue, as he knows the Chair of the Board of Trustees, Bill Jones, and most of the other board members are not supportive, and do not want any public discussion of this issue. They are fearful that Oaktree University will lose public support from the state legislature if they take any actions that might be considered supportive of LGBT issues.

Mary Doe knows this is a volatile issue for Oaktree, for her president, for the board, and for her own future as a vice president. She also knows the strong and sincere feelings of the LGBT students and has empathy for their feelings of isolation, rejection, and insecurity. Finally, since the LGBT student organization has decided to make its report and recommendations public in a few days, there will be a lot of publicity and public discussion in the media no matter what the president and board do.

Discussion Questions

1. Should Vice President Doe assure the LGBT student organization that it has her support?
2. How can Vice President Doe help President Smith resolve this issue without creating a major problem for him and for the university?
3. Recently, Vice President Doe created a committee on student affairs consisting of faculty members and student affairs professionals. How could this committee be of help in resolving the issue?
4. How can Vice President Doe, with the president's support, help to inform and educate the Board of Trustees' Chair, Bill Jones, and other board members about LGBT issues?
5. What should Vice President Doe do if Smith and Jones order her to reject the LGBT report and inform the students that Oaktree University will not support any of their demands?
6. What alternative forms of institutional commitment to LBGT students might Vice President Doe suggest if she realizes that there is no chance of the students' proposal being accepted?

Research Activities for Further Exploration

1. Review the policies and support services for LGBT students at similar public universities to determine the scope of these programs.
2. Contact selected student affairs vice presidents to learn how they were able to bring about change and improved services for LGBT students.
3. Contact the Association of Governing Boards and learn about the various LGBT education programs they conduct for members of governing boards.

Chapter 3

RACE AND ETHNICITY CASE STUDIES

CAMPUS, COMMUNITY, AND CONFLICT

WILLIE J. HEGGINS, III

Description of the Institutional Environment

Belmont University is a four-year public research university located in a rural college town. Approximately 19,000 students attend this predominantly white institution. The racial demographics of the university are as follows: 75 percent white, 2 percent American Indian, 4 percent African American, 4 percent Hispanic, 6 percent Asian American/Pacific Islander, and 9 percent unreported racial identity. The average SAT scores of incoming first-year students are about 1100 with an average GPA of 3.5.

Description of the Surrounding Community

Belmont University is a symbol of strength for Dewey County, which is located in a rural town in the Northwest with approximately 35,000 residents. The institution provides about 16 percent of the town's employment. The community environment is supportive of and dependent upon the university for its stability and economic growth. The racial makeup of the town, not including the students, is about 3 percent nonwhite. The closest urban center is approximately 100 miles away.

Primary Persons Involved in the Case

- Nick Brown is a middle-class white senior majoring in business and accounting. He is the president of the Inter-Fraternity Council.
- Victor Sanchez is a native of Spain. He is a first-year student living in a residence hall.

• Beth Simmons is the Vice President for Student Affairs.

Information Germane to the Case

• This year a study was commissioned by the university to assess the perceptions of minority students on campus. The study found that minority students felt a sense of alienation on campus. The results of the study also indicated that minority students perceived the institution as unwelcoming and hostile.
• On campus the students are "tolerant" of diversity issues, but there is not an overwhelming desire to move beyond general recognition that there are diverse students on campus.

The Case

A university multicultural student group organized a "Welcome Back Fundraiser" showcasing local performers. The concert was held in a downtown dance club following a university football game. Those targeted and in attendance included university students, faculty, staff, and community members, and more specifically members of the multicultural community. Recognizing that he has had limited exposure to an activity similar to this, Nick Brown and some of his friends from the Greek community decided to attend the event. More important, this event was Victor Sanchez's first social gathering as a new student.

The downtown club is a well-known establishment in Dewey County. Many university student groups have utilized this club for multiple purposes. Capacity of this particular establishment is limited to 150; however, on this evening, the establishment contained over 300 individuals. Overall, this event was successful from the perspective that it brought together representation of all groups within the university community. As the night began to come to an end, an argument started between Nick and Victor over Victor's perceived interest in Nick's girlfriend. As their argument began to become somewhat physical due to racial and homophobic slurs and innuendos exchanged between the two parties, the club staff instructed their bouncers to step in and quell the disruption.

The bouncers grabbed Nick and Victor and began to escort them to the main door. Their friends followed behind to help calm the situation. As the men came to the main entrance, Nick and Victor began to push and shove one another until they both were restrained.

As a result of this situation, Beth Simmons called a meeting with students, faculty, staff, and community members impacted by this incident. Overall, this meeting was convened for the purposes of developing a strategy on how to handle this incident as well as to discuss the perception of past campus climate issues that has affected the minority community in Dewey County.

Discussion Questions

1. What steps should Beth Simmons utilize to obtain information from individuals who were impacted by this event? How will this information be used to support the university's policies on conflict resolution?
2. Describe some of the intervention techniques that you would recommend for Nick Brown and Victor Sanchez.
3. What are some applicable theories of development that would apply to actions and reactions of the key players in this case?
4. Imagine this scenario at a Hispanic-serving institution in an urban area. From your perspective, does this change the case?
5. How do you feel this event has changed the perceptions of an inclusive community?
6. If you were a parent of a first-year student who attended this event what concerns would you have? How would this event change your opinion of the institution?

Research Activities for Further Exploration

1. Conduct research on your campus to explore your university's policy on diversity and research some alternatives on how to better publicize this policy.
2. Research the diversity policies in your city government, university, and campus law enforcement to determine if these policies are similar and collaborative.
3. What are some of the historic rulings or events on race relations that are pertinent to the above case study? Document your sources.

THE EXPERT ON DIVERSITY

H. RICHARD MILNER

Description of the Institutional Environment

Williams State University (WSU) is a public institution in the northwestern U.S. with approximately 17,000 undergraduate students. The institution is not the main state university; however, it graduates the largest number of teachers in the state, and it has several competitive graduate and undergraduate level education programs, including the elementary education program, which ranks in the top 50 in the U.S. Approximately 86 percent of the faculty members at WSU are white, 6 percent are Asian, 4 percent are Hispanic, and 4 percent are African American. Similarly, 84 percent of the students are white, 3 percent are Asian, 4 percent are Hispanic, 7 percent are African American, and 2 percent classify themselves as "other."

Description of the Surrounding Community

WSU is at the heart of the small town of Williams County with a population of 43,000 residents. The university employs many of these residents, who typically embrace and support the students who attend school there and the institution in general. This support is most evident at football and basketball games.

Primary Persons Involved in the Case

- Janine Lee is a first-year international student from Taiwan majoring in elementary education.
- Dr. Lauren Scott is an assistant professor of education at WSU. This is her third year teaching at WSU, and this is her first job as an academician. She is white and in her early thirties. She earned her doctorate in pedagogy and philosophy from a large research institution in the northwestern part of the country.

Information Germane to the Case

- The college and faculty of education at WSU offer no courses on diversity and/or multicultural education. The college and faculty maintain that they are not in opposition to issues of diversity but have not made any conscious, assertive efforts to build a program that addresses these issues.
- The college and faculty are very supportive of students, and they are committed to students' needs. Indeed, the faculty members approach their teaching as well as their research quite seriously, and they seem to embrace the balance of teaching and research.

The Case

Janine was excited to attend her first class, Introduction to Education. Janine already had outlined questions concerning some of her interests for the very first day of class. During the first few class sessions, however, Dr.

Scott, the instructor in the course, talked very generally about the nature of schools, communities, and parents. Janine was the only Asian American student in the course, with the remainder being white. In the third week of the class, Janine began to question why diversity issues were not being addressed in the course. She decided to speak to Dr. Scott in order to voice her concern.

Janine was a bit nervous as she went to see Dr. Scott. This would be her very first meeting with a professor. The meeting began with Dr. Scott talking about her perception of the success of the course. Dr. Scott was very cordial and smiled as she reflected on an example she had used in class the evening before. Janine was still nervous, but she finally admitted to Dr. Scott that she was hoping that the Introduction to Education course would address some issues around diversity. She wanted to learn about some of the academic achievement disparities among students from various races and cultures, for instance. To Janine's surprise and relief, Dr. Scott was quite receptive to this idea. She informed Janine that for years she had had an interest in these topics but had not read much or conducted empirical research around the topic of diversity. Nonetheless, Janine left refreshed, thinking that some of her interests and concerns would be addressed in the course in the future.

Dr. Scott began the next class discussion by asking Janine to inform the class about "minority" students and some of their issues. Janine was perplexed because she did not feel comfortable speaking on behalf of "minority" students in general, and she had not expected this type of request from Dr. Scott.

Discussion Questions

1. What are the primary issues in this case from Janine's perspective? From Dr. Scott's perspective?
2. Why do you believe Dr. Scott asked Janine to speak for "minority" students?
3. Was it appropriate for Dr. Scott to ask Janine to speak on behalf of all minorities? Why or why not?
4. If you were a college counselor, what developmental theories would assist you in understanding Janine and Dr. Scott? How could those theories be used?
5. Why is addressing and understanding diversity important to Janine?
6. As an academic advisor, what would you advise Janine to do in this situation?

Research Activities for Further Exploration

1. Why has the term "minority" become problematic to many underrepresented and marginalized groups?
2. How are diversity issues incorporated into undergraduate and graduate programs on your campus? What are some ways that policies, programs, and practices could better reflect and attend to diversity?
3. What is the role of the student affairs professional in promoting and supporting academic attention to diversity issues?

LIVING AND LEARNING IN A DIFFERENT WORLD

OCTAVIA MADISON-COLMORE

Description of the Institutional Environment

Mays University is a state-supported liberal arts and sciences institution, which offers undergraduate and graduate degrees in 38 disciplines: 20 disciplines at the undergraduate level and 18 disciplines at the graduate level. Approximately 5,000 students attend this historically black university. Twenty-five percent of incoming first-year students earn an SAT verbal score over 500 and 19 percent earn an SAT math score over 500. The racial demographics of the institution are as follows: 1 percent Native American, 1 percent Hispanic/Latino, 2 percent Asian American, 8 percent white, and 88 percent African American. Mays University is considered one of the top historically black colleges and universities in the nation and is known for its excellence in education.

Description of the Surrounding Community

Mays University sits on more than 300 acres of land in a small, secluded town, just ten miles from a city with approximately 50,000 residents. The city is known for its wide range of museums; its recreational, educational, and cultural offerings; and its family-oriented community. Ninety-two percent of the students at Mays University are residents of this city.

Primary Persons Involved in the Case

- Lisa Thomas is a first-semester student at Mays University.
- Mark Williams is a first-semester student at Mays University.

- Marsha Peters is Lisa's roommate and a first-semester student at Mays University.

Information Germane to the Case

- Lisa grew up in a small, rural, predominantly white community with nearly 14,000 residents. Approximately 92 percent of the county's students enter the workforce after high school graduation, mostly in blue-collar, low-skill jobs, while around 8 percent continue their education beyond high school. Lisa is the elder of two siblings. Her father is a part-time butcher at the local supermarket, and her mother is a nursing assistant at the county's only hospital. Neither of Lisa's parents completed high school.
- Mark is an only child. His father, a former college football star, is a self-employed Certified Public Accountant and a retired military officer. His mother is a science teacher at the local high school. His parents both are graduates of Mays University and are very active in the alumni association.
- Mark and Lisa attended the same high school, where he performed well academically and athletically. His grade point average ranged from 3.75 to 3.98 (on a 4.0 scale) throughout his high school years. Football was one of several sports Mark played in high school and the one sport that brought him the most fame.
- Lisa and Mark met at a social event during their junior year in high school and began dating in secret shortly thereafter.

The Case

As Lisa Thomas began her senior year in high school, she began to worry about her relationship with Mark Williams, wondering whether or not the relationship would continue after graduation. She was aware of Mark's plans to attend Mays University, but she had no idea what she was going to do. She had hoped to go to a technical school to study computer programming, but due to her parents' financial situation, she knew that they could not afford to cover the cost. Mark also was afraid that the relationship would end. He was aware of Lisa's interest in computers and encouraged her to apply to Mays University. Not knowing much about college, Lisa took Mark's advice and, a few months later, she received a letter of acceptance, along with a full academic scholarship offer.

Days passed before Lisa gained enough courage to tell her parents about the letter of acceptance. She was afraid that her parents would say "no" because of its location, approximately 300 miles from home. Much to Lisa's surprise, both parents were just as elated as she was about her decision to go to college.

Finally, the day arrived for Lisa to leave for Mays University. Her parents loaded the car, while Lisa said her good-byes to neighbors and friends. As the family approached the campus, Lisa's mother noticed a lot of African American students and very few white students walking around the campus. Lisa's mother stated, "Boy, there are a lot of black kids here. Where are the white kids, Lisa? I have only seen one or two so far? Is this one of those schools for poor blacks?" Lisa responded to her mother by saying, "Mom, I am sure there are plenty of white kids here. We just have not seen them yet." Lisa, following the directions on the map, guided her father to the dormitory. The family unloaded the car and assisted Lisa with unpacking her belongings. As more and more students arrive, Lisa's father turned to her mother and stated, "You know, Mary, I haven't seen many white people here either. I better see some soon or I'm taking my daughter out of here." Lisa assured her parents that she had researched the school and found a number of white students attending the university.

A few hours later, Lisa's parents decided to leave and head back home. Lisa escorted them to the car and said her tearful good-byes. She returned to her room, gathered a map, and searched for directions to the football field. As she got closer to the field, she noticed Mark standing on the sidelines. She stood patiently at the fence waiting for him to turn around. Ten minutes later, the two of them made eye contact, followed by huge smiles. Knowing that Mark would be practicing for another hour or so, Lisa decided to walk back to her residence hall. As she approached her room, she noticed the door to her room was open and her roommate, Marsha Peters, had arrived. Marsha, an African American female, extended her hand to Lisa and introduced herself. Lisa was a bit surprised by Marsha's appearance: the braided hair, the African print scarf around her head that matched her pantsuit, and the three-inch spiked heels. She was also surprised by the hip-hop music that resonated throughout the room and into the hallway, and the posters of African America celebrities taped to the walls.

Marsha invited Lisa to join her on a tour of the campus. Halfway through the tour, Lisa noticed that she had not seen a white female and only two white males. She also noticed the hundreds of eyes that stared at her, which made her feel uncomfortable. Shortly after the tour, Lisa ran into Mark, who was sitting with a group of football players in the cafeteria. As Lisa walked over to greet him, she noticed an unusual look on his face, as if he was startled by her presence. After a moment of silence, Mark introduced Lisa to the guys at the table and identified her as his "home girl." At this point, Lisa began to feel uncomfortable, wondering if she had made the right decision to attend this university and wondering if Mark really was the right person for her. As Lisa and Marsha headed back to the residence hall, Lisa began questioning herself saying, "What have I gotten myself into? I feel so alone, so isolated, and so out of place. I cannot believe Mark's reaction toward me. What did he take me to be? And, this place, this college, this university, it is surrounded by black people. Where did they all come from? Surely not from my hometown, where there are only a handful of blacks. How could I be so stupid to select a college that I knew absolutely nothing about? Maybe I should just pack up and go home. But I can't because I would disappoint my parents. I would let my friends down and my community. More important, I would be letting myself down. What should I do?"

Discussion Questions

1. What are the main issues in this case?
2. If you were a student affairs professional at this particular historically black institution, what would you recommend to assist students with the transition from high school to college?
3. Although Lisa dated and fell in love with an African American, male student, she seemed to have little insight into African American culture. What would you recommend to educate Lisa about the African American culture?
4. What steps would you take to educate the parents of first-generation students about college?
5. If you were in Lisa's shoes, what would you do? What resources would you tap into?
6. What kind of programs could be developed for students with backgrounds such as Lisa's? What would be the incentives for participating in such programs?

Research Activities for Further Exploration

1. Interview white students who are currently attending a historically Black college or university and ask the following questions:
   a. What made you decide to attend a historically black college or university as opposed to a predominantly white college?
   b. Did you have difficulty adjusting to the campus environment? If so, what were these difficulties and how did you deal with them?
2. Conduct interviews with high school counselors to see what they are doing to encourage more students to consider college, especially students in rural areas.
3. Develop a model program that would assist college officials and minority students with transitioning from high school to college.

a. What would be the goal and objective of this program?

b. How would you measure its efficacy?

WHO AM I?

ROBERT E. MEEKS, JR.

Description of the Institutional Environment

Pleasant Hill University (PHU) is a private four-year liberal arts institution. Approximately 9,385 students attend. The average incoming first-year student earns a 24 on the ACT. The racial demographics of the school are as follows: 1 percent American Indian, 4 percent African American, 6 percent Hispanic American, 5 percent Asian American, and 84 percent white. The majority of African Americans who attend PHU have moved there from other parts of the country. The school is divided into two separate campuses: the main campus with the business and liberal emphasis, and the law school campus.

Description of the Surrounding Community

The main campus is located in an upper-class neighborhood south of a large metropolitan city. From PHU the students have easy access to the downtown area and have easy access to ski resorts on the weekend. PHU employs most of the residents in this city.

PHU and the surrounding community have had their share of problems that are typical with neighborhoods that border college areas, such as loud and unruly students. The neighborhoods that surround PHU are mostly middle to upper class.

Primary Persons Involved in the Case

- Thad Watson, a Hispanic American, is a first-year student studying theater. He finished the first quarter on academic probation.
- Donald Kent, a Hispanic American student affairs professional, works in the Center for Academic Resources as an Academic Advisor. His main duties are to give general advising to all PHU students.
- Ronald Mitchell, an Asian American student affairs graduate student, is doing his internship in the Center for Academic Resources and works closely with Donald Kent.

Information Germane to the Case

- Traditionally, Hispanic American students as a group have been severely isolated on campus.
- There are 34 Hispanic American professors on campus.

The Case

During the spring semester, Donald Kent received a letter from one of Thad Watson's professors stating that Thad had plagiarized a 12-page paper and subsequently had received an "F" for the paper. Donald and his intern, Ronald Mitchell, organized a meeting with Thad to discuss the issue. In the meeting, Thad stated that he did not plagiarize the paper and felt as if he was being wrongly accused.

Because Thad was still on academic probation, this allegation definitely put him at risk for suspension if found guilty. Accordingly, Donald called the professor and explained Thad's situation to see if he would be willing to give the young man another chance. The professor refused and told Donald that he reported Thad to the Community Citizenship and Standards Board for disciplinary action.

Donald and Ronald both agreed to attend the hearing. Before the hearing Ronald and Thad had an interesting conversation about the dilemma he was facing. During the conversation, Thad confessed to the plagiarism. In addition, Thad explained to Ronald that he plagiarized the paper for the following reasons: (a) the competition to excel is so great on campus that he felt he had to do this to keep up, (b) he felt inadequate as a minority student on campus, and (c) he felt that there were not enough mentors on campus to provide support or guidance. Following the hearing, Thad was placed on academic suspension for one year.

Discussion Questions

1. What are the primary issues in this case?
2. How could the advising center offer more to its minority students on campus? Be specific.
3. Has the competition for grades caused college students to become successful at all cost? Explain.
4. How could student development theories be used to better understand Thad's situation?
5. What advice would you give to Thad during orientation for coping with the academic demands of college? During the first semester? After being placed on probation?

6. How would you design a workshop for academic advisors to help prevent academic dishonesty?

Research Activities for Further Exploration

1. Conduct an ethnographic study of a university that has a majority white population to explore the experiences of Hispanic American students on campus.
2. Research the meaning of the term "academic dishonesty" and describe the mechanisms and resources at your institution to respond when it is alleged to have occurred.
3. What are the demographics of Hispanic American students, faculty, and staff on your campus? What services are in place to support Hispanic American students? What are the expectations of Hispanic American faculty and staff regarding mentoring Hispanic American students? How are non-Hispanic faculty and staff trained to provide support for Hispanic American students?

GIVEN A SECOND CHANCE

SHEILA WITHERSPOON

Description of the Institutional Environment

Latimore College is a four-year land-grant college. Approximately 5,000 students attend this historically black college. The average incoming first-year student earned an 850 on the SAT. The racial demographics of the school are as follows: 2 percent Hispanic American, 8 percent white, and 90 percent African American. Latimore College recently was ranked #1 among all colleges for graduating African-American teachers.

Description of the Surrounding Community

Latimore College is held in high esteem in the African American community in Morris, a small southern community of 10,000 residents. Morris is surrounded by rural and suburban residential neighborhoods. Many African Americans support Latimore College because of its high academic standards, alumni giving, and community connections. Latimore also is supported by a history of winning athletic teams and the college's famous Marching Band.

Primary Persons Involved in the Case

- Monique Odom is an 18-year-old high school senior.
- Malik Johnson, Monique's boyfriend, is a student at Latimore College.
- Brenda Smith is the director of the Office of Admissions and Recruitment at Latimore College.
- Evelyn Cameron works in the Office of Admissions and Recruitment at Latimore College. She specializes in the recruitment of scholarship recipients.
- Kia Johnson is a work-study student and tour guide in the Office of Admissions and Recruitment at Latimore College; she is Malik's older sister and also attends Latimore College.

Information Germane to the Case

- Efforts to enhance Latimore College's capital campaign were launched through a recent scholarship recruitment event. The goal was to research the list of potential National Merit Achievement Scholarship recipients within the country and organize a recruitment event for the college.
- The campaign organizers sponsored a "Latimore College Day." Prospective scholarship students and their parents toured the college and attended a brunch and a football game.

The Case

Monique is very interested in attending college out of state, particularly a historically black college or university. Monique has expressed an interest in Latimore College because her boyfriend Malik is a student there.

Monique currently is enrolled in a college preparatory curriculum at her high school. Though Monique's SAT score is 1,400, she knows that her current cumulative grade point average of 1.47 might hinder her from being accepted at many colleges. In addition, Monique often is absent from school because she gets off work late.

Malik's older sister, Kia Johnson, is a student at Latimore College who works in the admissions office. Kia has a good working relationship with Brenda Smith and Evelyn Cameron and is interceding on Monique's behalf regarding her possible consideration for "special" conditional admission into the college. Kia's hope is that Monique will be granted admission for the first year with a partial scholarship or work-study opportunity. The idea is that if Monique does well, she may have an opportunity to receive a full scholarship through the honors college as a sophomore.

Discussion Questions

1. What concerns might Brenda Smith and Evelyn Cameron have regarding conditional admission for Monique?
2. What issues may affect Monique's academic and social life on campus if accepted?
3. As Director of Admissions, Brenda Smith has the option of interviewing prospective students with exceptional circumstances. If you were the interviewer, what important issues would you take into account to help you render an admissions decision regarding Monique?
4. As a financial aid counselor, explain to Monique what the college can offer to her financially if she is admitted as a conditional student.
5. If you were Monique's academic advisor at Latimore College, what strategies would you recommend to Monique for achieving and maintaining academic success in college?
6. Monique has been offered conditional admission status. She must enroll in lower level, noncredit courses for one academic year and cannot receive less than a "C" in any class. Based on information given in the case study, discuss Monique's anticipated response to her conditions. If you were a student affairs professional in the counseling center, how might you respond?

Research Activities for Further Exploration

1. The concept of the extended family or kinship network is not uncommon to African American families and is not limited to blood relatives. Interview five African American students and have them identify who else can be included in the extended family set and why.
2. Research the term "low-income first-generation" college student. Discuss the issues and obstacles that are associated with these students, as well as programs that have been designed to assist this population.
3. It is often assumed that African American college students are given preference through special admission programs that lower standards for admission. Based on your experience with Monique, write a mock defense to a legislator about why, though many African American college students are eligible for "regular" admission, it is important to maintain current programs that assist students like her.

ADVISING AFRICAN AMERICAN STUDENT ATHLETES

JOY L. GASTON

Description of the Institutional Environment

Woodstone University is a large research university with an enrollment of approximately 35,000 students. Minorities constitute approximately 12 percent of the total student population (5% African American, 1% American Indian, 2% Asian American, 4% Hispanic).

Description of the Surrounding Community

Woodstone University is located in the heart of an urban city on the East Coast. The population of the city is approximately 1.2 million. The community surrounding the campus consists of predominantly African American, working-class residents. A number of suburbs around the perimeter of the city consist primarily of middle-class to affluent white and some African American residents.

Primary Persons Involved in the Case

- Ricky "Torpedo" Brown is an African American sophomore at Woodstone University. He is an All American running back on the football team.
- Leo Conroy is a white, male academic counselor in the athletic department at Woodstone University. He has been an academic counselor at the university for 11 years and advises athletes in men's basketball, football, wrestling, baseball, and women's track and field.

Information Germane to the Case

- Woodstone University is very competitive in its admissions process. The average ACT score is 26 and over 60 percent of the students rank in the top 30 percent of their high school class. Ricky's academic performance was fairly good during his first year at Woodstone and his cumulative GPA for the year was 2.85.
- Ricky, a first-generation college student, grew up in a predominantly black neighborhood and attended a predominantly black high school. He scored a 19 on the ACT, had a 2.5 high school GPA, and finished in the 50th percentile of his high school class. Although Ricky's test scores, rank, and GPA were lower than average, he was admitted to the university because of his status as a highly recruited football player.

The Case

During the first week of the fall semester, Leo Conroy called Ricky Brown in for an appointment to discuss majors. During the meeting, Ricky expressed great interest in the business program, which is one of the most competitive programs at the university. Students must earn a 2.9 GPA and complete a number of core courses with a grade of "B" or better for admission into the program. Ricky told Mr. Conroy, as well as his parents, about his desire to be a sports agent and own a business one day.

Based on Ricky's high school background, test scores, and status as a high-profile athlete, Leo encouraged Ricky to pursue sociology or physical education because those majors are not as competitive as business at Woodstone. He concluded the meeting by telling Ricky, "You only need a 2.0 GPA to stay eligible, so why pursue a major that is so competitive? We really need you this season and cannot afford to have you off the team because of poor grades!"

Discussion Questions

1. Identify and summarize pertinent and conflicting issues in this case.
2. What kind of message do you think Leo Conroy's advice sent to Ricky about his ability to succeed in business? Why might this be problematic?
3. Assume the role of Ricky's academic counselor. Create a culturally responsive plan of action to help Ricky achieve his academic goals and stay eligible. Discuss what Leo could have done differently (according to your plan) in advising Ricky about choosing a major.
4. Give examples of other factors Leo could have taken into consideration in determining Ricky's future academic success. What, if anything, should Leo know about predicting academic achievement for African American students?
5. Identify and describe some of the psychosocial issues African American students (particularly student athletes) might encounter at a predominantly white college or university. Determine how these issues might affect African American students.
6. Describe what type of intervention(s) you would suggest for Leo and other academic counselors to increase their cultural competence in working with diverse student populations.

Research Activities for Further Exploration

1. Survey and evaluate the literature on predictors of academic achievement for African American students. Identify noncognitive predictors and dis-

cuss how this information might be incorporated in advising African-American students.

2. Interview an African American student athlete about his or her academic experience and expectations. Then, interview an academic counselor about his or her experience in advising African American student athletes. Compare and contrast the responses from the two individuals. Make recommendations for culturally responsive advising based on your conclusions.

3. Research the term "stereotype threat" and explain its importance and impact on the academic achievement of African American students.

NIA'S STORY

Dionne M. Smith

Description of the Institutional Environment

Lambridge University is a public four-year university located in the northeastern part of the United States. Approximately 20,000 students attend this predominantly White institution. The racial demographics of the university are: 70 percent white American, 14.1 percent Asian American, 8 percent African American, 4.0 percent international, 3.6 percent Hispanic American, and 0.3 percent Native American. Lambridge University is considered one of the most prestigious universities in the United States.

Description of the Surrounding Community

Lambridge University is the centerpiece of a small, yet thriving city with a population of 45,000 residents. Beautiful mountains and sculptured countrysides surround this small town. The city has a rich history, sponsors annual cultural events, and is a growing attraction for both national and international tourists.

Primary Persons Involved in the Case

- Nia Allen, an international student from Costa Rica, is a first-year student at Lambridge University.
- Dr. Melinda Jones is the Coordinator of the Honors Program at Lambridge University.
- Dr. Gloria Neilson is the Staff Psychologist at the Student Counseling

Center at Lambridge University.

Information Germane to the Case

*   Lambridge University promotes diversity; however, few proactive steps have been taken to diversify the campus environment.
*   Very few mechanisms are in place to enable new students of color to meet and interact with other students and faculty of

The Case

During her first semester at Lambridge University, Nia Allen began to experience feelings of isolation because she was not very successful at forming meaningful relationships with students and faculty of color. She was hundreds of miles away from home and felt that her support system was fading away. Although she received verbal support from her parents via telephone, it did not seem to be enough for her. The lack of support and absence of meaningful relationships caused Nia to lose interest. As a result, her desire to participate in organizations and activities began to diminish. The one thing that Nia held dear was her academic status as an honor student. Toward the end of her first semester, Nia realized that she was failing many of her courses. During this time, Nia totally lost hope, motivation, and interest in continuing her education. She completed the academic semester with a 1.3 GPA.

Upon receiving Nia's end-of-semester grade report from the registrar, Dr. Melinda Jones, Coordinator of the Honors Program, contacted her via telephone to inform her that she was placed on academic probation. As a part of this process, Nia was required to visit the office to discuss her options and to begin working on her academic probation intervention packet. On the day of Nia's visit to the office, she sat down with Dr. Jones, and they discussed her situation in detail. Midway through the conversation, Nia began to cry and started sharing her feelings with Dr. Jones. She explained that she was really having a rough time adjusting to the new environment and that she felt extremely isolated. She then shared with Dr. Jones her disappointment with faculty, administrators, and peers, particularly those of color, who seemed disinterested in reaching out to her to help make her experience a success.

Nia also reported that she was struggling financially and that she was tired of having to deal with racism from white faculty and students. She then shared several personal stories of racism that she had encountered during her first semester at the university. She also complained of stomach cramps, headaches, and sharp pains in her heart at times. Nia reported losing 20 pounds within a two-month period.

Nia also stated that her high school experience was so different and that she could not understand what was happening to her. Losing interest in people and academics was very depressing to Nia because she had always been an extroverted person. She reported feeling horrible because she felt as if she was letting her family down. After expressing most of her feelings, Nia began to cry uncontrollably and murmured in a very low tone that she wished that it were "all over."

Having been trained as a psychologist, Dr. Jones, with Nia's permission, called a colleague, Dr. Gloria Neilson, at the Student Counseling Center to make an appointment for Nia. Although Nia consented to an intake session at the Student Counseling Center, she was somewhat apprehensive about the appointment because she was not sure if she could trust Dr. Neilson or any of the other staff members at the counseling center. After further consultation with Dr. Neilson via telephone, the three of them agreed that Dr. Jones would sit in on the initial intake session with Nia. Dr. Neilson conducted the initial intake session with Nia and Dr. Jones within hours of the telephone consultation.

During the intake session, Nia disclosed her thoughts, feelings, and actions as they related to her experience at the university. Although Nia was a bit uncomfortable with counseling in general, she was very honest with Dr. Neilson about how she was feeling and coping with problems in her life. Dr. Neilson conducted a suicide assessment based on Nia's comment regarding wanting things to be "all over," and concluded that a written safety contract was warranted. Upon gathering all of the pertinent information from Nia and Dr. Jones, Dr. Neilson recommended that Nia begin individual counseling with a therapist at the counseling center. She also recommended that Nia join a counseling group that focused on international students' experiences at Lambridge University. Nia then told both Dr. Neilson and Dr. Jones that she would think about pursuing counseling and would follow up with both of them within one week. Nia left the office in a very depressed mood and did not follow up with Dr. Neilson or Dr. Jones by the end of the week.

Discussion Questions

1. What is the next step that both Dr. Melinda Jones and Dr. Gloria Neilson should take on behalf of the Honors Program and the Student Counseling Center, respectively? What responsibility does the university in general and the Honors Program and the Student Counseling Center in particular have to Nia?
2. Based on this case study, what are the issues that Nia will have to sort out and deal with in order to feel better about her situation? Be specific.
3. What resources exist at your institution and in your community to help students like Nia?

4. Place Nia's problems in rank order based on severity and provide the rationale behind the ranking decision (i.e., which issue should be addressed first, second, third, etc.). Develop a list of interventions that you could recommend for Nia or other minority students in similar situations. These interventions should utilize university resources, community resources, familial resources, etc.

5. Based on your knowledge of mood disorders and stressors related to international students on college campuses, develop an initial treatment plan for use in individual counseling as well as a follow-up plan for Dr. Jones and the Honors Program.

6. How can Nia's family be a part of this process? What are the legal and ethical responsibilities, duties, and limitations of involving family on the part of Dr. Jones, Dr. Neilson, and the university? Cite relevant legislation where appropriate.

Research Activities for Further Exploration

1. Identify, review, and discuss relevant research (both quantitative and qualitative) that has been conducted on stressors, needs, and interventions of international students.

2. Conduct a qualitative research study using semistructured interviews with first-year international students who are also first-generation college students. The purpose of this study is to ask participating students about their experiences at the institution. Give the students an opportunity to tell their stories in their own words.

3. Using the information gathered from the literature review in question #1 and the results of the qualitative study in question #2, write a report that can be presented to administrators, divisions, and programs, responsible for the recruitment and retention of international students.

ON SACRED GROUND

JAY CORWIN & MYRON L. POPE

Description of the Institutional Environment

Byng University is a four-year private research institution, which enrolls approximately 18,000 students and is located in the Southwest. The institution was founded in 1871 and has for many years been affiliated with the Presbyterian Church. Due to its national academic reputation, Byng

University enrolls students from around the country. However, about 65 percent of the institution's enrollment consists of students who are residents of the state. The student enrollment of the institution is 53 percent women, 74 percent white, 14 percent Native American, 9 percent Hispanic, and 3 percent African American.

Description of the Surrounding Community

Byng University is located in Pushmataha, a city of 105,000 people. Along with the campus enrollment, the city has grown exponentially during the last 30 years due to affordable and comfortable living. The city's history includes a significant amount of Native American influence, which also impacts the overall culture of the area. It is located within an hour's drive of the heart of the Sioux Nation. The city attracts a substantial amount of tourists throughout the year who come to take in this culture and to camp in the picturesque mountains that are just 30 miles outside the city limits.

Primary Persons Involved in the Case

- Jonathan Barefoot is a senior at Byng and is also the President of the American Indian Student Association (AISA).
- Brad Thompson is President of Alpha Beta Gamma (ABG), a traditional Inter-Fraternity Council organization on campus.
- Diane Backus is the Dean of Students.
- George Gibson is Chief of the Byng University Police Department (BUPD).
- Tom Billings is the Coordinator of American Indian Student Services and Byng's Campus Judicial Affairs Coordinator.
- Chief Flying Eagle is the local leader of the Sioux Nation.
- Dr. Hayes Woodward is the President of Byng University.

Information Germane to the Case

- Recently, Chief Red, the schools mascot, was replaced with another mascot. In the past, campus officials as well as students had recognized Chief Red as a representation of pride. However, in recent years pressure to find a new mascot was created by Native American student marches and protests in the community led by Chief Flying Eagle.

The Case

It was well after midnight on a Friday morning during American Indian Awareness Month. The outskirts of Byng University were beginning to quiet down. Like many universities, the weekend begins on Thursday evening and students were returning home after a long night. As part of the awareness month, a large teepee was erected on campus in an area that once was a sacred location of Sioux hunting grounds. That evening AISA hosted a traditional ceremony that ended around 1:00 a.m. in the teepee. Three student volunteers from AISA were going to sleep there that night. Some members of the ABG fraternity were in the area.

Diane Backus received a phone call from Tom Billings at 2:15 a.m. George Gibson had informed him that BUPD received a phone call reporting a group of young white males defacing the teepee. While one of the witnesses called police, the other two chased the males back to the ABG fraternity house. All three witnesses are members of AISA. BUPD was dispatched to the fraternity house and to the teepee. Due to the circumstances, Billings recommended that Dean Backus go to the campus immediately. Since Billings also is the coordinator of American Indian Services, Backus asked him to meet her there. They arrived on campus to find that the police seemed to have things under control. Backus called Dr. Hayes Woodward and the university spokesperson to update them on the situation before returning home.

By morning, word of the night's happenings already had traveled throughout the campus and the local community. The incident was the lead story on the morning news. AISA was outraged, as they perceived the incident to be a direct insult to their heritage and ancestry. The students who witnessed the incident were very willing to talk. The police were still investigating, the university was just beginning to sort things out, and the AISA students were becoming more and more impatient with the way the situation was being handled.

By 10:00 a.m. meetings to interview the witnesses and ABG members had begun. Brad Thompson was in Backus' office. While he initially had no interest in divulging names, he did end up giving the names of the six students who were at the scene—all first-year students and ABG pledges. Thompson said they were "out and about" and not doing anything fraternity-related. One by one, the six students were called into Backus' office. All six relayed the same story. All admitted that they had been inebriated, but said they did not deface the teepee.

President Woodward, who wants a statement from Dean Backus for the media by the end of the day, already saw the first media reports, and realized that the institution cannot afford to sit by as its image is further damaged. Additionally, he has received several phone calls from Chief Flying Eagle who has threatened to boycott the institution and encourage Native American students not to enroll there. Woodward wants action but does not want the fraternity closed. However, with disciplinary actions from the university pending against the organization due to reports of hazing and underage drinking at organizational socials, he has little tolerance for the fraternity at this point.

Discussion Questions

1. What are the issues or problems presented in this case?
2. What are the options for the resolution of these issues by not only Dean Backus, but also the rest of the administration? What strategies should be utilized in bringing harmony to the campus?
3. What should the statement that President Woodward is requesting include? How should the media be dealt with to desensitize the situation now? How should they have been dealt with initially?
4. As there was not clear evidence that the six students involved defaced the teepee, how should the institution proceed in handling this situation?
5. How much pressure from external individuals, including the media, should the administration consider in making decisions related to diversity issues in this case?
6. What can the university do from here to mitigate racial tensions on campus? What role, if any, should Billings play in that plan?

Research Activities for Further Exploration

1. The usage of Native American mascots in athletics has been an issue for several years. Many institutions of higher education have since changed their mascots to more politically correct ones. Conduct research on some of the past images and names that were used prior to these changes at institutions of higher education around the country.
2. Write an annotated bibliography on articles and books that focus on using mascots that have offended cultural groups.
3. On your campus, determine who is responsible for representing your institution when it comes to multicultural relations? Interview this individual and determine their training in multicultural student issues and their approach to addressing the media when issues related to multicultural student issues arise?

SHATTERED DREAMS AND BROKEN PROMISES

James L. Moore III

Description of the Institutional Environment

MCC (MCC) is a public two-year institution with nearly 10,000 students, located in southeastern Florida. The community college is very diverse, i.e., 45 percent white, 35 percent Hispanic American, 15 percent African American, 3 percent Asian American, and 2 percent other. It adheres to an "open admissions" policy.

Description of the Surrounding Community

MCC consists of three commuter campuses: one main and two satellite sites. The main campus, where most students take classes, is situated in a very large, diverse city. It is located just 35 miles from one major four-year research university and 10 miles from three private four-year liberal arts institutions. Compared to the other institutions of higher education, MCC is positioned closest in proximity to the downtown area of the city. Hispanic Americans, African Americans, and Asian Americans comprise 46 percent of the city's population. The urban center attracts tourists from all over the world as a result of its rich cultural ambiance. Fiestas, parades, and other cultural events are presented annually.

Primary Persons Involved in the Case

- Juan Caesar Ramos, a Dominican student, is a second-year student-athlete. In high school, he was a two-time All-American in both basketball and football, and during his senior year, he was the National High School Player of the Year in basketball.
- Joe Bowdan is the head basketball coach for MCC.
- Dr. Gladys Lois Peake serves as the Director of Office of Academic Support for Student-Athletes (OASSA) at MCC. She specializes in working with minority student-athletes who are on academic probation.

Information Germane to the Case

- Recently, OASSA was established to provide advising, tutoring, and so forth for students who participate in intercollegiate sports. This office was created to improve retention of student-athletes.

The Case

In his second and final year of eligibility at MCC, Juan Caesar Ramos started the basketball season as a preseason All-American. Many college basketball coaches were recruiting him heavily. In addition, many National Basketball Association (NBA) scouts were beginning to take notice of him. During the first week of school, one well-known NBA analyst stated in a national newspaper, "Juan Caesar Ramos is the best basketball player eligible for the NBA draft." As a result of this statement, sports agents, college scouts, and fans began to bombard Juan with telephone calls, mailings, and unexpected visits.

Two weeks later, MCC played the team ranked fifth in the country and last year's national champion. This was a game in which Juan had to perform extremely well. Three or four NBA scouts were expected to attend this game. Also, Coach Joe Bowdan told him that 20 to 30 different college scouts also were expected to come to the game. Throughout the first quarter, Juan made several exciting acrobatic plays that definitely impressed the roaring fans in attendance. However, 30 seconds before halftime, Juan injured both knees after attempting to do a very acrobatic slam-dunk. He was carried off the basketball court and rushed to the emergency room.

After thoroughly examining Juan's knees, the team's doctor realized that Juan had severely damaged his knees to the point that he would never again be able to play basketball. The doctor first told Coach Bowdan, and together they told Juan. After hearing the news, Juan broke down in tears in Coach Bowdan's arms. Juan listened reluctantly as they told him that he could still fulfill his dreams by becoming a basketball coach.

Three months after having two knee-replacement surgeries, Juan learned that he had lost his basketball scholarship after re-enrolling in MCC. Hearing this heartbreaking news made him feel like giving up, but before doing this, he decided to stop by Dr. Gladys Lois Peake's office. Although she was not in her office, he decided to wait for her return in the waiting area.

After Juan had waited several hours, Dr. Gladys Lois Peake returned to her office, where she found Juan in tears. He told her that he felt disrespected and exploited by the athletic program. He also stated that he was tired of being viewed on campus as a poor Dominican who was incapable of doing college work. He confessed that he previously had not taken his academics seriously because of the implicit messages from coaches, instructors, and peers that academics were secondary to basketball.

Discussion Questions

1. Based on the issues presented in the case, what questions need to be raised in order to work effectively with Juan?
2. As you review the case study, consider issues that are unique to (a) college students, (b) student-athletes, (c) and minority students who attend predominately white community colleges. Which information would you use to assess the problem? How would you use the information to help Juan?
3. If you were working with Juan, what student affairs professionals and outside professionals would you need to involve in this case?
4. Given the facts, do you think that MCC should provide additional services for student-athletes like Juan? What commitments should MCC make to student-athletes in general and Juan in particular? What procedures do you recommend that MCC follow?
5. Based on your knowledge of student development and career development theories, how would you help Juan? What specific advising and/or counseling interventions would you use to assist Juan? What issues do you see that call for professional counseling or psychotherapy?
6. As the director of an athletic academic advising center, would you develop specific services and programs for athletics of color? If so, why and what would they be? If not, why not?

Research Activities for Further Exploration

1. Create an annotated bibliography on college student-athletes. Use the following headers to organize your annotated bibliography: counseling student-athletes, student development theory and student-athletes, and career development theory of student-athletes.
2. Using information from the library, write a research paper on factors that influence retention and academic achievement for student-athletes enrolled in two- and four-year institutions. Be sure to include athletes of color in your discussion.
3. Conduct interviews with several student-athletes on your campus. Include questions about the obstacles and challenges endured by college student-athletes. Present a summary of your findings.

IN THE LAND WHERE TRADITION
AND FOOTBALL ARE KING

MYRON L. POPE

Description of the Institutional Environment

South State University (SSU) is a four-year regional institution with approximately 12,000 students located in the Deep South. It is the oldest state-supported institution in the state, and it has had a tradition of strong academic programs producing many of the top state leaders, including the immediate past governor, a current U.S. Senator, and several current upper-level state legislators.

Description of the Surrounding Community

SSU is the pride of Sweet Water, a small, southern town of about 35,000 residents. SSU is the largest employer in Sweet Water and contributes significantly to its economic base especially during fall weekends when supporters flock to the small town for football games. The town is fairly conservative with a population base that is reflective of the state, which is 81 percent white, 16 percent African American, and 3 percent Hispanic.

Primary Persons Involved in the Case

- Monica Jones is a senior with a 4.0 GPA. She is President of the Black Student Association (BSA) and has been active in various campus activities during her matriculation at SSU.
- Marcus Harrison is the starting quarterback for the SSU Bulldogs. He is an all-conference player and a significant leader for the team. He is an African American and a member of BSA.
- Dr. Charles White, the Vice President of Student Affairs, supervises all student organizations and activities as well as the athletic department.
- Dr. Sherry Small is the President of SSU. She is an SSU graduate and is a major supporter of its football program.
- "Mean" Gene Howard is the fiery head coach of the Bulldogs. He has been at SSU for 12 years and has claimed four conference championships and one national championship during his tenure.
- Scott Hawkins is the leader of the largest Greek organization on campus, Kappa Nu Iota.

Information Germane to the Case

- Despite it being the oldest institution in the state, SSU was the last state institution to open its doors to African American students almost 45 years ago. This integration came about only after a strong stand from both the federal courts and the SSU executive administration against the governor of the state, who also was an SSU graduate.
- The Greek system at SSU is very prominent, with 20 percent of the student body being active members in 12 traditionally white organizations. Due to the nature and size of these organizations, they have controlled campus student politics for over 30 years. Presidents and executive committee members of the student government association, as well homecoming queens have come from these organizations during this period.

The Case

Monica Jones has been quite verbal regarding race relations on campus, and after deciding to run for BSA president, promised to pursue the institution's administration until the environment for African Americans on campus changes. After winning the election for the BSA presidency in the spring, she returned to campus in the fall with many plans to change the "system." During the first BSA meeting, Monica encouraged the students in attendance to begin thinking about the homecoming queen elections. She encouraged African American students to vote for a preselected candidate just as the white Greek organizations do. Everyone agreed, and subsequently they nominated and selected Monica to be that candidate.

The elections were held at the beginning of homecoming week. Charles White had heard about the BSA coalition efforts and was not surprised when election turnout was very high, in terms of Greek membership and African American students. However, he was not sure about what outcome to expect, as the executive assistant to the president and the president are the only individuals who know the results of the election until the day of the game.

That weekend, Marcus Harrison had a spectacular first half, and the crowd was very excited about the upcoming conference game the following week, as well as the announcement of the homecoming queen. As an SSU tradition, the governor of the state announced the homecoming queen at halftime. Monica, along with the other five finalists, was on stage behind him as he started the introduction of the new queen. As he called Monica's name, the crowd was shocked, as she was the first African American homecoming queen. Most of the stadium began to cheer, but the Greek section, led by Scott Hawkins, began to jeer and turned their backs to the field as she was paraded around the field in a convertible. As the second half began and Marcus and the team returned to the field, the Greeks cheered them on.

The BSA held an emergency meeting on Sunday and suggested that a sit-in be held in the president and vice president's office until the white Greeks apologize for jeering Monica. They also included a demand that the administration increase its recruitment and retention efforts for African American students, an issue that had not been a priority at SSU in the past. Marcus, who was at the meeting and was still particularly angry, suggested that the African American football players not practice or play in any games until an apology was received. There was significant attendance at this meeting, and both suggestions were well received.

Dr. Charles White was informed about the African American students' demands and he dreaded Monday morning. As he reached his office, he encountered Coach Howard who told him about the African American student-athlete walk-out. Coach Howard demanded that something be done immediately because his job would be on the line if he did not win the conference championship this year. After Coach Howard left, Dr. White's administrative assistant informed him that the president was holding for him on the phone. Dr. Sherry Small wanted to know what he was going to do about the situation because she had received several phone calls from alumni who were embarrassed by the national media coverage of the homecoming incident. She stated that the incident, if not handled swiftly, would hurt African American recruitment as well as financial support for the institution. She also emphasized that Dr. White's actions had better not do anything to jeopardize the chances of the Bulldogs winning the championship.

Discussion Questions

1. What are the issues or problems presented by this case? How does the history of the institution impact these problems? Be specific.
2. What are Dr. White's options in terms of solutions for this case? For each of these options, what steps should he take to resolve this case? How much consideration should he give to the impact of the status of the football team and the conference championship?
3. Would you suggest diversity training for any of these students? If so, which group(s) of students? How should this training be conducted, and what should be included in the content of this training? How long should the training last?
4. How do external and internal constituencies affect decision making regarding diversity affairs in this case and overall on this campus?
5. Should Dr. White pursue efforts to diversify the Greek organizations? What would be the implications of this decision on the student body? On

his career?

6. A diversity plan, which could address some of these issues regarding recruitment, retention, and education, was not mentioned in this case. How important would such a plan be in addressing the present and potential problems at SSU? What should be included in this diversity plan? How should employees and students of SSU be informed and educated about this diversity plan?

Research Activities for Further Exploration

1. Research the concepts of campus climate and campus community. What do they mean? How do these concepts impact minority students? Talk to administrators on your campus about things that they have done to achieve positive campus climate and campus community for minority students.

2. Research a predominantly White institution of higher education that has a pageant or homecoming queen contest which is affiliated specifically with a minority group on campus, such as Miss Black South State University or Miss Asian American South State University Homecoming Queen. Ask a student affairs professional on your campus about the history and significance of such programs.

3. Many will argue that if white students were punished for the jeering incident, the institution would be violating their freedom of speech and expression rights. How does the Constitution define these rights in the First Amendment? What are the limitations of freedom of speech and expression?

WHAT'S IN A COLOR?

SHARON K. ANDERSON

Description of the Institutional Environment

North Burns State University (NBSU) is a land-grant institution whose history dates back to the late 1800s. It began as an agricultural college and still claims to be the state's premiere institution in agriculture as well as leading university in business, education, and natural sciences. Although NBSU strives to be a multicultural campus, a majority (82%) of the 20,000 students identify themselves as " white." The next largest group is Hispanic (5%). To demonstrate support for students of color, NBSU sponsors several advocacy offices within the Division of Student Affairs (i.e., Black Student Alliance, Asian and Pacific American Student Services, and El Centro) with limited budgets. NBSU has worked hard to recruit and retain faculty and staff of color; however, a majority (90%) of the faculty and staff also is white. It is interesting to note that NBSU's president is a Native American who has led the institution for 10 years with vision and clarity in many areas, including multicultural awareness and sensitivity.

Description of the Surrounding Community

The campus is located in the city of Burlington. A majority of the 100,000-plus residents (94%) identify themselves as white; the median household income is $53,600, and 43 percent of the population reports completing four and more years of college. The major employers in the area are high-tech companies and the university. The city is located on a river near the foothills of the Smoky Mountains. With easy access to winter and summer activities in the mountains, NBSU's geographical location is a huge drawing card for out-of-state students.

Primary Persons Involved in the Case

- Department of Education faculty (over 40 professors and instructors from the education and student affairs higher education program) are seated around tables for a department faculty meeting.
- Dr. Steven Professor Willis is a white male and a full professor in the department. He has been asked to present information during the faculty meeting about his teaching experience with the honors program.
- Dr. Ellen Davis is a white female and an assistant professor in the department. She has been asked to present information during the same faculty meeting about her upcoming coedited book on issues of privilege and oppression.
- Dr. Mary Thompson is an African American female on the tenure track in the department. She coedited the book on issues of privilege and oppression.
- Dr. Luisa Cardona, who identifies as Chicana, holds the office of Vice President for Student Affairs and teaches one course for the student affairs higher education program. On several occasions she has shared with the faculty how students of color feel invisible or are continually called upon in class to be the voice for all students of color on campus or in the classroom.

Information Germane to the Case

- A majority of the people who are tenured or tenure-track professors in the education program are white. Most of the assistant professors are white females.
- From Ellen Davis' perspective, Mary Thompson has received limited support from the faculty regarding her progress toward tenure. For example, she received minimal mentoring support and structure from senior faculty while other junior faculty (usually white females) were assigned to and worked with faculty who offered to collaborate on writing projects.
- Several years ago at a different university, Luisa Cardona directed an Upward Bound project and Ellen Davis was the assistant director. At that time, Ellen didn't understand her white privilege. Luisa was very patient in trying to help her "get it," but many of Luisa's comments just didn't make sense at the time.

The Case

The faculty was seated at tables set up in a U-shaped configuration. Steven Willis, who is recognized as an outstanding teacher by the department as well as the university, shared his experience with the First-Year Seminar. All first-year students are required to take this seminar. Steven, who is noted for his creative and innovative techniques in teaching, decided to talk about activities he found to be helpful tools to engage students in discussion and self-exploration. In one such activity, pieces of paper in a variety of colors are passed around the room and students are encouraged to select a color that represents how they are feeling at that time. He described the different emotions students shared and the corresponding colors they selected to represent those feelings, including the color black. He then asked the faculty what they thought those students were feeling. There was a chorus of responses with words like "sad," "angry," or "lonely"–representing negative feelings or emotions. He confirmed the replies and went on to tell more student stories. Ellen Davis scanned the room to observe the reactions on her colleagues' faces. To her, Mary Thompson's expression seemed to say, "Here we go again: My color is the negative color."

As Ellen waited to speak about the upcoming coedited book on privilege and oppression, she wondered what to do. Should she share her observation with her colleagues? If yes, how could she address what appeared to be a glaring lack of cultural sensitivity? To not address the connotation people unwittingly associate with colors (black equals bad, white equals good) seemed intolerable. She had become aware of her white privilege a couple of times and was learning more and more about the issue because of the book. But, she felt like a "rookie" who was just getting this "privilege thing." Ellen thought something had to be said, but how? And by whom? She wondered if Mary would say something. Luisa Cardona caught Ellen's eye and motioned to meet her outside the room in the hallway.

Discussion Questions

1. Ellen Davis sees her colleagues as being culturally insensitive. Do you agree? Why or why not?
2. If you were Ellen Davis, what would you be feeling and thinking?
3. If you were Luisa Cardona, what would you say to Ellen Davis in the hallway?
4. If you were Ellen Davis, what would you do?
5. If you decided to address the group as a whole, what would you say? If you discussed the issue with Steven Willis individually after the meeting, what would you say?
6. How would your knowledge of Helm's white identity development model help you construct your response?

Research Activities for Further Exploration

1. Do a literature search on the issue of white privilege or other types of privilege.
2. Write a reflection paper on your own areas of privilege (e.g., skin color, gender, socioeconomic status, sexual orientation) and how your privilege results in oppression for others.
3. For a week, keep a log where you record phrases, comments, or conversations where the language used is "typical" and accepted but culturally insensitive. Share your results with the class.

DAWN WU'S JOURNEY OUT OF DEPRESSION

WALTER RANKIN, DORIS BITLER & DONNA FOX

Description of the Institutional Environment

Independence University (IU) is a public four-year institution with an enrollment of nearly 25,000 undergraduate and graduate students. Ranked as one of the most diverse institutions in the country, IU has a minority enrollment of 35 percent, of which 13 percent are Asian, Asian American or

Pacific Islander; 9 percent are African American; 6 percent are Hispanic American; and 7 percent are nonresident international students. IU is primarily a commuter institution with 12 percent of students living on campus. Approximately 53 percent of students are enrolled full time in one of 55 undergraduate or 68 graduate programs.

Description of the Surrounding Community

IU primarily serves the large suburban population of the Washington, DC metropolitan area. Sigmund County lies within 20 miles of the national capital and has a population approaching one million residents. Its ethnic population closely mirrors that of the university (13% Asian, Asian American, or Pacific Islander; 11% African American; and 8.4% Hispanic American).

Primary Persons Involved in the Case

- Dawn Wu is a 23-year-old sophomore at IU. She was born in Korea and her family speaks only Korean at home. She is the first member of the family to attend college. She has no siblings. English is her second language, but it also is her major, and she speaks and writes it with native fluency. She also works as a reporter for the IU student newspaper.
- Brian Smith is the Director of IU's Learning Services and Student Affairs Office. He has developed a successful series of workshops to help students better understand their individual learning styles and to help them refine their study skills.
- Dr. Rebecca Day is a psychologist employed at IU's Counseling Center.
- Dr. Alex Williams has served as an academic dean within the College of Arts and Sciences for seven years. He advises students in academic jeopardy and reviews requests for exceptions to academic policies.

Information Germane to the Case

- IU students must earn a 2.0 GPA (C average) each semester to remain in good academic standing. Students who earn below a 2.0 GPA in two consecutive semesters are placed on suspension for two semesters. Students can request an early return from suspension, however, and the deans encourage their return if they are willing to take steps to improve academically. Some of these steps might include meeting with a counselor to address personal issues and/or meeting with an academic advisor to plan an appropriate course load. After returning for suspension, students who earn below a 2.0 GPA in subsequent semesters can be dismissed. Dismissal typically is considered a permanent academic action, and thereafter students may not enroll again at the university.

The Case

Academically, Dawn Wu performed adequately during her first two semesters of study, maintaining a C average. In her sophomore year, she stopped attending classes in the middle of the semester, and she earned failing grades in all of her classes. During this time, she realized that she was experiencing great emotional distress, and she contacted Dr. Rebecca Day in the Counseling Center. While undergoing treatment for clinical depression, she enrolled in additional classes and performed poorly. Following that semester, she was placed on academic probation for one semester. When she returned to school, she did not continue with counseling, nor did she take medication that had been prescribed. During final exam week, Dawn realized that if she did not score well on her exams, that she could be dismissed from the university.

Dawn contacted Dr. Day and explained her situation fully. Dawn explained to Dr. Day the severity of her untreated depression and the impact her emotional well-being had had on her academic progress. Dr. Day referred her to Brian Smith to discuss her study habits and learning style. She also encouraged Dawn to meet with Dean Alex Williams to discuss the possibility of being withdrawn from her unsatisfactory classes until she felt better.

Brian Smith administered a series of learning assessments and helped Dawn discover that she was an auditory learner who would benefit greatly from class lectures. She also learned that she could tape a number of her lectures (with the instructors' permission) and play them back to help her pick up any missed information. He also helped Dawn review her time commitments with regard to her family, her classes, and the student newspaper, and they developed a clear calendar for her to follow over the coming months.

In his meeting with Dawn, Dean Williams carefully reviewed the information provided by Rebecca Day and Brian Smith. He assured her that withdrawals would be a possibility, but that academic policies would not allow additional withdrawals in the future for similar reasons. He explained that she also would need to meet with him and with Brian Smith throughout the remainder of her studies so that they could follow her academic and personal progress carefully and provide appropriate guidance. He reviewed IU's suspension and dismissal criteria with her and encouraged her to enroll part time for the next few semesters so that she could do her best academically, with the goal of improving her GPA and her self-esteem simultaneously.

Dawn stated that she now understood the importance of counseling and medication for depression. Since her return, Dawn has averaged a 2.80 GPA in 31 hours of coursework, and her cumulative GPA has increased to above a 2.0.

Discussion Questions

1. Define the term "model minority" with regard to the Asian and Asian American student population and discuss its relevance to Dawn's situation.
2. What aspects, if any, of Dawn's Korean American background might have prevented her from requesting academic and personal guidance earlier?
3. In a large university setting, what specific steps could the institution take to help reserved, reticent students like Dawn stay on track?
4. Compare the approaches taken by the three university representatives in their attempts to help Dawn.
5. Dawn tells you that she does not want her parents involved in her educational career. Her parents have been calling you, however, asking you to tell them about her situation. Their English skills are limited, and they do not read the language well. How should you address this issue while protecting the student's right to privacy?
6. What would you do if Dawn were to fall back into her old pattern?

Research Activities for Further Exploration

1. Conduct research to find five academic institutions with relatively large Asian and/or Asian American student populations. Cite and discuss statistics on their retention and graduation rates, and support services (if any) offered specifically for these students.
2. Research the occurrences of depression on college campuses in relation to specific minority groups.
3. Research the history of U.S. involvement in Korea, including President George Bush's inclusion of North Korea in his "Axis of Evil." What is the impact of the current U.S.-Korean political situation on Korean and Korean American students?

A NEW PROFESSIONAL'S DILEMMA

J. Shay Davis & Ralphel L. Smith

Description of the Institutional Environment

Southeastern State University (SSU) is a large public state-supported institution with approximately 22,000 students located in a small southern town. Currently, the ethnic and racial background of the student population is 72 percent white, 23 percent African American, 2 percent Hispanic, 1 percent Asian, 1 percent -multiracial, and 1 percent not specified. SSU is known for its bird sanctuary on the south end of campus and the school mascot is the Falcon. Seven residential areas on campus house 1,000 to 1,500 students each, for a total of 10,000 beds in the entire residence hall system.

Description of the Surrounding Community

SSU is located in Collegeville and is the second largest employer in the county. The largest employer is an agricultural center located on the outskirts of town. Collegeville has a population of approximately 50,000 people. Many small businesses in town rely on university events for their primary income.

Primary Persons Involved in the Case

- Daniel Boland, an Asian American student, is a fifth-year senior. He is a third-year Minority Assistant (MA) and is the informal leader of the 20 MAs on campus.
- Selena Starks, a Latina student, is a junior in her first year as an MA. She worked as a Resident Assistant (RA) last year.
- Nichole Hall, a Hawaiian student, is a sophomore and a first-year MA.
- Susan Lewis is a white entry-level professional in her first year as a Residence Hall Director (RHD) after completing her Master's degree. Susan supervises Daniel Boland, Selena Starkes, and Nichole Hall.
- Rachel Jones is an African American RHD in her third year in the position. She coordinates the MA program and the training for the MAs, and provides campus-wide oversight of nine other supervisors.

Information Germane to the Case

- The MA program began in 1982. At that time, no office of multicultural affairs or minority programs and services existed. The housing staff created the MA program in an attempt to recruit more students of color and to create a more supportive environment in the residence halls for the small numbers of minority students on campus.

- The 20 MAs are responsible for a designated area of the residential community in which they live. This could include several floors in one building or several small residence halls. The MAs serve as mentors or resource persons for the minority students living in their designated area of responsibility. In this role, they advise their peers, educate all students on issues of diversity, and plan social and educational programs. Each MA visits his or her residents twice a week to discuss issues such as college adjustment, academic success, and programming one-on-one with each resident.

- The MAs have a campus-wide meeting with Rachel Jones at least once a month. The nine MA supervisors are invited to these meetings as well. Supervisor attendance varies from month to month. Susan Lewis has not attended a meeting in three months. Along with these monthly meetings, the MAs in each area attend a weekly staff meeting with their supervisor. MAs also visit the RA staff meetings regularly.

- Susan Lewis is managing her area very well and the RAs report that she is a good supervisor and support system for them. As a new MA supervisor, Susan participated in staff training over the summer where the history and role of the MA program were discussed.

The Case

Daniel Boland, Selena Starkes, and Nichole Hall just completed a weekly area staff meeting with Susan Lewis in which several student issues and upcoming programs were discussed. Susan asked the MAs if they needed anything from her to complete their responsibilities for the programs; they all said they were doing fine. After the meeting, Susan met with Rachel Jones.

Rachel told Susan that during the last campus-wide MA meeting, several MAs stated that they did not feel like Susan was supporting the MA program because she missed the last three campus-wide meetings and seldom attended an MA program in her area. The MAs also wanted Susan to visit their residents more often. In addition, Susan recently addressed a roommate conflict between a white woman and an African American woman, but she never asked the MA to assist in the process of resolving the conflict. The MAs perceived this as a lack of support and understanding of the importance of the MA program.

Rachel also was frustrated because she feels like she has taken on an extra task in coordinating the MA program. She cannot be the supervisor for all 20 MAs and she wanted Susan to take on a more active role and show the students she is concerned and supportive of the program. Rachel also told

Susan that because she is white, she must work harder to show the MAs that she is supporting them.

Discussion Questions

1. Complete a SWOT (Strengths, Weaknesses, Opportunities, Threats) Analysis of this case.
2. What do you think about the way Rachel confronted Susan? Was this appropriate for her to do?
3. Design a recruitment and selection process to hire Residence Hall Directors who can effectively supervise traditional residence life staff and the MAs.
4. Explain what actions Susan should take in following up with the MAs to work on their relationship and how she should follow up with Rachel.
5. Based on your knowledge of identity development theory, what training should the RHDs receive before supervising the MAs? What training should the MAs receive?
6. How would you assess the readiness of entry-level professional staff of various ethnicities to supervise undergraduate staff of color?

Research Activities for Further Exploration

1. What is the history of race relations and desegregation on your campus?
2. Conduct focus groups of minority students living in your residence halls to investigate their interest and opinions about having a special program such as the Minority Assistance Program described in this case.
3. Conduct research on current methods (or instruments) for assessing racial identity development and their use with student affairs professionals.

DYNAMICS OF ASIAN AMERICAN IDENTITIES

ALVIN ALVAREZ

Description of the Institutional Environment

Prestige University is a private 150-year-old urban campus of approximately 15,000 students. As a highly competitive institution, students have an average SAT score of 1200. Although predominantly white for much of its history, students of color are becoming an increasingly visible presence on campus: 9 percent are African Americans, 7 percent are Latinos, 3 percent are Native Americans, and 2 percent are Asian Americans.

Description of the Surrounding Community

Prestige University is located in the heart of a large metropolitan city. Although located in a historically African American neighborhood, the area is being transformed with the influx of new immigrants from Asia, Central America, and Eastern Europe. In general, Prestige has been perceived by the surrounding community as an isolated "ivory tower," removed from the neighborhood.

Primary Persons Involved in the Case

- Santi Lee is the president of Asian Americans for Justice (AAJ), a small sociopolitical student organization dedicated to advocating for Asian American issues.
- Daniel Kim is the President of the Korean American Students Association (KASA), a large, primarily social and cultural student organization.
- Charissa Pei is the President of the Chinese American Association (CAA), the largest and oldest Asian American student group at the university.
- Carol Taylor is the President of the Black Students' Coalition (BSC), the largest and oldest African American student organization on campus.
- Angelita Ramirez is the Director of the Cross-Cultural Center (CCC). The mission of the CCC is to provide advocacy, operational support, organizational consultation, meeting facilities, and performance space for all of the organizations for students of color.

Information Germane to the Case

- Prestige University was the first school in the area to create an African American Studies program as a result of the Civil Rights Movement. Currently, no other ethnic studies programs exist on campus.
- Historically, "ethnic minority" issues on campus have been framed within the context of black-white relations.
- Historically, the 14 Asian American student organizations have been focused around distinct ethnic groups (e.g., Chinese, Japanese, South Asian) whose primary purpose has been to promote social activities such as dances, ski trips, museum outings, etc. In general, there has been minimal collaboration among these groups.

The Case

During the first part of the semester, Santi Lee and a small group of AAJ members began developing a proposal for a new pan-Asian umbrella group (the Asian Pacific American Network or APAN) with representatives from each of the 14 Asian American student organizations. Santi and other AAJ members feel strongly that there are issues of common concern to all Asian American students at Prestige University, such as the underrepresentation of Asian American faculty and staff, the underrepresentation of certain segments of the Asian student community (e.g., Southeast Asian and Filipino students), the lack of services for Asian American students, and the creation of an Asian American Studies program. Although AAJ typically has advocated for these sociopolitical issues in the past, Santi has argued that an umbrella organization of various Asian American student groups would be a more effective and representative advocacy group. Lately, Santi has begun speaking with the presidents of various Asian student groups to gather their support.

Other student groups within the Cross-Cultural Center have heard of APAN and have had mixed reactions. Daniel Kim dismissed the idea of APAN and suspected that this was yet another way that "militant" types like Santi could get attention and gain more power. According to Daniel, most of his constituents saw themselves as Korean rather than Asian American and wouldn't identify with APAN's "activist" agenda. Indeed, Daniel privately felt that Santi was creating trouble where there was none. Charissa Pei, however, felt that APAN might be complementary to the mission of CAA. She was intrigued by the possibilities that APAN could create by uniting the Asian American community. Carol Taylor already has discussed the creation of APAN with her executive board. Some of her officers felt strongly that APAN could be a threat to African American students and the BSC by cutting the "slices of the pie" even smaller than it already was. They argued that Asian American students already were overrepresented at Prestige and didn't require the same support as African American students. Other BSC officers, however, felt that an alliance with APAN could create a stronger and larger force for advocacy for students of color at Prestige.

Two days ago, Santi Lee informed Angelita Ramirez of his ideas about APAN. He asked Angelita if she would be willing to convene and facilitate a meeting of the various student organizations at the Cross-Cultural Center to discuss the possibility of creating APAN. Representatives from a number of groups, including Daniel Kim, Charissa Pei, and Carol Taylor, all have expressed an interest in attending the meeting.

Discussion Questions

1. What are the major concerns of each of the individuals in the case? How do these concerns complement or compete with one another?
2. What does Angelita need to know about Asian Americans, both on campus and in the larger society, to put this case into perspective?

3. What role should Angelita and the Cross-Cultural Center play in this process?

4. What student developmental theories might be useful in conceptualizing the developmental issues and group dynamics in this case? How would these theories inform the type of interventions available to Angelita? How would these interventions be modified for Santi, Daniel, Charissa, and Carol?

5. What comments and group dynamics would you anticipate at the meeting? How would you respond to each of the individuals if you were the director of the CCC?

6. What are the possible outcomes of this meeting in the short term and the long term? Evaluate the pros and cons of each outcome. How might each of the participants react to these outcomes?

Research Activities for Further Exploration

1. Research the history of the term "Asian American identity" and how this identity evolved. How have Asian ethnic groups historically related to one another? What is the significance of the term in relation to the Asian American civil rights movement?

2. Research the types of programs and services offered to Asian American students at several small, prestigious private colleges and universities in different parts of the U.S. What features do they have in common? What needs appear to be unmet?

3. In teams, prepare for a debate on the issues raised by Santi and Asian Americans for Justice (e.g., underrepresentation of Asian American faculty and staff, the need for services for Asian American students, etc.). That is, conduct research and collect information that supports and refutes these issues. Conduct the debate.

VANESSA'S VISION

Michael K. Herndon

Description of the Institutional Environment

Vector College (VC) is a public, four-year, liberal arts institution, with a private institutional ambiance. Enrollment is just above 3,500 students. The racial demographics of this institution consist of American Indians (1%), African Americans (2%), Hispanic Americans (2%), Asian Americans (3%), and white Americans (92%). VC is nationally recognized for its academic programs, especially in anthropology, business, and education. The institution has a very active and supportive alumni association.

Description of the Surrounding Community

Located in the heart of the mid-Atlantic region of the United States, VC is one of the largest employers in Ignatius, a suburban town. The town population hovers around 25,000 residents. Although the institution is predominately white, the demographic composition of the town is culturally diverse.

Primary Persons Involved in the Case

- Vanessa Rodriguez Arroyo, a first-generation, third-year student majoring in political science, is the only Latina Resident Assistant (RA) at VC.
- Kyle Carson, a Puerto Rican male, recently graduated from a leading student affairs program and is now the Director of Multicultural Affairs at VC.
- Marcia Webster, who is white, is the Director of the Office for Residence Life. Marcia is dedicated to her job and to the students at VC.
- Clark Houston, who describes himself as biracial, is the Director of Alumni Affairs.

Information Germane to the Case

- This institution has struggled over the past ten years to create a multicultural environment. Despite several plans to recruit and retain students of color, faculty and administrators have been unsuccessful. Senior administrators claim that VC's location and its degree options are not appealing to minority students.

The Case

VC administrators, faculty, and alumni pride themselves on the varied traditions at their institution. One of the most popular traditions at VC is the theme floor program, sponsored by the Office for Residence Life. The theme floor program allows students to develop their own housing assignments centered on a particular topic. Residents typically work throughout the year advancing theme floors through programs and service learning projects. Occasionally, faculty and members of the local community are invited to participate in activities on the theme floors.

Currently, the institution has five theme floors: (a) Sons and Daughters of the Confederacy, (b) Students Against Noise in the Environment, (c) the

Writers' Guild Floor, (d) Peace and Globalization Floor, and (e) an alcohol-free floor. Students requesting a new theme floor option must complete a group application, justifying the need for the newly proposed theme floor. There is no limit to the number of theme floors in the residence halls. The Office for Residence Life has recently announced the deadline for completed theme floor applications for the next academic year.

Vanessa envisions being the RA of a theme floor. She fantasizes about a theme floor devoted to addressing issues of race, class, and social policy. To generate student interest in her idea, Vanessa distributed posters, sent emails, and made announcements in all of her classes inviting students to become residents of her newly proposed theme floor.

Later in the term, Vanessa held two interest meetings related to her vision. Forty students (25 Latinos, 8 African Americans, and 7 Asian Americans) attended the meetings and expressed a genuine commitment to be a part of Vanessa's theme floor. For Vanessa, this was a bittersweet victory. On one hand, she was elated that a total of 40 students wanted to join her in advancing discussions related to race, class, and social policy on Vector's campus. On the other hand, however, she was disappointed that many of her white classmates who promised to support this initiative bailed out and did not attend either one of the interest meetings. Nevertheless, Vanessa was determined to submit a comprehensive application before the deadline set by the Office for Residence Life. Shortly after the second interest meeting, students started developing the theme floor application and the application was submitted three days prior to the posted deadline.

When Marcia Webster reviewed the application for a theme floor on race, class, and social policy, she immediately contacted Vanessa and requested a meeting to discuss the proposal. Marcia informed Vanessa that the Office for Residence Life could not support the proposal, although it was well written and submitted on time. She expressed her disappointment that no white students were included in the application. She then proceeded to give Vanessa a lecture about how it was illegal to house students by race and that a floor committed to confronting issues like race would appear to be "too ethnic." Vanessa explained that she exhausted multiple options to include all students in the application process, but Marcia stated that Vanessa's application for a theme floor would not be considered.

After meeting with Marcia Webster, Vanessa walked across campus to seek assistance from Kyle Carson in the Multicultural Affairs office. Kyle listened to Vanessa's concerns and suggested that the two of them go back to Marcia's office and further explore this issue. As they arrived at Marcia's office, both Kyle and Vanessa overheard Marcia discussing Vanessa's proposal with Clark Houston. Clark exclaimed, "We can never have a theme floor like that at VC! What will our alumni think? A floor like that could jeopardize alumni fundraising efforts."

Discussion Questions

1. Why is Vanessa frustrated and confused?
2. What are the potential ramifications of this case if Vanessa's theme floor is not approved?
3. How could Vanessa ensure the approval of the theme floor application?
4. Given the historical legacy of VC and its unsuccessful efforts to recruit students of color, how can the student affairs professionals help to implement Vanessa's vision?
5. List and describe the kinds of interventions, training, and skills that student affairs and higher education administrators need to respond to issues of race and racism on campus.
6. How would you evaluate the campus climate at VC for change in the area of race relations?

Research Activities for Further Exploration

1. Research the history of Latinos on predominantly white campuses. In general, what issues and concerns are typical for this population of students?
2. Conduct a literature review on theme housing in residence halls. Discuss the implications for theme housing on diversity, social responsibility, and service learning.
3. Conduct a needs assessment for a theme floor related to race and social class.

BIENVENIDOS A TODOS

Maricela Alvarado

Description of the Institutional Environment

The university is a public land-grant institution, which was established in the latter part of the 19th century. The student population of nearly 13,000 includes approximately 10 percent multicultural and international students. The four most prevalent ethnicities are Native American, African American, Asian American, and Hispanic/Latino. International students comprise approximately 2 percent of the overall student population. Fewer than 5 percent of all university employees identify themselves as multicultural or international.

Description of the Surrounding Community

The university is located in a northwestern logging community situated at the base of a mountain. Most of those not involved in the logging industry work for and/or support the university in some capacity. Local recreation includes horseback riding, rodeos, farmers' markets, fairs, and so forth. The community is located about 90 miles from a major city. The total population, including university students, reaches 25,000. The local community seems to thrive from the university's presence.

Primary Persons Involved in the Case

- Doris Rivera-Perez, a Chicana, is a second-year student majoring in comparative American studies. She is the first person in her family to attend college. Although she is bilingual, she cannot read or write in Spanish. Her parents were migrant workers who met while completing their General Education Degree. Doris is a member of Latinas Unidas on campus. She works in the evenings as a student assistant in the Multicultural Student Center.
- Robert Nelson is a third-year journalism student and reporter for the campus newspaper.
- Scott Wilson, a white transfer student from Los Angeles, is majoring in management information systems.

Information Germane to the Case

- It is common knowledge that a White supremacist group is active within 60 to 100 miles of the university.
- The case takes place during an election year in which an antiaffirmative action proposal has been added to the state ballot.
- An underground student coalition is being formed, involving primarily students of color and lesbian, gay, bisexual, and transgender students. Doris Rivera-Perez is a new member of this coalition.
- The Multicultural Student Center is open until 9:00 p.m. on weeknights.

The Case

Right before the Thanksgiving break, several anonymous hate signs consisting of White supremacist propaganda decorated with swastikas were posted on campus, targeting African American and Jewish faculty members. University officials denounced these acts in the campus newspaper and the multicultural affairs office hosted discussions about what had happened and how students were feeling. The multicultural community quickly came together and created new signs illustrated with a menorah and captioned in Spanish with "Bienvenidos a todos" (welcome to all). The signs were posted everywhere. However, the semester ended shortly thereafter and when classes reconvened in January, campus life resumed as if nothing had happened.

However, the multicultural community had not forgotten the signs, which stimulated discussion of other issues, such as faculty and staff diversity, multicultural student recruitment, and, above all, the campus climate. The campus newspaper became the forum for the voices of the multicultural community. Although the newspaper was flooded with opinion columns about these issues, the staff had to balance these with other issues on campus that seemed important to the majority of readers, such as a fraternity house closing or becoming a "dry" campus.

One day an editorial by Robert Nelson appeared in the newspaper opposing the multicultural community's endorsement of equal multicultural faculty and staff representation on campus. He argued that there weren't enough people of color with the proper credentials to fill position vacancies and asked, "Why do multicultural students feel they need instructors who look like them? These students must look beyond color and see the credentials and mentoring opportunities that the current faculty and staff can offer." He also stated, "These students shouldn't be complaining when they all receive special grants and scholarships, as well as the benefits of getting into college with lower admission standards to pursue their education."

This editorial sparked anger in Doris Rivera-Perez and many others. She responded by submitting her own article to the newspaper. The article was published without any kind of contact information for Doris, but the next day, Scott Wilson stopped by the Center and asked to speak with her. He was informed that she usually worked in the evenings and he was invited to leave a message in her box at the Center. He left a letter that had a tone of curiosity and seemed to express a need to be educated about the subjects Doris addressed in her article. She found his letter to be kind and looked forward to speaking with him.

Scott called Doris at the Center one evening and began the conversation with questions about her ethnicity and where she grew up. He also asked if she was attending the university on a scholarship. After she answered his questions, he commented on her article by saying, "I came to this university because it is 90 percent white. If you want faculty and staff representation of your people, go to California." He angrily accused multicultural students of getting a free ride while also receiving the benefits of lower admission standards.

Doris defended herself by explaining how her parents had fought during the 1960s so she could have a good education. When Scott began using profanity, she hung up on him. He called back several more times and she continued to hang up on him. She then called a friend to come sit with her in the Center until it closed. She reported the incident to the university police department (UPD) and they took a statement from her, but she never heard from them again. No one from the university contacted her to make sure she was okay. She was tormented by the incident and frustrated that nothing had been done about it. Her primary support came from student organizations and the underground coalition. For them, this incident was yet another example of the insensitivity and inequality experienced by multicultural students.

Discussion Questions

1. What are the primary concerns of the two main characters in this case?
2. How might their concerns be explained by identity development theories?
3. Based on information given in the case, discuss how Doris's family history may influence her reactions to this experience.
4. Which university offices should follow up on Doris's statement to the UPD? How should this be done? What services should be offered?
5. Would the situation and/or reaction(s) have been different if Doris were male?
6. What issues might multicultural students encounter when going through the college search?

Research Activities for Further Exploration

1. Doris's father identifies himself as a Chicano, but her mother prefers the term Mexicana. Research the history of these and other terms that have been used to describe people whose roots are in Mexico or Central America (e.g., Hispanic, Latina/o, etc.). Write a report that includes their definitions as well as controversies that have arisen regarding their usage.
2. The Southern Poverty Law Center's Intelligence Project monitors the activities of hundreds of racist, neo-Nazi, and "Patriot" groups in the U.S. Research the impact of white supremacist groups on college and university campuses. Then select a group that has been active on your campus (or elsewhere in the state or region) and prepare a report about its history, philosophy, organizational structure, membership, recruitment practices, and other activities both on and off campus. What has been your institution's response to this group's on-campus activities?
3. Interview fourth-year or graduate Latina/o students on your campus to develop a grounded theory on factors that may influence their retention and persistence.

A BALANCING ACT

Cyrus Williams

Description of the Institutional Environment

Armstead College (AC) is a large public land-grant, research institution. AC is the state's oldest, largest, and most comprehensive university. It is among the nation's most academically diverse public universities. AC is one of only 17 public land-grant universities that belong to the Association of American Universities. AC operates six apartment villages for eligible graduate students and students with families.

Description of the Surrounding Community

Armstead College is the pride of Springdale, a small town with 35,000 residents. Springdale offers a picturesque view, complete with several lakes and spacious farms. The community is very supportive of AC because most of the residents in this town are employed by the school and are blue-collar workers (lower to middle class).

Primary Persons Involved in the Case

- Richard Lee is a senior majoring in art history. He and his wife, Suzy (whose English skills are limited), live in one of the apartment villages with their two children, Ricky (7) and Donna (2).
- Mary Smith works for the Department of Housing as a Residence Assistant (RA); she lives next door to the Lee family.
- Barbara Lewis is the Victim Advocate for the University Police Department.
- John Hart is the Director of Housing.
- Phyllis Cantrell is the Director of the International Center.
- Robert Hill is the Assistant Dean for Student Judicial Affairs.

Information Germane to the Case

- The Lee family is in the United States on an educational visa. Richard Lee must be a full-time student to remain in the country. He may not work while in the U.S.
- Housing policy at AC stipulates that any students involved in a domestic dispute must be removed from housing.

The Case

Mary Smith suspects that her next-door neighbor, Suzy Lee, is being bat-
tered by her husband, Richard Lee. Mary has been observing the family
since the start of the semester and has noticed that Suzy usually walks behind
her husband. Mary believes that Richard intimidates Suzy; she has heard
them arguing on many occasions. Mary has attempted to speak with Suzy;
however, she does not open the door when Mary knocks and she does not
answer the telephone.

One morning, while Mary and Suzy are waiting at the bus stop, Mary
notices bruises on Suzy's arms. Mary asks Suzy how she is adjusting to the
university and the country and informs her that if she needs anything to call
on her. Suzy, who does not speak English well, tells Mary that she is not
allowed to speak to anyone without her husband's permission. Suzy tells
Mary that her husband would be very upset if he saw her speaking with a
university official. After this conversation, Mary is sure that Richard is abus-
ing his wife and reports this to John Hart.

The next day, John calls a meeting with Phyllis Cantrell and Barbara
Lewis to get their advice. Phyllis informs them that Richard Lee's views on
women and marriage are a common, recurring issue with students from different countries. Barbara is very concerned about the health and safety of
Suzy and the children. Phyllis tells Barbara and John that she knows the family well and she does not feel that Richard is a threat to his wife or children.
The three of them decide that Phyllis should speak with Richard and encourage him to seek counseling at the University Counseling Center. A week
later, Mary Smith hears Suzy and Richard Lee arguing in their apartment.

At 8:00 a.m. the next morning, John Hart contacts Robert Hill to initiate
an intervention with the Lee family. At 9:00 a.m., Barbara Lewis, Phyllis
Cantrell, Richard Lee, and Suzy Lee arrive at Robert Hill's office to discuss
the incident. Suzy tells Robert that there is no problem in her home. She says
that Richard found out that she had spoken with Mary last week and that is
why they were arguing. She explains to the entire group that Richard is overwhelmed with his classes, but he is a good husband and father.

Discussion Questions

1. What are the issues in this case?
2. Do you think Mary Smith did the right thing by reporting the situation to
   the Director of Housing?
3. What were some of the cultural assumptions Mary Smith used as a basis
   for her actions?
4. Based on your knowledge of student development theory, what interventions would you recommend for Richard Lee?
5. Should cultural differences be taken into consideration when there are

conduct violations on campus?

6. How would you proceed if you were Robert Hill?

Research Activities for Further Exploration

1. Develop a comprehensive training program for student affairs practitioners for dealing with the issues discussed in this case.
2. Develop an educational module on domestic violence and child abuse and neglect for the orientation sessions provided to new international students.
3. Research articles and court cases that discuss universities' duty and responsibility to address and sanction students in a culturally sensitive way.

THE SPECIALIZATION OF MINORITY SUPPORT SERVICES

EMMANUEL (SONNY) AGO

Description of the Institutional Environment

Grand University (GU) is a large private research institution. It boasts medical, business, and law schools as well as various graduate and professional schools encompassing numerous disciplines and fields, including education, social work, and engineering. Among approximately 11,000 undergraduates who attend this predominantly white institution, 22 percent are Asian American, 11 percent are African American, and 8 percent are Latino. GU consistently has been ranked among the top 10 research universities.

Description of the Surrounding Community

GU has a tumultuous relationship with the surrounding urban neighborhood in the large northeastern city in which it is located. Residents of this low-income area continually grapple with the dilemma of gentrification and rising costs of living due to the expansion of the GU campus. However, some residents recognize that the university has created jobs and, through its various graduate programs, has provided an array of social services as a part of its community outreach.

Primary Persons Involved in the Case

• Marilyn Watson is the current Director of the Minority Cultural Center at

GU. The Center is a freestanding three-story building at the edge of campus. Historically, the center has been the primary support and cocurricular programming hub for all minority students. Marilyn is the advisor for the undergraduate Minority Student Coalition (MSC), which was established 15 years ago and formerly served as an umbrella organization that represented about a dozen minority student organizations on campus.

- Simone Talbot is a junior and the current Chair of the MSC.
- Miguel Teja is a senior and the founding and current Chair of the Latino Empowerment Coalition (LEC).
- Dr. Paul Rodriguez is the current Director and only staff of the newly established Hispanic Resource Center (HRC). Rodriguez also is the Chair of the Latino Studies Program.
- Gloria Hyun is a first-semester junior and the founding and current Chair of the Asian Student Coalition (ASC).

Information Germane to the Case

- Since the peak of minority student protests, which took place after the Rodney King verdict in 1992, GU has been receptive to institutionalizing diversity on campus.

The Case

The LEC was formed two years ago when the Latino student groups seceded from the MSC. The LEC currently consists of the Puerto Rican Nationals, Latinos United, and the Latina/o sorority and fraternity. As a result of its secession from the MSC, there is animosity between the LEC and some of the other non-Latino minority student organizations on campus. As defined by Miguel Teja and his board, the LEC's primary mission was to establish separate student resources utilizing the general Diversity Fund set aside for programs and services for minority undergraduates. After a year of petition writing, meeting with the university president, and three public protests, the LEC was successful in creating a proposal for the HRC, which recently was inaugurated and boasts a library, computer room, and general meeting space. It is located in an old fraternity house at the center of campus sharing a floor with the Lesbian, Gay, Bisexual, and Transgender Center, and one flight above the African American Resource Center.

The ASC was established last year. Similar to the LEC, Gloria Hyun and the ASC board seek resources from the general Diversity Fund and a centralized resource center for Asian American students on campus. The ASC consists of the Chinese Student Organization, the Korean Contingent, the Asian American fraternity and sorority, the Filipino Student Organization, the Taiwanese Student Organization, and Japanese Americans United. However, during the process of creating a proposal for an Asian American Resource Center, the ASC still remains under the MSC umbrella and shares resources and space with other minority student groups at the MCC.

Marilyn Watson recently attended a MSC meeting, during which Gloria Hyun requested that the MSC and its members sign a petition in support of ASC's proposal to establish a new Asian American Resource Center. The petition and proposal will be presented to the University Advisory Board (UAB) at next month's general meeting.

Simone Talbot responded on behalf of the MSC, saying "Gloria, while we agree that it is necessary to address the issue of the growing number of minority students on campus and the need for increased resources for all our individual ethnic communities, we feel that it is actually counterproductive for each community to establish separate spaces and resources. We need to seriously contemplate the effects of the LEC leaving the MSC as we decide whether or not to support ASC's cause. As we told Miguel Teja a couple years ago, separating our distinct ethnic communities only serves to diminish MSC's voice. Since LEC's departure, we can no longer fully represent the entire minority student population's concerns at UAB meetings. Because of this, the administration already sees us as fragmented and, in the future, might not consider our needs as a collective minority community. Once we're all physically separated and acting as individual political coalitions, it will be nearly impossible to address general minority concerns like minority recruitment as part of the UAB. Right now, under the MSC, the Asian American community has a direct link to the president and administration. Do you want to risk losing that like the Latino groups have?"

Hesitantly, Marilyn Watson concurred with Simone: "There's a lot of history involved here. I need to make it absolutely clear that the MCC and the MSC already are part of GU's mainstream campus culture. While the LEC has its space, it isn't part of the formal UAB. It has taken years for the MSC to win a seat on the UAB and, because of this, can function in the actual voting and decision-making process as a part of the administration. Because the LEC doesn't have a seat, the only way they could formally voice their future concerns and needs would be through Dr. Rodriguez. Also, we all need to consider the issue of the Diversity Fund and the future of the MCC. I already can tell you that because of the Latino students leaving, the president is considering reducing the MCC budget–displacing some of our money from the Diversity Fund to support the HRC. At this point, we're not sure how many of our services we can sustain if we lose more resources. Essentially, if new centers are established for each ethnic community, we'll all be fighting for pieces of the same pie."

The MSC voted against supporting the ASC's efforts to acquire a new center on campus, as it had done with the LEC two years earlier. Reflecting on these recent events, Marilyn Watson predicts that, as with the LEC, the ASC will now begin the lengthy process of sit-ins, protests, and further petition writing if the UAB rejects their proposal. As new ethnic-specific coalitions form, fuelled by a political agenda to gain institutional recognition of distinct minority communities on campus, she foresees a dilemma that will soon face the MCC and MSC. With the institutionalization of the HRC—and, predictably, the efforts of the ASC not far behind—she has noticed the emergence of a highly specialized and fragmented campus culture when it comes to minority student support. She has resolved that the MCC must redefine its role in order to sustain its budget and resources. To the administration, it must demonstrate its relevance as an office that can still provide a valued service as a part of implementing diversity, as well as coexist with the new ethnic-specific centers. She laments that the MCC can no longer focus on its traditional role of being the primary support and programming hub for all minority groups on campus. Similarly, according to Simone Talbot, new challenges face the MSC—in particular, trying to devise new strategies that will allow a unified minority student voice to emerge once again at GU.

Discussion Questions

1. What are the major issues that prevent the MSC from supporting the LEC and the ASC?
2. Do you see the MSC's refusal to support the ASC and LEC as being justified? Explain.
3. You are the MCC Director and advisor to the MSC. Role-play as to how you would go about advising the MSC Chair in preparation for meetings with the LEC and the ASC.
4. What are the possible issues and conflicts minority cultural centers and minority student coalitions face once ethnic-specific student coalitions and centers are established?
5. Based on your knowledge of campus culture and climate, what strategies would you recommend in order for the MCC to maintain its relevance as a part of GU's campus?
6. Create a mission statement proposing tangible new programs minority cultural centers might undertake in order to coexist with ethnic-specific centers.

Research Activities for Further Exploration

1. Research the history of race relations on your campus. How does this con-

tribute to the problems of creating a unified minority student voice or coalition?

2. Write a report, using data from library resources and individual interviews with student affairs administrators on selected campuses, which focuses on the push toward specialization of multicultural centers.

3. Survey the missions, roles, structures, and programs of other minority cultural centers at research universities nationwide.

CULTURE CLASHES IN THE RESIDENCE HALL

SHARON L. HOLMES & SARAH L. WILLIAMSON

Description of the Institutional Environment

Gunthers College (GC) is a moderately selective private liberal arts college for women located in Arkansas. Incoming students have SAT scores in the 1400s; 67 percent rank in the top 10 percent of their high school graduating class, 94 percent rank in the top quarter, and 100 percent in the top half.

Description of the Surrounding Community

Gunthers College is located in a small town on the Arkansas-Missouri border with a population of 33,000. People like having the college located in their town because they feel it increases the prestige of their community. However, some residents have concerns about the growing minority population on campus, which naturally spills over into the local community.

Primary Persons Involved in the Case

- Angela Jones is a white first-year student from a small community in southern Arkansas, located approximately 60 miles from the college. She is a first-generation college student and the first of her four siblings to attend college.
- Tara Jefferson is a first-year African American student from Detroit, Michigan. She is a second-generation college student.
- Rusty and Sue Jones are Angela's parents. They raised their children to believe that abortion, alternative lifestyles, hard drinking, profanity, and race mixing are sins written about in the Bible.
- Norma Jefferson, Tara's mother, is a divorced single parent who lives in Detroit, Michigan.

- Candace Coleman is the Hall Director (HD) of Coopers Hall. She has been charged by the dean of students to work with her staff to configure living arrangements that promote diversity and cross-ethnic and cross-cultural involvement.
- Mary Smith is the Resident Assistant (RA) assigned to the floor where Angela Jones and Tara Jefferson will be roommates during their first semester at GU. One of her primary responsibilities as an RA is to assist the new incoming students in making the transition to college during their first year.
- Dr. Donna White, an African American woman, had been at GC in various student affairs positions for six years before becoming the Dean of Student Affairs four years ago.

Information Germane to the Case

- In an effort to assist students in learning about ethnic and cultural differences, all students are required to live on campus during their first year of enrollment in preassigned residence halls.
- It also is a hall policy that incoming students live in their assigned halls for at least the first year, and students must remain with their assigned roommate for at least the first semester. After the first semester, they are free to change roommates or move to another room in the hall if they desire. Incoming students are assigned to rooms at random without regard to race, religion, or other demographic characteristics to enhance the possibility of cross-ethnic and cross-cultural interaction.

The Case

At the beginning of the school year, GC held its annual "Fresh Start Day." The vice president for student affairs hosted a welcome reception for students and their parents along with the faculty, staff, and other administrators. Activities for the day were designed to provide new and returning students with an orientation to campus, distribute room keys, and introduce the leaders of campus organizations.

After the activities were over, Angela and her parents began to move her things into her assigned room. By mid-afternoon, Angela was completely moved in. As Mr. and Mrs. Jones were about to leave, Mr. Jones gave Angela a present with a card on which he had written, "Don't forget us back home." The present was a large Confederate flag, which she and her father immediately hung on the wall by the bed she had chosen. After her parents left, she continued to busy herself unpacking her things as she anxiously awaited her roommate's arrival. When Tara put her key in the door, Angela opened it for her and they both stood in shock for a moment as they realized the other's race. Tara introduced herself, and then she and her mother began moving her things into the room. It was then that Tara noticed the Confederate flag hanging on the wall. She was immediately bothered, but decided to wait to see if, out of respect, Angela would remove the flag now that she knew the race of her roommate.

As the semester got underway, both women began to make new friends, yet they spent very little time getting to know each other. Angela associated with other white students, while Tara befriended other black students. Angela and Tara spoke to each other only when it was absolutely necessary, and neither seemed interested in developing a relationship with the other. They traveled in their own racially homogeneous social circles, which did not interact with students of other races on campus.

Finally, after days of being bothered by the flag, Tara asked Angela to take it down. Annoyed by the request, Angela asked her why she should. Tara explained that to African Americans, the Confederate flag is offensive and is viewed as a sign of racism. Angela told her that to her and her family, the Confederate flag represents a sense of pride in cultural heritage. Tara told her that she was offended by what the flag stood for and that she should not have to be subjected to such things in her room. Angela replied that she should have known what she was getting herself into when she decided to attend a college in the South. Again, Tara asked Angela to remove the flag and again Angela refused. When Tara left the room, Angela immediately called her father and told him about what had just happened. He reassured her that she had every right to hang whatever she wanted in her room, and if that black girl didn't like it, she could just move out.

After several more weeks of silent tension in the room, Tara approached her RA, Mary Smith, to discuss the problem. Mary asked her if she and Angela had tried to work out the situation on their own. Tara told her that they rarely spoke to each other unless it was absolutely necessary. She also told Mary that she refused to allow such an offensive symbol to hang in her own room any longer and that she should not be forced to accept it. Mary asked Tara to try once more to talk to Angela, and if they still could not reach a compromise, then the three of them would discuss the matter with the HD, Candace Coleman. Tara did not try to talk to Angela again.

A few days later, Angela approached Mary. She indicated she felt nervous to be in the room with Tara and that she did not see why she should have to take her flag down. With this, Mary asked both students to meet with her in Candace's office. After hearing both sides, Candace suggested that they all meet with Dr. Donna White. In the meeting, Angela expressed how angry she felt that Tara wanted her to remove the flag. Tara replied that she too was angry because she considered Angela's flag a racist symbol. During the meeting, both women became emotional while trying to argue their case and a compromise could not be reached. A second meeting was called for the next week with the hope that the roommates could work out their problem themselves.

After several days of heated telephone calls from Rusty Jones, a meeting was arranged to include the students, their parents, Mary Smith, and Candace Coleman. In the meeting, everyone sat quietly while Rusty Jones used colorful language to explain why his daughter had every right to hang whatever she wanted on the walls on her side of the room and that he was outraged that the college supported these type of living arrangements anyway. When he was reminded of the college's room policy, he screamed that he didn't care about policy; he didn't like what was going on and somebody had better do something about it. Norma Jefferson, on the other hand, remained calm as she shared her concerns about her daughter's emotional state of mind and the impact this situation could have on her first-semester grades. She also pointed out that there was no reason why the college should permit such blatant forms of racism in this day and age. Both parents demanded that the college allow their daughters to change rooms to escape the tense living environment.

Discussion Questions

1. Was it appropriate for the RA to ask Tara to try to resolve the situation with Angela without her immediate assistance? Overall, do you believe the residence hall staff handled the matter appropriately?
2. Considering race relations in America, and specifically in some southern states, is the residence hall policy reasonable? Explain why it is or is not.
3. How would you resolve each aspect of this case? Explain in detail.
4. Discuss the implications of the residence hall's room assignment policy as a method to increase cross-ethnic and cross-cultural involvement.
5. Using relevant theories of college student development identity, discuss where Angela and Tara may be in terms of their individual identities.
6. Discuss other initiatives the college might use to enhance cultural and ethnic involvement and interaction between diverse student groups?

Research Activities for Further Exploration

1. Conduct research at your institution to investigate their free speech policy and how it is implemented in the residence halls.
2. What is the distribution of ethnic and cultural student groups on your campus? What initiatives has your institution implemented to bring the various groups together as community?

3. Identify five to seven undergraduate students from diverse ethnic groups on your campus. Invite them to participate in a focus group in order to discuss the case. Summarize your findings.

RESPONDING TO TENSION ON CAMPUS

Dennis M. Baskin & Jerlando F. L. Jackson

Description of the Institutional Environment

Green University (GU) is a public institution with a student enrollment of approximately 10,500. The student to faculty ratio is ten to one. This institution prides itself on being a comprehensive regional university that offers 42 undergraduate and 14 graduate degree programs. The student of color population is approximately 9 percent, of which 4 percent is African American, 2 percent is Latino, 2.5 percent is Asian, and 0.5 percent is Native American.

Description of the Surrounding Community

Green University is located in a rural community of 12,000 people. The town has a very small diverse population that does not exceed 3 percent. However, it is within 30 minutes of several large urban cities. The university and the community have a good working relationship and many university employees reside in town.

Primary Persons Involved in the Case

- Sally Smith is the Assistant Director of Student Activities and the staff coordinator of the homecoming weekend committee.
- James Johnson is the President of the Coalition for Unity. The coalition includes members from the Native American Student Union, Black Student Union, Latino Student Organization, Asian Student Union, and the Gay and Lesbian Student Union.
- Mark Mashi is a full-time administrator in student affairs at GU and serves as the faculty advisor for the Native American Student Union.
- John Stevens is the student president of the historically white Trident Fraternity.
- Dr. Roger Billary has been the Chancellor of Green University for three years.

Information Germane to the Case

• Recently, the Native American Student Union submitted a formal letter to Dr. Roger Billary outlining racial problems that have occurred on campus. The letter requested that GU make a concerted effort to hire and attract more faculty and staff members of color.

The Case

Each year during the first week of October, GU hosts a variety show during homecoming weekend. As usual, students rallied to put on the variety show with the theme of "Don't Touch That Channel." The idea was to identify commercials that stood out over the years. Many student organizations participated in the contest. One particular organization, Trident Fraternity, decided to do a Native American skit. The audience booed loudly when a white member of Trident Fraternity, went on stage in "War-Face." This insensitive incident caused great protest on campus. The students interpreted the skit to be making a mockery of Native American culture.

The following morning, Sally Smith filed a complaint with the homecoming steering committee requesting that the fraternity receive a written reprimand. Many of the multicultural organizations found this request to be a mere "slap on the hand" and decided to form a committee and address the issues directly with the chancellor. The coalition members felt that the chancellor did not take their concerns seriously and they decided to march to the chancellor's office to protest the insensitive portrayal of "War-Face" and the chancellor's careless response to the incident. The students led a successful march that included approximately 200 students; many television and newspaper reporters were in attendance. Many of the media outlets portrayed the issue as racial problems at Green University. The student leaders solicited state Native American leaders as a resource base to give greater statewide attention to the problems.

The following day, the chancellor issued a statement announcing that he planned to host three campus-wide meetings to address the perceived racial problems on campus. At the first meeting, tensions were high. Coalition for Unity members had a shouting match with members of the Trident Fraternity. The coalition members expressed that "War-Face" was offensive and offered history to back up their claims. Fraternity members insisted that their variety show skit was done in complete fun and that it was not their intention to offend any person or group. The first meeting ended with nothing constructive being accomplished. At the second meeting, there was less tension and each participant was able to educate the others about their perceptions. After the third meeting, the chancellor and the Coalition for Unity members decided to create a task force whose mission was to improve race relations on campus.

Chancellor Billary called Mark Mashi and asked if the students would march again. He also asked if the students now felt that his actions demonstrated an understanding of the seriousness of the issue. Dr. Billary asked Mark to play a major role on the task force and to ensure him that the students would not march and publicly embarrass the university again. Mark informed the chancellor that he could not assure him that the students would not march again. He also stated that he saw the march as a learning experience rather than a public embarrassment. The chancellor said he disagreed with Mark's opinion but would welcome the opportunity to work with him and with the Coalition for Unity.

Later, the chancellor was shocked to learn that Sally Smith and several multicultural students had advised and pleaded with the white student not to go on stage with "War-Face," but the student decided to do so anyway. The student eventually was placed on probation, and Trident Fraternity was sanctioned and had to fundraise nearly $2,500 to pay for a national speaker to come to GU to talk about fostering better race relations.

Discussion Questions

1. Identify the issues or problems presented in this case. Be specific.
2. Did the multicultural students overreact to the incident and embarrass the university?
3. Explain what each party involved did right and/or wrong in the case?
4. How would you describe race relations and campus culture in this case?
5. Do you believe the chancellor provided solid leadership in response to the situation?
6. If you were the chancellor, how would you have handled the situation?

Research Activities for Further Exploration

1. Research similar cases that have occurred in recent years on college campuses. While conducting research, be sure to note how each case/incident was resolved. Write a report based on your findings.
2. Interview a student affairs administrator regarding his or her views about your university's campus climate. Focus your interview questions on the current campus community, how the campus community could be improved, and ways to better evaluate student perceptions of the campus community.
3. What is your university policy on diversity? How does your diversity statement or policy compare with other colleges and universities in your state?

DEE'S GRADE APPEAL

Gypsy M. Denzine

Description of the Institutional Environment

Northland University (NU) is a public four-year institution with moderately selective admission criteria. Approximately 25,000 students attend NU, which is a predominantly undergraduate residential institution. The racial and ethnic demographics of the university are as follows: 23 percent Native American/American Indian, 8 percent Hispanic American, 6 percent African American/Black, 2 percent Asian American/Pacific Islander, and 61 percent white.

Description of the Surrounding Community

Three very large Native American reservations are within 90 miles of the campus. The tribal demographics are 60 percent Navajo, 35 percent Hopi, 2 percent Apache, and 3 percent other.

Primary Persons Involved in the Case

- Dee Begay, is a second-year human services graduate student at NU. Dee also is an academic advisor at Pineridge College, a two-year tribal college located 90 miles from NU.
- Dr. Gail Turin is an Assistant Professor and serves as Coordinator of the Student Affairs graduate program at NU.

Information Germane to the Case

- The Student Affairs Masters degree program at NU is considered to be a very strong program. Graduates of the program receive several job offers upon graduation and a large number of students go on to earn doctoral degrees in student affairs. Dee chose to enter the 36-hour human services program rather than the 48-hour counseling-based student affairs program because of her full-time job at Pineridge College and her two-hour roundtrip commute to take classes at NU.

The Case

Dr. Turin integrated a qualitative research project into her course on college student development theory. As stated in the syllabus, the purpose of the research project was to provide students with an opportunity to: (a) learn more about resilient college students, (b) gain knowledge and skills relative to qualitative inquiry, and (c) simulate the experience of presenting at a professional conference. Students were required to have their topic approved in advance by Dr. Turin prior to submitting a proposal to the Institutional Review Board (IRB). For this assignment, students were to conduct at least five semistructured interviews with undergraduate students from a specific subpopulation. As indicated in the syllabus, students were to transcribe two of the five interviews verbatim in order to gain qualitative methodological skills. The transcribed interviews were to be attached to the handout students would share with their classmates during their presentation. Dr. Turin spent an entire two-hour class period discussing the importance of tape-recorded interviews in qualitative research. In addition, she provided an opportunity for students to interview each other briefly during class and illustrated how to complete an interview transcription. Students were not required to write a research paper; instead, Dr. Turin required the students to submit a handout, which is a common practice in conference presentations. Dr. Turin provided students only 15 minutes of class time to present their research because 15 minutes is the typical time frame for graduate student presentations at national student affairs conferences.

The research project counted for 40 percent of the student's grade in the course. Dr. Turin did not itemize the percentage points for each component of the project (i.e., topic selection, review of the literature, IRB proposal, data collection, interview transcriptions, handout, and oral presentation). The research project for this course is considered to be one of the capstone experiences of the student affairs graduate program and is used for program assessment of student learning outcomes. Dee chose to explore the experiences of students who transferred from Pineridge College to NU. Specifically, she was interested in understanding the experiences of transfer students who were conditionally admitted and later thrived and became highly academically successful at NU. Dr. Turin agreed with Dee that this would be an ideal subpopulation for understanding the experiences of resilient Native-American students. Dr. Turin frequently asked the students for project updates in class. Dee repeatedly shared that her project was going very well but did not report any details. Dr. Turin invited Dee to stop by during her office hours, but Dee stated that none of Dr. Turin's scheduled office hours fit her work and commute schedule.

Students were scheduled to present their research findings during the last night of class. Dee began her presentation by stating, "My husband's family had a ceremony today so when I am done, please do not clap or ask questions. Thank you." Dr. Turin suspected that several of the students in the class were not familiar with the role of ceremonies in the Native American culture and did not know how to respond to Dee. Although Dr. Turin believed this could be an ideal learning opportunity for the other students in the class, she decided not to ask Dee to share anything during her presentation about the ceremony she attended. Dee chose not to share with the group that the ceremony was held because her husband's brother recently died in a car accident. During the ceremony, the medicine man asked that all family members honor their lost family member by engaging in quiet reflection for a period of 48 hours. After Dee requested that her class members not clap or ask questions, she then shared her name, tribal affiliation, and clan identity from both her Navajo and Hopi heritage. Following this five-minute introduction, Dee stated that she had not tape recorded her interviews because her first interviewee believed that tape recording or "capturing one's voice on tape" was insensitive in the Navajo culture and reminded Dee that she should know better. Therefore, Dee chose not to use a tape recorder in her subsequent interviews. Dee did not explain that this individual was from a very traditional Navajo background and his elders had raised him to not share his voice on tape because it could contribute to the loss of their native language.

During her presentation, Dee briefly stated that the interviews were interesting but from a Navajo perspective, it was much more important to tell one's own story. Dee used the remainder of the presentation time to share her own experience of attending Pineridge College and later transferring to NU. Dee also provided a very rich and interesting description of the student services provided at Pineridge College. However, she did not discuss the topic of resiliency among college students, nor did she provide a handout. She stated that because she did not have transcriptions to share she did not think a handout would be useful. Instead she chose to share college brochures and other informative materials from Pineridge College.

Dr. Turin met individually with students after class to discuss their research project and presentation. Dr. Turin was unsure about discussing the course project and providing feedback to Dee because of Dee's statement about respecting that she had attended a ceremony earlier that day. After meeting with several students, Dr. Turin returned to the student lounge and was informed by other students that Dee had gone home. Dr. Turin planned to contact Dee prior to submitting her grades, but she ran out of time and submitted her grades without having met with Dee. Dr. Turin decided Dee earned a "C" for the project, which resulted in a "B" for her overall course grade.

Soon after receiving her grades, Dee met with Dr. Turin to share her concerns about her grade for the course. Dee believed she earned an "A" for her research project and presentation and should receive an "A" for the course. Dr. Turin informed Dee she would not change the grade because Dee did not follow the requirements for the qualitative research project. Dee has filed a formal grade appeal with the department chairperson.

Discussion Questions

1. How important are the syllabus requirements for this case study?
2. Is Dee's grade appeal a typical or unusual situation?
3. Did Dee have a responsibility to inform Dr. Turin in advance of her research project revisions?
4. In what ways did Dr. Turin's knowledge of Native American culture limit or enhance her ability to effectively manage this situation?
5. Create a mock dialogue with Dee that shows what types of questions would be most important for the chairperson to ask in order to make a decision regarding this grade appeal.
6. Should Dr. Turin consider changing the qualitative research assignment in order to be sensitive to the needs of Native American students? Why or why not?

Research Activities for Further Exploration

1. Conduct semistructured interviews with three faculty members on your campus to discuss the extent to which they believe a cultural immersion program would be useful to new faculty members.
2. Read five research articles on the topic of student-faculty interaction. Discuss the implications of these studies relative to the issues underlying this case.
3. Design a survey instrument to measure the quality of Native American students' interactions with faculty.

SAVAGE DIFFERENCES

ELLEN M. BROIDO & MICHAEL DANNELLS

Description of the Institutional Environment

Sizemore College was established in 1913 primarily to serve the needs of Idaho residents who wanted to remain in state and attend a private liberal arts college. Today only about 60 percent of Sizemore's 2,200 students are from Idaho; the rest of the student body is largely from West Coast cities. The "Out-Staters," as the locals sometimes call them, are attracted by the clean, fresh air; the availability of outdoor activities; and an increasingly liberal faculty. The enrollment is 52 percent women and 48 percent men, of whom 90 percent are white, 5 percent are Native American, 3 percent are Latino/a, and 2 percent are African American. Most of the Out-Staters come from fairly affluent families and have politically liberal and activist leanings. Most of the students from Idaho are from middle-class and blue-collar families, and their political orientation tends to be conservative.

Description of the Surrounding Community

Sizemore College is located in the foothills of the Idaho mountains, in the isolated town of Jessup (pop. 25,000). Apart from the college, Jessup is an almost entirely white, working-class, and conservative town.

Primary Persons Involved in the Case

- Lewis Clark is the newly elected president of Native Americans for Campus Action (NACA). At 28, Lewis is older and more of an activist than his predecessors.
- Lori Newton is beginning her second year at Sizemore as the Assistant Dean of Students and Director of Campus Activities as well as advisor to the Student Government Association (SGA). As a liberal white woman raised in San Francisco, Lori has experienced some struggles in her adjustment to life in Jessup.
- Franklin Bernard, an African American, has been the Associate Dean of Students for five years, with primary responsibility in the areas of student judicial affairs, residence halls, dining services, and crisis intervention. He serves as advisor to the Homecoming Committee, which is comprised of representatives of various student groups, faculty, alumni, and local businesspersons. He finds the Sammy and Samantha Savage mascots deeply offensive—a "despicable example of racist stereotyping"—but he has been quiet on the matter because he loves his work and fears that if he takes a stand, he might lose his job, leaving African American students with one less support person and role model (of which there are few).
- Dr. Neil Bowman is the Dean of Students and has worked at Sizemore for 32 years. He served as the Sammy Savage mascot from 1964 to 1966, and

after a tour of duty in the Army (and Vietnam), he returned to Sizemore to finish his Bachelor's degree and to serve as president of SGA in 1970-1971. "Dr. Sammy," as he sometimes is called, is famous for his ability to raise funds.

- Gaylord Wilson, a powerful alumnus and a former president of the foundation, is a current member of the Board of Trustees and an influential businessperson in the community. He is the founder and CEO of a diversified company that owns many local businesses that cater to students. All of his businesses have names related to the Sammy Savage mascot.

Information Germane to the Case

- Since the founding of Sizemore, the mascots have been Native American caricatures named Sammy and Samantha Savage, who are highly visible at athletic events, various booster functions, and other public gatherings to raise school spirit. Many campus and community traditions are based on the Savages.
- Over the past 15 years, various individuals and campus groups have pressured Sizemore to change the mascots, but until recently, the initiatives had not been sustained or broad based. The local townspeople, the council leaders of the nearby Shoshone tribe, the central administration, most of the students, and the alumni association were resigned to, if not thrilled by, the Savages. Dean Bowman argued that the cost to the college would be enormous in terms of changing signage, uniforms, and logos, and also in terms of reduced alumni and donor support. He pointed to letters from alumni who, insisting that the Savages were noble and forceful mascots, often threatened to stop making donations to the foundation.
- *The Tomahawk* is the student newspaper at Sizemore. Besides being the voice of the more conservative students on campus, *The Tomahawk* is heavily dependent on revenue from its sale of advertising space to local businesses.
- NACA, the only student group devoted to the Native American students at Sizemore, had not weighed in on the mascot issue until recently. Late last spring its new president, Lewis Clark, announced that NACA would be taking a firm stand against the mascots. This fall, Lewis Clark sought out and found a strong advocate and personal friend in Lori Newton.
- Franklin Bernard and Lori Newton both report directly to Neal Bowman, although Dean Bowman often designates Franklin to take the lead in key projects and expects Franklin to supervise Lori as his assistant on such projects.

The Case

Opposition to the Savages recently coalesced in both the SGA and the Faculty Senate. During the spring semester, each organization passed a resolution decrying the racist and demeaning image of the Savages and called for the president to appoint a blue-ribbon panel to study the issue and find a new and inoffensive mascot. Further, the SGA has threatened to withhold funds, taken from student fees and administered by SGA, from any student group that used the Savages in a public way, such as on floats in the Homecoming parade. *The Tomahawk* has reported on these events but has been highly critical of the student government and the faculty, in one editorial labeling them the "knee-jerk liberal, political-correctness police," and calling for respectful observance and honoring of campus history and traditions.

At the fall retreat for Sizemore administrators, the president announced that the Annual Giving Campaign would be built around a donation of $5,000,000 by Gaylord Wilson, to be given in $1,000,000 increments over the next five years. Mr. Wilson attended the retreat, and in his remarks to the group, made several references to the "troublesome few outsiders" who fostered disrespect for time-honored campus traditions. He implied that his support of the campaign might be reconsidered if the administration took seriously efforts to change the mascot.

The following Monday, Lori Newton went to Franklin Bernard's office and "went off" on the subject of Wilson and financial and political power. She railed against the demeaning mascots, the shame and disgrace they brought upon the college, how they prevented the college from attracting and retaining more Native Americans, and how they infuriated student leaders like Lewis Clark. She could no longer stand by and let the college continue with its racist ways. She vowed to support in every way possible NACA's and SGA's efforts to get the mascots changed, including meeting with *The Tomahawk's* advisor to help him see how the student newspaper is "led by rightwing reactionaries who have no respect for minorities" and helping NACA and SGA build an alliance with the Faculty Senate on this issue.

At the Homecoming Committee's first meeting of the fall semester, when it was time to put the finishing touches on the Homecoming schedule, the mascot issue arose, dividing and sidetracking the committee. Now, with only six weeks until Homecoming, the parade, in particular, is in jeopardy. SGA has threatened to refuse funding to any student group that uses the Savages on its float. NACA has threatened to boycott and picket the event, with some members suggesting that they may try to block its progress by lying down on the street. There has been a war of letters to the editor in *The Tomahawk* on the issue, with some white in-state students in favor of keeping the Savages and some out-of-state students arguing against it.

Discussion Questions

1. Describe the issues raised by this case study and the major points of contention.
2. Are Native American mascots by definition racist, or might they be symbols of pride and respect?
3. What forms of challenge and support would be appropriate (developmentally and ethically) for Lori Newton and Franklin Bernard to provide to the students of NACA and SGA? How might they justify these to Dr. Bowman? Have their actions to date been appropriate?
4. Chickering and Reisser (1993) discuss the final vector of Developing Integrity, as including, in part, the congruence of one's values and actions. What circumstances in this case might challenge one's ability to do this?
5. Frame the issues in this case study in light of both Lawrence Kohlberg's and Carol Gilligan's theories of moral decision making. Where might you place each actor in this case study in terms of these theorists' models? What insight does this provide into their behaviors?
6. As an outside consultant hired by Dr. Bowman to mediate this crisis, what strategies would you use to help to bring resolution and reconciliation to this campus?

Research Activities for Further Exploration

1. Research the experiences of campuses that have considered changing their Native American mascot (e.g., University of Illinois), those that already have done so (e.g., Stanford University), and those that have obtained permission from the Native American nation in question (e.g., Florida State University, Miami University). What have been the major points of contention? What arguments and influences led to decisions to change or not change the school's mascot?
2. Interview several Native Americans about the mascot issue. What differences are evident among the people with whom you spoke? Do the opinions of Native Americans who are college students differ from those who are not?
3. Interview several senior campus decision makers to gain insight into how they resolve tensions between the wishes of alumni, donors, community members, and students.

A FIRST-YEAR CHINESE STUDENT'S

EXPERIENCES AT COLLEGE

YANMEI ZHANG

Description of the Institutional Environment

Prominence University is a large southeastern institution that has a total enrollment of more than 40,000 students representing all U.S. ethnic groups and over 100 other countries. About 23 percent of the student body are minorities and approximately 5.6 percent are international students. The students are among the best in the nation. Over 90 percent of all entering first-year students score above the national average on standardized admissions tests.

Description of the Surrounding Community

The university is located in Evergreen, which has a population of about 80,000. The majority of the residents in the city are Prominence students, faculty, and staff. Others are in service industries and research institutes associated with the university. The residents are proud of the university in their neighborhood, and are very involved in activities sponsored by the university, such as cultural events, games, and festivals.

Primary Persons Involved in the Case

- Jiahui Li is a 19-year-old first-year international student from China. He studies in the Department of Business Management. His father is a government official and his mother is a professor. He has no siblings.
- Tom Johnson, Jiahui's roommate, is a first-year Native American student. He has just graduated from high school and entered the university as an honor student.
- Scott Corry, a Residency Hall Assistant (RHA), is a second-year graduate student in the student affairs program in the School of Education.
- Barbara Smith is the Academic Advisor in the Department of Business Management.

Information Germane to the Case

- The number of international students at Prominence is rapidly increasing. However, a recent survey of international students' perceptions and feelings at the university revealed that the majority of international students felt a lack of connectedness in the community. They reported difficulties in establishing positive relationships with other students.

- Though there are many student organizations on campus, most international students are not involved in these organizations and feel isolated from campus activities.

The Case

After arriving in the U.S., Jiahui found that college life is much harder than he had expected. Never having left home before, Jiahui is very homesick. He misses his family and his friends back in China. He has to adjust himself to a new life away from his parents, to learn to make decisions by himself, and to be independent. Being in a completely new environment, he feels very vulnerable. He finds that everything here is different from what he was used to in China. People are very busy every day. They don't seem to care about others. To his great frustration, he realizes that it is difficult to make friends with other students in the U.S. It seems that they are not interested in getting to know him.

Though he is able to speak and read English, he has trouble understanding others and cannot communicate very well, resulting in difficulties in his personal life as well as his academic life. Not knowing anything about higher education in the U.S., he feels lost. He didn't know which classes to register for, and has no idea to whom he can turn for help. U.S. professors teach classes very differently compared to what he is used to in China, where the teacher teaches and the students listen and learn. What's worse, he sometimes cannot understand his instructors and thus he is unable to take notes in class. He has the greatest difficulty with class discussions. While the other students are talking, he feels like an idiot sitting there, not saying a word, and not understanding what the others are talking about. Even when he does understand them, it is hard for him to speak up because he is afraid that the professor and the other students will not be interested in what he has to say. He thought about meeting with Barbara Smith, but he is afraid that he cannot make himself understood, and that Barbara will not be able to help him either.

At first, Jiahui was very happy to be living with his roommate, Tom Johnson. He saw it as a good opportunity to get to know an American and practice his English. Furthermore, because Tom is an honor student, Jiahui hoped that he could learn from Tom and that Tom would help him with his studies. But now he finds it hard for him to make friends with his roommate.

Jiahui has no knowledge about Native Americans except for what he has learned from American movies he saw in China. When he learned that Tom was a Native American, Jiahui was very curious and he wanted to know more about Tom and about Native Americans. However, he perceives a distance between Tom and himself, and it seems that Tom is not interested in making friends with him. As a member of several student organizations on campus, Tom has many friends and is busy with many activities. When he is at the residence hall, he doesn't talk much with Jiahui. Tom is not happy about living with an international student, as he feels it is difficult to communicate with Jiahui, who feels even more isolated when Tom invites his friends over to the residence hall. When they are having parties, playing, and chatting, Jiahui stays in his room alone, feeling more miserable and homesick.

When his parents called and learned that he was having a hard time with his roommate, they suggested that he move out of the residence hall to live with other Chinese students. He went to Scott, the RHA, to see if he could terminate the lease and move out. Scott could not understand why Jiahui wanted to leave, but said that he could not move out before the lease ends. Jiahui feels very bad.

Discussion Questions

1. What are the specific issues and problems that Jiahui encountered in his first year as an international student?
2. What do you perceive to be the barriers for Jiahui and Tom to understand each other and make friends with one another?
3. What can student affairs professionals and staff do to help improve relationships between international students and other students on campus?
4. Is there anything that Barbara Smith could do to help Jiahui with his difficulties?
5. Suppose you are the Director of International Student Services, how would you counsel Jiahui and help him with his situation?
6. Describe other issues and concerns that international students may have in their transition and adaptation to U.S. colleges and universities? How can institutions help them with their adjustment?

Research Activities for Further Exploration

1. Use the resources from your library to conduct a literature review on issues concerning international students in American higher education.
2. Conduct interviews with five international students at your institution about their learning experiences and their relationships with other students. Write a report of your findings.
3. Use library or online resources to conduct a research study on the support system for international students at other universities, and compare them with the services at your university. Write a report on how the system can be improved in your university.

SHARON'S DILEMMA

Quincy L. Moore

Description of the Institutional Environment

The University of Culver (UC) is a Division I-research institution. The average ACT score is 26. Approximately 26,000 students are enrolled at this predominantly white campus. The racial demographics of the school are as follows: 2 percent Asian American, 4 percent Native American, 6 percent Hispanic American, 8 percent African American, and 80 percent white.

Description of the Surrounding Community

Stockton, the town surrounding UC's campus, has a population of 40,000 residents. It is primarily a farming community with a large number of its citizens employed in various positions at UC. This rural community is comprised of mostly lower- to middle-class households. Stockton residents typically perceive themselves to be more well-rounded and "cultured" than most small town residents.

Primary Persons Involved in the Case

- Sharon Biggers is a first-year African American student from Chicago.
- Heather Small, also from Chicago, is an African American graduate student in English, working as an academic advisor in the UC advising center.

Information Germane to the Case

- UC has worked to establish a diverse environment for both students and faculty. By establishing recruitment and retention programs, UC has successfully enhanced the overall graduation rates of students of color. Academic support is provided via teaching assistants and academic advising designed to reflect the diversity of the student population. First-year and transfer students are randomly assigned academic advisors before they register for class.
- Sharon Biggers is from the inner city. She is the first person in her family and on her street to attend college. Her father was killed when she was just 12 years old. Consequently, Sharon's mother raised her and her two younger siblings while working as a department store salesclerk. As an

honor roll student throughout her four years of high school, Sharon also perceived herself as a role model for her younger brother and sister.

The Case

Sharon's first-year college courses are English, biology, history, and music appreciation. She is glad to see that her academic advisor, Heather Small, is also an African American student from Chicago. During the first three weeks of class, Sharon realizes that college is not just the "next level after high school," but also a higher level of reading, communication, comprehension, and writing. It is especially difficult for her to understand why she is having problems in English. As one of the best students in her high school, Sharon received all A's and honors in English courses. Surprisingly, her grades on college papers were C- and D's. Her instructor told her to just "edit, revise, and resubmit" and, most important, see a tutor in the writing center. To close the gap between what she "thought she knew" and what is now required, she decided to attend a study skills and time management workshop.

Sharon's advisor, Heather Small, attended a prestigious undergraduate college and was raised in an upper-middle-class, two-parent family. Heather has an impressive track record at UC. Her advisees adjust to college without any major problems and typically perform well. As a result of what Sharon learned about Heather at the group orientation, she considers her a role model as well. Although Sharon was now apprehensive about seeing her advisor for the first time, she scheduled an appointment anyway. Before her appointment she dropped off two of her graded English papers for Heather to review, and she hopes that Heather will give her some quick advice for improvement.

When Sharon arrived for her appointment, Heather seemed rather cold and distant. She began to criticize Sharon for submitting such "shabby work." She also made several remarks about the poor organization of Sharon's papers and the repetitive elementary sentence structure. She said, "When I was in high school, my work was much better than this. How did you even graduate?" Then she made a negative comment about "inner city" high schools. Eventually she asked Sharon, "Have you ever considered going to a community college?" Sharon became very nervous about any further discussion of her work and returned to her residence hall in tears. As a result, she was depressed and even more discouraged about her English papers and her future relationship with her advisor.

Discussion Questions

1. What are the key academic and socioeconomic issues presented in this scenario?

2. Was Heather's reaction to Sharon's work appropriate? Why or why not?
3. Outline criteria to assess Heather's advising competency? What should be the advising objectives for Sharon's first session? For follow-up?
4. Describe the dilemmas experienced in college by "high achievers" from low-achieving high school environments.
5. Why should advisors be required to understand multicultural counseling competencies?
6. How should student affairs graduate preparation programs evaluate students' levels of multicultural competency?

Research Activities for Further Exploration

1. Prepare an annotated bibliography of recent articles that address classism in higher education.
2. Use a participant-observation method to assess the strengths and weaknesses of traditional advising and counseling practices at your current campus.
3. Develop a presentation for student affairs professionals that discusses the Standards for Multicultural Competencies developed by the Association for Multicultural Counseling and Development.

UGLY GREEK TRADITIONS

WILMA J. HENRY

Description of the Institutional Environment

Unity University is a midsized state institution located in an urban area in the Midwest. Approximately 18,000 students attend this predominantly white institution. The average SAT score of entering first-year students is 1075, and approximately 70 students are National Scholars. Unity's mission espouses a commitment to diversity, and one of its strategic goals is to increase the number of minority students, faculty, and staff. The racial demographics of the student body are as follows: 1 percent American Indian, 3 percent Asian American, 7 percent African American, 5 percent Latino American, and 84 percent white. Unity is considered one of the top doctoral degree-granting institutions in the Midwest.

Description of the Surrounding Community

Unity University was established in 1964 and is the youngest of three public institutions in the state. A sizeable number of students (approximately

1,300) are involved in fraternities and sororities. The Greek organizations at Unity are organized under three separate campus councils. The National Greek Council governs the predominantly white groups, the National Greek-Letter Council governs the predominantly African American groups, and the National Greek Society Council governs the predominantly Latino groups. Many members of the Black Faculty and Staff Caucus and the Latino Faculty and Staff Alliance serve as mentors to African American and Latino students at Unity.

Primary Persons Involved in the Case

- John Frecker is the president of Beta Theta fraternity. John is a junior National Merit Scholar majoring in psychology. He has served as a Student Government Senator for three years. John volunteers on the advisory board to the Office of Multicultural Affairs. The National Greek Council governs Beta Theta.
- Eric Miller is a sophomore majoring in engineering, and is enrolled in the Honors College. He is an active member of the Black Student Union and was recently elected president of Chi Pi Chi fraternity, which is governed by the National Greek Letter Council.
- Jen Shorter, the Director of Greek Affairs, was recently appointed and has served in her position for only three months. Jen reports to the Dean of Students.
- Lorie Concord is the Dean of Students who oversees the offices of Judicial Affairs, Multicultural Affairs, Student Disabilities Services, and Greek Affairs. Lorie reports to the Vice President for Student Affairs.

Information Germane to the Case

- Minority faculty and staff members charging the institution with discrimination have filed several lawsuits. Three of the most recent cases were highly controversial and received national attention.
- A university-wide committee was recently appointed by Unity's president to conduct an equity and climate study. The findings and recommendations from the study should be available next year.
- During the past year, the Offices of Diversity Initiatives and Multicultural Affairs have sponsored training workshops to promote cultural awareness and appreciation among students, faculty, and staff.

The Case

During the fall semester fraternity rush week, Beta Theta, a predominantly white fraternity, was showing a videotape of various activities that included scenes of a Halloween party. In the 20-minute video, approximately 15 seconds showed two men with colorful serapes draped across one of their shoulders and wearing large sombrero hats. The brims of the hats were artfully decorated with shiny sequins that formed the inscription "wetback." A couple of Beta Theta members also were captured in this scene wearing their fraternity symbols. Upon leaving a Latino Student Union meeting that was held two doors down from the fraternity rush gathering, two Mexican American females observed the 15-second portion of the video. They were outraged and immediately sought out Latino faculty mentors for advice. The next morning, Dean Concord received 70 emails from Latino students, faculty, and staff expressing concerns and demanding that the fraternity members be suspended. Dean Concord immediately called Jen Shorter to discuss the incident and develop a strategy for responding to the situation. Jen spoke with John Frecker who informed her that the video was not made at a Beta Theta party; he did not know the two men dressed in offensive costume, and he was not aware that the scene was a part of the videotape being shown.

The same evening, during the National Greek Letter Council's annual step competition, members of the Chi Pi Chi fraternity performed a skit that included members dressed as prisoners on a chain gang. Two members were playing the role of overseers with sticks symbolizing guns, mimicking white dialect and displaying a raccoon (stuffed animal) to represent a human baby. The skit portrayed the overseers seeking to find which of the chain gang members would admit to owning the "coon." The next day, two African-American and two white students told Jen Shorter that the skit had offended them. They also reported that some members of the audience "booed" the fraternity and left the event. The next day, the president of the Black Faculty and Staff Caucus phoned Dean Concord demanding that an African-American Greek Advisor be hired to advise black Greeks at Unity. When Jen Shorter spoke with the president of Chi Pi Chi about the incident, he informed her that that the skit was based in part on a movie that depicted the reality of black men working on chain gangs. It was not intended to be offensive, but rather to provide facts as well as entertainment.

Discussion Questions

1. Identify and discuss the meaning of specific stereotypes in the incidents involving both Beta Theta and Chi Pi Chi fraternities that could be offensive to individuals observing the events.
2. Should the Greek governing councils assume any responsibility for the actions of either Beta Theta or Chi Pi Chi fraternities? Explain your answer.
3. Does the University have a responsibility to educate students about issues

of stereotypes and racism in America? Explain your answer.

4. Should Dean Concord pursue disciplinary action for either one of these incidents? Explain your answer.

5. Describe some of the intervention strategies you would recommend to Dean Concord for responding to (a) the emails from Latino groups, (b) concerns from the Black Faculty Caucus, and (c) the incidents involving Beta Theta and Chi Pi Chi.

6. As a result of the incidents, what recommendations would you make to Jen Shorter for creating a more culturally aware, unified Greek program at the institution?

Research Activities for Further Exploration

1. Research news releases of incidents of fraternity involvement in racially offensive behavior during the last five years. Briefly summarize and discuss your reactions to each incident.

2. Research racial stereotypes of African Americans and Latinos and discuss how specific terms have been used to denigrate these groups. Discuss the importance of racial sensitivity and appreciation.

3. Interview a faculty or staff member on campus who has participated in cultural awareness or diversity training. Using information from the interview and other resource material, outline a cultural awareness or appreciation training workshop that might be presented to members of the Beta Theta and Chi Pi Chi fraternities.

THE WRITING ON THE WALL

Robert Coffey & Mary Taylor

Description of the Institutional Environment

The University of Hamilton (UH) is a midsized competitive public university that draws students primarily from its home state and the surrounding region. Though its focus is on undergraduate teaching, selected graduate and doctoral programs in engineering, business, and education have raised the institution's national profile over the past ten years. The average SAT score for incoming first-year students is 1100. Fewer than 4 percent of the students attending UH are ethnic minorities, with 1.6 percent Asian American, 0.9 percent African American, 0.9 percent Hispanic, and 0.3 percent Native American.

Description of the Surrounding Community

Hamilton enjoys a bucolic campus setting, located in a picturesque New England village of 4,000 not far from the Atlantic coast. Though historically tied economically to the sea, the surrounding region has diversified considerably in the past 50 years and now supports burgeoning technology and financial services industries. The tech boom has been aided by the region's close proximity to a major northeastern city. Residents extol the pleasures of rural New England life with convenient access to urban cultural opportunities.

Primary Persons Involved in the Case

- Wendy Hubbard, a white woman, is a junior majoring in women's studies at UH. She is a leader of the local chapter of the Women's National Organization (WNO), which began organizing in late fall and decided against seeking university recognition as a student organization.
- Kelly Mills, a white woman, is a sophomore majoring in mathematics.
- Jenny Wong, an Asian American woman, is a junior majoring in psychology. She and her family emigrated to the U.S. from Hong Kong five years ago. Jenny was a leader in the Asian Student Union (ASU) last year.
- Manny Padilla, a Latino senior, is the chairperson of the Diversity Alliance, a student organization that works across identity lines for diversity and multiculturalism.
- Marcius Walters is the Director of the Office of Multicultural Affairs (OMA), which was established several years ago to provide resources and support to students of color and sponsor campus events that address issues of diversity. In addition to supervising diversity-related programming, Marcius also addresses student retention for the office's constituent groups. He is an African American man and has been at UH for two years.
- Janice Pendleton is a white woman who has been at UH for five years. She is the Director of the Rape Crisis Center (RCC), which was established in 1984 following a very public rape case on campus. Janice coordinates and supervises all sexual harassment and rape responses as well as all education and prevention programs. The RCC also provides advocacy and crisis response for survivors of sexual and partner violence and their allies.

Information Germane to the Case

- Although UH recruits students from cities and towns across the northeastern U.S., the number of matriculating students of color remains small. In a recent UH survey, many students of color cited feelings of isolation or marginalization in the classroom and uneven treatment by white peers. In contrast, white respondents reported a high level of satisfaction with their experience at UH.

- The relationship between UH and its host state is characterized by tension and conflict. The state's political leadership historically has preferred to underfund public higher education. An unsympathetic editorial board at the state's most influential newspaper also has criticized efforts to promote diversity at UH as "useless exercises in political correctness." This tension, combined with the state's small size and population, ensures that news emanating from the campus frequently receives statewide media coverage.

The Case

Two weeks before the spring semester ended, three students from WNO (Wendy Hubbard, Kelly Mills, and Jenny Wong) put up a display on a wall inside the student union. Using foot-long letters placed next to an image of a person being lynched, the statement "Rape is to sexism as lynching is to racism" was attached to a wall five feet from the Office of Multicultural Affairs and ten feet from the main entrance to the building. Before a group can hang a display, the student union office must approve a form indicating the title and sponsoring organization.

Last year, WNO organized several actions that focused on a certain fraternity with members who were the alleged perpetrators in a recent date-rape case. Many students believed that UH failed to hold the alleged perpetrators and the fraternity as an organization responsible for this incident. The actions that Wendy, Kelly, and Jenny organized at that time included wearing tee-shirts that read "My name is Heather and I was raped at UH," chalking "I was raped at UH" on sidewalks across campus during first-year student orientation, and spray painting "We rape" on an exterior wall of the fraternity house. The university did not take any action in response to these activities.

In addition, Wendy has had difficulties with a number of students and staff from the OMA. These incidents range from strained conversations to charges of harassment. At one point, Wendy had been allied with a number of these students, but a series of incidents has damaged these relationships. Jenny talked with Marcius Walters following these incidents and indicated that she felt torn between her alliance with Wendy and Kelly and her commitment to the ASU. Marcius encouraged her to talk with other students from the OMA and work to build bridges between these two communities. Marcius also recommended that Jenny talk with Janice Pendleton, as the OMA recently had begun to collaborate with the RCC on programs.

Prior to their affiliation with WNO Wendy and Kelly had numerous meetings with the Vice Chancellor for Student Affairs and the Chancellor as a result of their activism against rape on campus. After several unproductive meetings with these students, the Chancellor asked the RCC director to advise and help "mainstream" these students. Janice Pendleton met with Wendy at the Chancellor's request. Wendy said that she was mistrustful of most UH officials and was "fed up" with the university's lack of commitment to addressing violence against women on campus. She said that strong action needed to be taken. She also said that the administration and the student community needed to be "shaken up." Janice encouraged Wendy to get involved with the RCC peer education program.

Manny Padilla is organizing a speak-out in the food court of the student union. He said that students are outraged about this incident and are demanding that the university do something. The display was hung up at approximately 10:00 p.m. on Wednesday evening. At 9:00 a.m. on Thursday morning, the director of the student union covered the display with paper as a result of numerous complaints. A group of university officials will meet at 10:00 a.m. in order to discuss this issue.

Discussion Questions

1. What are the specific issues or problems presented in this case?
2. What were the WNO students trying to accomplish by comparing one kind of oppression to another? What does it mean when one does this?
3. Given contemporary understandings of the relationship between different kinds of oppression, how might the Vice Chancellor for Student Affairs respond? The OMA director? The RCC director?
4. What policies or procedures might you develop or revise in response to this incident?
5. What support, if any, should the university provide to the WNO students? What support, if any, should the university provide to communities of color in response to this incident?
6. If you were organizing this meeting, whom would you invite? What would you do to prepare? What are some of the difficulties you might anticipate?

Research Activities for Further Exploration

1. Research the laws governing freedom of speech and the ability of higher education institutions to regulate time, place, and manner for individuals to exercise this right. What are the differences between public and private institutions in this regard?

2. Does your institution have a policy for responding to bias-related incidents on campus? What is this policy? Is the policy and protocol clearly laid out? How does the campus community access resources available to those who feel they have experienced discrimination or bias?

3. Research the history of the relationship between communities of color and the women's community on campus. Explore the points of tension between these groups. What recommendations would you offer these groups to help them foster understanding and develop alliances?

MIGUEL AND THE SIGNIFICANT OTHERS

Schevaletta M. Alford

Description of the Institutional Environment

Daniel Webster College is a four-year comprehensive urban commuter institution. Students attending Daniel Webster are primarily interested in careers related to law, law enforcement, corrections, and the courts as well as fire and forensic sciences. In addition, students also study forensic computing. Presently, the racial demographics of the 10,000-plus students are 26 percent African American, 4 percent Asian/Pacific Islander, 35 percent Hispanic (including Puerto Ricans), 22 percent white, and 13 percent other (or not identified). A little over 60 percent of the students are female.

Description of the Surrounding Community

Daniel Webster, located in one of the largest cities on the eastern seacoast, is one of seven senior colleges in a university system comprised of junior and senior schools. Because of its location, many racial and ethnic groups, the largest of which are Latino/Hispanic, African American, and Caribbean islanders, populate the city.

Primary Persons Involved in the Case

• Miguel Ortega is a 19-year-old junior honor student, majoring in forensic science. He came from an elite public high school, most graduates of which attend Ivy League institutions. Although he is very respectful of his parents, he has begun to have difficulty communicating with them. They are middle-income Cuban immigrants who do not particularly like other Hispanic groups. They want Miguel to become a doctor like other members of their family.

- Mercedes Rodriguez, Miguel's girlfriend, has stopped attending the college. She originally was from Mexico. However, her mother is from Nicaragua. She is the eldest of three children and the first person in her family to begin college.
- Dr. Lenora Eggerman is the fifth child of a divorced woman. She lived in Puerto Rico until she was 14 and, since arriving in the U.S., has returned to Puerto Rico every summer for approximately two months. She is Miguel's counselor. She also directs Daniel Webster's Women's Center.
- Dr. Juan Martinez is Puerto Rican by birth; his parents moved to the mainland when he was three years old. He is the counselor for one of Miguel's friends. His office is a lively place in which students discuss everything from politics to sexual freedom. The students consider him to be "real cool."

Information Germane to the Case

- Most of the counselors at Daniel Webster are white and African American. There are only five Latinos, two male and three female. Three are Puerto Rican, one is Mexican, and one is Dominican. One counselor is Japanese. The counselors are divided into two camps, conservative and modern.
- New students are randomly assigned to the counselor who teaches their first-year seminar classes. If they wish, students may switch counselors after a discussion with the counselor to whom they were originally assigned.

The Case

When Miguel Ortega entered college he had excellent grades until the end of his sophomore year, when his grades began to drop. When Dr. Eggerman asked him about this, he spoke about his new girlfriend, Mercedes Rodriguez. After Miguel started dating Mercedes he began to spend all of his free time with her. Although she is very intelligent, she came from one of the worst high schools in the city and her foundation was weak. In addition, she spent much of her time helping her mother. Mercedes had only average grades and she was advised to seek tutoring help, which was how she met Miguel. Their relationship developed as he tried to help her with mathematics. As time passed, their relationship became romantic.

When Miguel tried to explain his relationship to his parents, they were not very pleased. Miguel's mother stated, "She is not the right type for you.

Besides, her family is not Cuban." Miguel wanted his parents to accept the young woman, but this semester things have become worse. Mercedes dropped out of school. She has been unable to find a job and recently she announced that she is pregnant. She says she wants to keep the child because her mother wants a grandchild. Miguel found a part-time job and works extra hours because he wants to provide for the child. However, he did not plan to have children until he completed his degree. He wants to end the relationship, yet he feels obligated to remain in it. His parents are unaware of the pregnancy and want him to stop working. He constantly argues with them.

Although strongly encouraged by his friends, Miguel will not speak with Dr. Eggerman, who is a champion for women's rights. Recently, she gave a presentation entitled "Women's Rights and Male Obligations: An Unequal Equation." Although she has strong views on male-female relations, she is an extremely good and conscientious counselor, with whom Miguel has always had good rapport. However, her traditional family values often conflict with the modern views of some students. She does not like other counselors advising her students and she becomes confrontational when they attempt to help her students with even minor matters. She is aware of Miguel's situation because Mercedes has told her about it, and she has been waiting for Miguel to come and talk to her.

When Miguel accompanies his friend to see Juan Martinez, a conversation begins about Dr. Eggerman's presentation. As a result of comments made by Dr. Martinez, Miguel decides to talk about his problem. Dr. Eggerman observes this and hears Martinez tells Miguel "You need to get out of the relationship! It's going nowhere. If she and her family want this baby, let them have it."

Discussion Questions

1. Identify the key issues in this case that relate to the students' relationships.
2. Identify the key issues in the student-counselor relationships.
3. In this case, are there racial, ethnic, and gender issues that appear to be at crossed purposes? If so, what are they? If not, why not?
4. Based on your understanding of the issues, what factors will impede the resolution of the problem between Dr. Eggerman and Dr. Martinez?
5. Develop a mock dialogue between two individuals in this case, for example Miguel and Dr. Eggerman after Miguel leaves Dr. Martinez' office, or Mercedes and Dr. Eggerman before she announces the pregnancy.
6. Discuss the impact of race, ethnicity, and cultural values on the attitudes of some of the primary persons.

Research Activities for Further Exploration

1. Write a paper on the effects of social or cultural divisions between group members from similar ethnicities (e.g., American-born Chinese [ABCs] and Mainland Chinese).
2. Using surveys or interviews, identify the key factors students consider when selecting a counselor or mentor on your campus.
3. Write a reflection paper on the significance of the counselors' understanding of intraracial or intracultural issues on his or her ability to counsel students.

FLYING HOME

LEE COVINGTON RUSH

Description of the Institutional Environment

Uppercrust College (UC) is a highly selective liberal arts college with a small student body of 3,000 undergraduate students. Because the college is selective, most first-year students have combined SAT scores between 1250 and 1400. UC offers 20 majors in five colleges and has an early admissions policy, a study abroad program, and a Phi Beta Kappa chapter. The student faculty ratio is 10 to 1. Demographically, the school is composed of 89 percent European Americans, 5 percent Asian Americans, 3 percent African Americans, 2 percent Hispanic Americans, and 1 percent American Indians.

Description of the Surrounding Community

Uppercrust College is located in a midsized residential New England community of 75,000 within 45 minutes of a major metropolitan area. The community's minority population is small (only 10%), and the major industry is tourism during summer and fall. Most of the residents commute to the larger metropolitan area for employment.

Primary Persons Involved in the Case

• Danny Twobears is an American Indian sophomore from another northeastern state. He is a member of the Iroquois nation. He grew up on the reservation and fully subscribes to the traditional cultural values, norms, and worldview of his heritage. He earned excellent grades in high school and had a combined SAT score of 1350.

- Sylvia Hand is an American Indian senior who came to UC from the same state as Danny. She is also a member of the Iroquois nation. Unlike Danny, she did not grow up on or near a reservation, and is more bicultural in her outlook. Though bicultural, Sylvia and her parents maintain close ties with their ancestral home and traditions.
- John Charles Worthington is an Academic Advisor at UC and graduated from the college (as did his parents and grandparents).

Information Germane to the Case

- Uppercrust College has a rich tradition of academic excellence and competitiveness among its students and is known as a feeder college for the top graduate and professional universities in the country.
- Only in the last few years has the college begun to place emphasis on the recruitment, retention, and graduation of students of color. The majority students at UC generally are pleased about having some students of color attending the college, though their attitudes are more that of noblesse oblige rather than any deep commitment to diversity issues.

The Case

In reviewing Danny Twobears' academic progress at Uppercrust, John Worthington learned that Danny's grades were barely acceptable during his first year and have been declining since then. He is additionally alarmed upon reading Danny's professors' comments that he has missed classes this year while returning home three times in a four-month period, he is reticent in his classes, he often comes late, and he appears unmotivated and depressed. Based on his concerns, John calls Danny and schedules an appointment to meet with him.

Given Danny's preference for communal decision making, he discusses the upcoming meeting with Sylvia Hand and asks her to accompany him there. Mr. Worthington is not pleased when Danny comes late to the meeting with Sylvia in tow. He asks her to wait in the outer office while he meets with Danny. During their meeting Danny does not look directly at Mr. Worthington, often looks away, is silent for long periods of time, and gives minimal verbal feedback that he understands Mr. Worthington's concerns. He does, however, tell Mr. Worthington that there was a flood on his reservation and his parents' home was severely damaged. He relates that he has been going home to help with the house restoration since he feels it is his duty and responsibility to help his family. Mr. Worthington explains to Danny that while he respects him and his people, it would seem to him that his family should be able to handle the home situation without his assistance.

He then chides Danny about his inattention to his schoolwork and his reticence in his classes. He reminds Danny that in order to remain at UC and have the bright future he is capable of he must improve his grades.

Discussion Questions

1. Why does Danny continue going home while doing poorly in his schoolwork? What were his reasons for asking Sylvia to attend the meeting with him? Explain both parts of the question.
2. Are Danny's responses to both his family situation and his apparently lackadaisical attitude toward his schoolwork anomalies? Discuss the significant variables involved.
3. If you were Danny's academic advisor, how would you work with him? Would your approach be similar to or different from Mr. Worthington's? Why?
4. Analyze and explain from a cultural and sociopolitical context, the implications for Danny in his attempt to negotiate the higher education system.
5. Provide a detailed intervention strategy that you believe to be culturally appropriate for work with American Indian college students as well as other students of color.
6. Articulate what you have determined are the most important factors necessary from both the institutional and academic affairs perspectives that would aid in the retention and graduation rates of American Indians from predominantly white institutions.

Research Activities for Further Exploration

1. Write a research paper comparing and contrasting the cultural values and worldviews of American Indians with those of the dominant American culture.
2. Write a report on the history and current status of an American Indian nation in your area.
3. To fully comprehend the significance of American Indian customs, traditions, and rituals, visit and interview individuals in a culturally appropriate manner at an American Indian reservation for a firsthand account.

SHALINI'S DATING DILEMMA

JOHN MOORE & MELANIE RAGO

Description of the Institutional Environment

Health Science University (HSU) is a small private university with a health science focus. Approximately 2,500 students are in preprofessional programs in pharmacy, physician's assistant studies, physical therapy, and premedicine. The racial and gender makeup of HSU is as follows: 30 percent Asian, 8 percent African American, 2 percent Latino/a, 56 percent white, 1 percent Native American, and 3 percent international students. Approximately two-thirds of the students are female. About half of the students live on campus.

Description of the Surrounding Community

HSU is an urban university in a large northeastern city with many other colleges in the area. The neighborhood is a blend of predominantly African-American families that have lived there for generations and housing rented by local college students. The city is very ethnically diverse. Racial groups, however, tend to live together in neighborhoods that are homogenous. The region has a high concentration of hospitals, pharmacies, and biotechnology firms, all of which employ the students and faculty of HSU.

Primary Persons Involved in the Case

- Shalini Matthew is a 20-year-old, third-year pharmacy student at HSU. She is a Resident Assistant (RA), is highly involved as the vice president of Lotus, the Indo-Pak Cultural Alliance, and is treasurer of the HSU's student chapter of the American Pharmacological Association.
- Harold Jones is the Resident Director of a 600-bed building for first- and second-year students. He supervises eight RAs, including Shalini. He is white, two years out of college, and has never been in an environment as diverse as HSU.
- Chacko Jacob is Shalini's 24-year-old boyfriend. His family immigrated to the U.S. about 25 years ago. Chacko works for an investment firm in the city. He and Shalini have been dating for $2^{1}/_{2}$ years.
- Abi and Rinu Matthew are Shalini's parents. Abi is a civil engineer for the city. Rinu is a nursing supervisor at an area hospital. The Matthews immigrated to the US from India 21 years ago. They expect Shalini to adhere to many traditional roles, especially those pertaining to dating and marriage.

Information Germane to the Case

- Many of the city's Indian immigrants work in highly technical or specialized fields in medicine or engineering, and HSU is a popular destination for their children.

The Case

Since the beginning of the semester, Shalini Mathew, one of the returning RAs, has concerned Harold Jones. Although she is a wonderful student, heavily involved in activities, and a well-liked and hard-working RA, she has several personal issues that are troubling her this semester. She is getting pressure from her family to marry; her parents are actively working to assist her in finding a suitable mate. Shalini is not interested in marrying yet, although she is dating Chacko Jacob, a young man whom her parents do not know about. Every time her parents come to visit, at least once or twice a week, she has to pack up all evidence of her boyfriend and hide it in a box under her bed. She is convinced that her parents would not approve of him because of his occupation as an assistant at an investment house. Her parents have told her that with her future career in pharmacy, the only appropriate match for her would be with someone in medicine or engineering. She has stressed to Harold, the rest of the staff, and her residents that they must be careful not to mention her boyfriend when her parents are around. Her parents' frequent and often unannounced visits place a lot of pressure on the staff; they feel like they have to lie to Shalini's parents or risk getting her in trouble.

Shalini is constantly suffering from the stress of her parents finding out about Chacko. She worries that other Indian students will tell their parents, who will then let her parents know. This is not unprecedented in the tight-knit Indian Christian community of which Shalini and her family are a part. Harold is concerned about Shalini's ability to continue splitting her life into two discrete parts as well as the effect that her behaviors are having on the staff and on her residents' perception of her. The Director of Student Life called him the other day about Shalini, noting that Shalini has appeared to be quite distracted and has begun to neglect some of her smaller responsibilities. Although she is still meeting all of her RA obligations, Harold has noticed that she is becoming less and less likely to take on additional responsibilities such as volunteering at the housing fair and covering for other RAs, things she used to do with enthusiasm.

Harold feels that all this may have something to do with her family situation but Shalini is reluctant to initiate discussions with him about what is going on. She will talk about the situation if prompted, but seems more and more discouraged about it working out. One day, however, Shalini comes to Harold quite upset. She was out with Chacko and friends of her parents saw them holding hands. She is concerned that her parents will make her choose between her family and her boyfriend. They have supported other families in the area that have threatened to disown their children for unsanctioned dating.

That weekend, Shalini's parents show up in an agitated state. She is not home, and they end up at Harold's door. They have called several times, and she has not answered. Harold knows that Shalini is out with Chacko but calms them down and convinces them to go home. When Shalini returns, and Harold informs that her parents are looking for her, she starts crying, and claiming that she knew this couldn't go on, that her parents know everything, and she has no idea what to do now.

Discussion Questions

1. List the competing forces that are putting stress on Shalini. Describe how they are doing so.
2. Write a paragraph that retells the scenarios from Shalini's perspective. Summarize aspects of U.S. culture that she seems to find most difficult to integrate into her Indian heritage.
3. How are the complaints Harold has received from Student Life and Shalini's co-workers related to his concerns about her? What other information might he need to assist Shalini?
4. What parts of his own culture might Harold want to be aware of when attempting to assist Shalini with her current situation? What can he do to keep himself neutral or unbiased in this dialogue?
5. What solutions would you suggest to Harold if he came to you for advice? Predict the points that Harold would need to address in an ideal conversation with Shalini, and what they might say to each other.
6. As a Resident Director, Harold must attend to many constituencies. Who are the constituents that Harold must take into consideration in this situation? How should they be prioritized? What action should Harold take with each regarding this situation?

Research Activities for Further Exploration

1. Using your library, find research on gay and lesbian students about the coming-out process. Although no developmental model exists for Shalini's dilemma, how might this information shed light on Shalini and her closeted relationship with Chacko?
2. Conduct an interview with an advisor from your institution's Office for International Students or the Counseling Center about his or her percep-

tions of the developmental challenges facing minority students in accommodating to both of their cultures. Write a paper to summarize what you learned and discuss how it can help you in understanding the needs of some of your students.

3. Research ethical codes from several professional student affairs organizations (e.g., ACPA, CAS, NASPA). Report how these codes may serve as guides for practitioners assisting students from backgrounds with which they are unfamiliar.

Chapter 4

RELIGION CASE STUDIES

IN THE CLASSROOM

VANESSA COOKE & OCTAVIA MADISON-COLMORE

Description of the Institutional Environment

Salem College is a privately endowed, nonprofit, coeducational, historically black liberal arts college. Approximately 6,000 students attend this institution, 72 percent of whom earn an ACT score over 18. The racial demographics of the school are as follows: 1 percent Native American, 2 percent Asian American, 2 percent Hispanic American, 5 percent international students, 3 percent white American, and 87 percent African American.

Description of the Surrounding Community

Salem College is situated on over 200 acres of land located in an urban city with approximately 146,000 residents. The city is recognized for its unique history, year-round entertainment, employment, education, culture, and diversity.

Primary Persons Involved in the Case

- Dr. Sharon Jones is a Professor in the Department of Psychology at Salem College. She is an outstanding academician who is well known both nationally and internationally for her work in the field of psychology. She has authored several texts and articles on topics related to psychology and spirituality. In addition to her scholarly work, Dr. Jones is actively involved in both professional and community organizations and has received numerous awards for her outstanding leadership skills.
- Dr. John Smith is the Chair of the Psychology Department at Salem

College.
• Sue Martin, a junior, is a psychology major and an atheist.

Information Germane to the Case

• The abnormal psychology course is required for all psychology majors.
• In the African American community, spirituality and religion are a cultural value viewed as providing a sense of hope. Students often rely—usually in very subtle ways—on their religion to get through the vigorous demands of college (e.g., a silent prayer before an examination).

The Case

During the first class meeting of her Abnormal Psychology course, Dr. Samantha Jones introduced herself and asked the students to do the same. She also asked them to say what led them to take the course, aside from the departmental requirement. Most of the students said that they were taking the course to learn more about abnormal individuals and how best to work with them. However, one student stated that he was taking the course to avoid being killed. After the drug-related deaths of two brothers, a cousin, and several friends, his mother apparently had told him, "I do not intend to bury the only son I have left. You are going to college and you are going to make something out of your life!" He concluded by saying, "So that is why I am here. I do not want to be killed and I certainly do not want to cause my mother any more pain. I want to make my mother proud and, more important, I want to be proud of me."

Dr. Jones responded by saying, "Praise God!" The students reacted to this exclamation with startled looks on their faces, as if something terrible had just been said. One of the students in the course, who is majoring in religious studies, said, "Excuse us, Dr. Jones, but this is the first time we have ever heard a professor say something like that. It is not a bad response; it is just one that we do not hear often, especially in the classroom. It feels really good to have a professor who values her religion." As the semester continued, the students' excitement about the course escalated. Statements such as "Amen, everybody," "Hallelujah," and "Thank you, Jesus" were heard quite frequently among the students.

Sue Martin became increasingly frustrated with the religious comments and finally decided to speak with John Smith. Sue explained her concerns to Dr. Smith, stating, "Until now, my courses have been fine. However, my abnormal psychology class has become ridiculous. Students are always saying things like 'Thank you, Jesus' or 'Amen, everybody.' This class is becoming more like a church than an educational experience. I have been in classes with most of the students and this is the first time I have had a professor who allows these sayings in the classroom. Perhaps if she had not said 'Praise God' in the beginning, this religious stuff would not be taking place now. Dr. Smith, I know that you are aware of the college's policy regarding the constitutional provision for the separation of church and state and I think you need to do something about this. It is becoming too much for me to deal with and I am certain that some of the other students feel the same way." Dr. Smith thanked Sue for sharing her concerns with him and assured her that he would look into it.

Dr. Smith later met with Dr. Jones and explained that a student in her abnormal psychology course had come to him expressing concerns regarding the religious phrases and statements she and some of the other students were making. Dr. Jones admitted she had indeed used the phrase "Praise God," and that several students also had used similar phrases and statements throughout the semester. Dr. Smith reminded her of the constitutional provision for the separation of church and state and suggested that neither she nor her students should continue making such statements in the classroom. A few days later, Dr. Jones responded to Dr. Smith in writing, stating, "I have taught at this college for ten years. I have used religious statements in the classroom before and no one has ever complained until now. I have a right to share what I believe with others and what you are asking me to do seems to be a violation of *my* constitutional rights. Given this, I have decided to seek legal counsel."

Several days later the students noticed a change in Dr. Jones. She appeared to be sad and frustrated, but when they inquired, she stated, "All is well. I'm just dealing with some personal concerns." As students exited the classroom they began speculating about what could be going on with Dr. Jones. Sue told a couple of the students about her meeting with Dr. Smith. When the other students heard about this, they reacted by staging a protest to express their desire to use religious statements in the classroom. The protest continued for nearly a week, and gained national media attention.

Discussion Questions

1. How would you conceptualize this case? List the facts and summarize the case.
2. If you were Dr. Jones, how would you handle this situation?
3. If you were a student in this class, how would you feel about this situation?
4. What are your thoughts regarding the separation of church and state?
5. Many public schools throughout the country are required to post signs that say, "In God We Trust." Do you think these signs should be posted in college classrooms or buildings? Why or why not?

6. What are your thoughts regarding the expression of one's cultural values in the classroom? Should students continue to practice their beliefs in a subtler manner or should they be allowed to speak more openly about their religious beliefs?

Research Activities for Further Exploration

1. Interview students, faculty, and administrators regarding the use of religious phrases and statements in the classroom.
2. Develop a survey (e.g., Perceptions of Religious Phrases and Statements in the Classroom) and randomly survey students, faculty, and administrators to determine their thoughts and perceptions regarding this issue. Compare and contrast their responses.
3. What does the research literature say about the separation of church and state at the college level?

MANDATED PREREQUISITE

Barbara J. Johnson & Adrienne M. Mustiful

Description of the Institutional Environment

Leland College is a private four-year liberal arts institution with approximately 8,000 students. The average ACT score for entering first-year students is 24. The racial composition of the student body at this historically black Catholic college is 93 percent African American, 3 percent white, 2 percent Asian, and 2 percent Latino. Non-Catholic students comprise 40 percent of the student body. Leland's student-faculty ratio is 20 to 1.

Description of the Surrounding Community

Leland College is the pride of Baker, a small southern town with 33,000 residents. Leland is located on the banks of the Mississippi River just a 45-minute drive to a sprawling metropolis. The college employs approximately 40 percent of Baker's residents. Baker is proud to be the home of Leland, the only historically black Catholic college in the nation.

Primary Persons Involved in the Case

- Taylor London, a Chicago native, is a white first-semester student on a full academic scholarship.

- Curtis Dorsett is the Director of the First-Year Advising Center at Leland College.
- Karen Rankin is the Admissions Counselor for the Great Lakes Region.
- Dr. Lavette Thompson is the Vice President of Academic Affairs. She has worked at Leland for more than 20 years.
- Bonnie Brown is the Academic Advisor in the First-Year Advising Center. Curtis Dorsett is her supervisor.

Information Germane to the Case

- The founder of Leland College, Father William Lee, ordained that at least 50 percent of Leland students should be practicing Catholics and that all Leland graduates satisfactorily complete a religion course with a minimum grade of C.
- To ensure a degree of consistency, the religion course has a prescribed curriculum (i.e., all faculty utilize the same text, assignments, and grading policies). Students complete a pretest to assess their awareness of various religions. The pretest scores are used to assess which two religions each student will be assigned for the final project. As determined by the pretest score, students are assigned two religions that they know little or nothing about for the final project. Requirements for the final project include completion of two observations of the assigned religions, comparison of the assigned religions with the student's identified religion, and a class presentation.
- Counselors in the First-Year Advising Center advise all entering students. Students must apply for admission to their major program in the spring semester of their first year at Leland. Conditional admission to the major is granted with the stipulation that students complete all general studies requirements prior to the fall semester of the sophomore year. Each spring, the First-Year Advising Center conducts an audit of all first-year students so that the files can be transferred to the appropriate program coordinator. Students who have not met the general studies requirements are asked to meet with their assigned academic advisor to discuss a plan for meeting the requirements by the start of the fall semester.

The Case

In a meeting with Bonnie Brown, Taylor London is advised that a religion course is required for all first-year students. Taylor informs Ms. Brown that he is an atheist and sees no need for a religion course. Ms. Brown reiterates that the religion course is mandatory for all students that graduate from Leland. Taylor refuses to enroll in the course and voices concern that it is an infringement upon his personal beliefs. However, Ms. Brown informs Taylor that he will not be able to graduate or be admitted to the College of Education without satisfactorily passing the religion course.

Bonnie Brown is quite disturbed by her meeting with Taylor and contacts Curtis Dorsett, who is perplexed that one of their "prized" recruits is refusing to accept the mandated policy and follow the prescribed curriculum. He then contacts the admissions office to determine which admissions counselor recruited Taylor. Finally, he is able to speak with Karen Rankin, the admissions counselor for the Great Lakes region. She indicates that Taylor was provided with the college's catalog and was made aware of the institution's religious affiliation. Additionally, she notes that Leland's status as the only historically black Catholic college in the nation is prominently displayed on all publications.

Curtis Dorsett then informs Dr. Lavette Thompson of the pending crisis with Taylor London. A day later, Dr. Thompson schedules a meeting with Taylor in an attempt to resolve the issue. Dr. Thompson begins the meeting stating, "She is a devout Catholic" and would like to hear more about Taylor's philosophical beliefs on atheism. Taylor explains his beliefs and is adamant that as an atheist that he should not be forced to take the religion course. Once Taylor is finished, Dr. Thompson explains in practical terms why the religion course is necessary and how it will assist in broadening Taylor's worldview. However, Taylor shows no signs of retreating and implies that he may have grounds for a lawsuit. Dr. Thompson concludes the meeting by restating that the religion course is mandatory and that he will be expected to enroll in the course for the spring semester or risk forfeiting his scholarship.

In the meantime, Taylor runs for vice-president of the incoming first-year class and pledges to challenge the policy on the mandatory religion class. Students from various religious backgrounds support Taylor's campaign and he consequently wins the vice-presidency by a landslide. Taylor immediately begins to explore ways to challenge the mandatory religion course, particularly from the perspective of an atheist who should be exempt from the mandate.

Discussion Questions

1. What are the issue(s) or problem(s) presented in this case? Be specific.
2. Discuss mandatory general studies requirements for first-year students. Does Taylor's situation differ from a first-year English major who does not want to take a math class because there is no perceived benefit? Explain.
3. Explain how Taylor's situation might affect other current and prospective students. How can the institution accommodate students who oppose the

religion course? Is there a way for Leland to integrate the material for the religion course into the curriculum so that it isn't a separate course?

4. Does Leland College have an obligation to ensure that the religious beliefs of students are not infringed upon?

5. Describe an intervention technique or activity you would recommend for Taylor and Dr. Thompson? Are there any other persons you would integrate into the intervention? If so, elaborate.

6. How would you evaluate the campus culture relative to religion?

Research Activities for Further Exploration

1. Assess the religious climate of your institution by reviewing the curriculum. Explore how the religious climate has changed since its establishment.

2. Conduct surveys of faculty, staff, and students (prospective, current, and former) regarding their perceptions of mandatory courses (e.g., first-year success courses, physical education, etc.). Report the findings across groups by gender, geographic region, and religious orientation.

3. Research other private institutions that require a religion class to ascertain if they have encountered a similar situation and if so, how it was handled. Compare your institution's policy with those of other private colleges.

UNCOMFORTABLE SARAH

Adam J. Kantrovich

Description of the Institutional Environment

Mid-South Mountain University is a public four-year state institution with approximately 7,000 undergraduate students and 2,000 graduate students enrolled in about 120 academic programs. The school's demographics are as follows: 94 percent white; 4 percent African American, Asian, American Indian, and Hispanic; and 2 percent international students.

Description of the Surrounding Community

The university lies in a small valley on the western side of the Appalachian Mountains in a town of about 12,000 people that is surrounded by federal or state-owned land. The nearest city with more cultural and religious diversity or access to an airport offering commercial flights is 60 miles away. The majority of the local community is employed through the university. The city contains 32 Christian churches and no mosques, synagogues, temples, or other places of worship.

Primary Persons Involved in the Case

- Sarah Stone is a junior studying animal science. She comes from a metropolitan area and is the middle of three children in a family that practices Conservative Judaism. Sarah strongly believes in and continues to practice her faith.
- Dr. Isabel Cortez is the Vice-President of Student Affairs. She is a native of Central America and received all three of her degrees in the U.S.
- Stephanie Jackson, an African American woman, is the Multicultural Center advisor. She is a 20-year veteran of postsecondary education.
- David Michaels is a student affairs professional who has been at the university for three years. He was born in a southern rural area and was educated in counselor education at a land-grant institution.
- Dr. Regina Smith is a faculty member and Sarah Stone's advisor.
- Jerry Johnson is a prelaw major in his senior year. Jerry was born and raised in a large New England city and has known Sarah since she arrived on campus as a first-year student.

Information Germane to the Case

- The Jewish religion does not believe in the New Testament and does not believe that Jesus is the savior. The three major Jewish denominations in the U.S. are Reform, Conservative, and Orthodox.

The Case

Sarah Stone has enjoyed much of her experience at Mid-South Mountain University because of the friends she has made and the outdoor activities that are available in the area. Shortly after arriving on campus, Sarah met Jerry Johnson, who invited her to become active with the Multicultural Center. Because of the lack of diversity on campus, he thought this would help make the environment feel more like home. Jerry and Sarah regularly attend Multicultural Center events.

However, Sarah sometimes becomes upset or depressed because of various incidents that occur on campus or in the surrounding community. Sometimes she feels like she should transfer from Mid-South Mountain University to a larger institution with more cultural and religious diversity. When Sarah begins to feel down she usually talks with her friend Jerry, her advisor Regina Smith, or Stephanie Jackson at the Multicultural Center.

For Sarah, the most disturbing events occur several times each year when a "street preacher" returns to the campus. This man almost always brings Sarah to tears when she hears him. He tends to be "in your face," aggressive, and blatantly ethnocentric, showing a complete disregard for all other religions and cultures. Sarah usually has to walk by the man on her way to class as he stands on a bench preaching at the top of his lungs about Jesus and the "gospel." His preaching about Christianity does not bother Sarah as much as his degradation of all other religions at the same time. He says that "all those who do not come to Christ will be doomed to Hell for eternity" and that they are "only dirt on an otherwise clean white tablecloth." He verbally attacks and harasses anyone who ignores him, and if they politely decline to become involved, he becomes even more abusive and steps up his degradation of all those who do not believe as he does. He usually preaches for an entire day and occasionally will spend several days at a central location on campus without any repercussion from campus security or administration.

Another event that makes Sarah uncomfortable usually occurs every semester when a religious organization comes on campus and posts one person at almost every building entrance. A person giving away copies of the New Testament greets everyone who enters or exits a building at the door. When people politely decline, this person questions them and their faith. The last time this occurred Sarah was on her way to meet with Regina Smith about her class schedule for the next semester. She began to tell Dr. Smith about how uncomfortable those individuals made her feel. Dr. Smith apologized and said that there was nothing they could do and advised her to try to ignore them. Sarah asked Dr. Smith if it was even legal for people to publicly preach or push a religious item on the students since this is a public institution. Dr. Smith suggested that it probably should not be allowed, but she did not think that the administration or others would do anything about it because almost 100 percent of the local population is Christian. This disturbed Sarah, so she went to see Stephanie Jackson to find out what she could do to prevent these activities.

Ms. Jackson told Sarah that she understood how she felt and she suggested that they meet with David Michaels. The three of them discussed the situation and how it affected Sarah as well as others on campus. Mr. Michaels was very sympathetic to Sarah and her situation and said that he would discuss this with his supervisor. Sarah thanked Mr. Michaels for his time and Ms. Jackson for her help. This conversation had helped to alleviate some of Sarah's anxieties. Now she hoped that the administrators would take action to resolve the problem of public events that degrade other religions or cultures.

Shortly thereafter, David Michaels reported on the situation to his supervisor, Isabel Cortez. They discussed various possible scenarios and their repercussions, such as (a) publicly denouncing these events and enforcing regulations and laws that do not allow public verbal or physical harassment towards minority cultures and religions, (b) creating new rules that prohibit any public religious activities on campus (e.g., a religious activity sponsored by a student organization would have to be approved by appropriate administration and held in an enclosed room out of the sight and sound of others), (c) reacting only when complaints are made, or (d) doing nothing about the present situation until the minority population grows and it is deemed absolutely necessary to change.

Discussion Questions

1. What are the primary issues in this case?
2. When advising Jewish students, what should administrators and faculty know about Judaism?
3. Does Mid-South Mountain University have an obligation to protect religious minorities attending or working at the institution? If so, in what way?
4. Define the term "ethnocentric" and explain how it relates to this case.
5. Discuss the options that the student affairs personnel created to resolve Sarah's situation. What are possible repercussions from the university and local community of each option?
6. Discuss how you would resolve the issues brought to light by this case (a) as a student advisor, (b) as a student affairs professional, and (c) as the vice-president of student affairs.

Research Activities for Further Exploration

1. Write a report on the appropriate federal and state laws that deal with religious rights in public education and the idea of "separation of church and state."
2. Conduct three to five interviews with Jewish students and faculty members about unintentional religious biases that occur, and how they deal with them.
3. Write a research paper on (a) religious freedom in America, and (b) how they relate to postsecondary public education.

CAMPUS RESTLESSNESS

James L. Moore III & Marcia L. Childs

Description of the Institutional Environment

Haybrook State and Technical University (HSTU) is a major public four-year research institution. Nearly 43,000 students (i.e., 32,000 undergraduates, 8,000 graduate students, and 2,500 professional students) attend this institution annually. The university was an original 1862 land-grant institution and is now considered to be the state's flagship institution. The demographic breakdown for the student population is as follows: 85 percent white American, 7 percent African American, 5 percent Asian American, 2 percent Hispanic American, and 1 percent other.

Description of the Surrounding Community

HSTU is a comprehensive research institution dedicated to serving the constituents of its state. In addition to the main campus, six regional campuses are located throughout the state. However, most of the students attend the main campus, which is situated in a small, college town located two hours from the nearest major city. Many of the students, staff, and faculty live within the town limits and in neighboring counties. Town officials are strongly invested in HSTU's growth, advancement, and overall success. The university has established various economic plans and community initiatives to attract biotechnical and computer-based companies to the area.

Primary Persons Involved in the Case

- Malik Muhammad is an international student from the Middle East. He is a sophomore and President of the Orthodox Muslim Association-Student Affiliation Branch (OMA).
- Dr. Elijah El Hajj is Dean of International Affairs at HSTU and serves as OMA's faculty advisor. He is a renowned scholar in world Islamic religious practices and rituals.
- Joseph Ellis is a white male majoring in political science theory and Western civilizations. In addition, he is President of the Equal Freedoms Organization, a political activist organization formed by white males with high IQs.

Information Germane to the Case

- Over the last five years, as part of its strategic plan to improve its nation-

al rankings, HSTU has aggressively recruited international students from the Middle East, Asia, and Africa for its graduate programs in math, science, and engineering.
- Recently, several Muslim organizations on campus made formal complaints to the president of HSTU about the lack of religious tolerance on campus. These students feel they are the victims of discrimination in the aftermath of the horrendous terrorist attack on the World Trade Center in New York City on September 11, 2001.
- When Dr. El Hajj was commissioned by the president of HSTU to meet with the Muslim organizations on campus, he learned that many of the Muslim students were dissatisfied with their experience at the university.

The Case

During early fall semester, preparations were being made for the annual cultural festival parade. Various ethnic student organizations were asked to submit proposals for showcasing their culture at the annual festival. The different organizations were sent personal invitations, by both the president of the university and Dr. Elijah El Hajj, to participate in the event.

Many of the Muslim student groups decided not to participate because they felt that the university had done little to address their concerns. However, the Orthodox Muslim Association–Student Affiliation Branch was the only Muslim group that decided to participate. After talking with Dr. El Hajj personally about the importance of participating, Malik Muhammad was influential in convincing his organization to participate. He urged his members not to be cowards and to step up and out. More specifically, Dr. El Hajj told Malik that it was important that the Muslim organizations become more active on campus so other student groups can learn more about the beauty of Islam.

Malik and several other active OMA members enthusiastically designed a float for the parade. They were proud of their Islamic beliefs and tired of the stereotypical beliefs held by non-Muslim students on campus. Malik suggested that the theme of their float be "Celebrating Unity through Differences." Flyers, posters, and emails were developed inviting students from different ethnic, cultural, and religious backgrounds to join them during the festival celebration in the student union for food, fellowship, and information about Islam.

Upon seeing the flyers and posters distributed around campus, Joseph Ellis felt outraged. He stated to fellow students, "These foreigners have gone too far." He immediately scheduled an appointment to see Dr. El Hajj. In the meeting, Joseph shared his organization's position on Muslim organizations and terrorism. Dr. El Hajj stated "all organizations will be treated equally at

HSTU." As a result, Joseph stormed out Dr. El Hajj's office and decided to take matters into his own hands.

The next day, Malik received a message on his cellular telephone warning him and his student group not to participate in the festival because there would be trouble, but Malik decided not to report these threats to Dr. El Hajj, campus police, or other university administrators. He became even more determined to participate in the cultural festival. The day of the festival parade finally arrived. Early that morning as OMA members put the finishing touches on their float, Joseph Ellis and ten of his followers arrived to protest against OMA and they completely sabotaged the group's float. A crowd of students, alumni, and friends gathered to observe what was happening. Many administrators and faculty, including Dr. El Hajj, were in attendance.

Discussion Questions

1. What are the main issues in this case?
2. How do you imagine the conflict was resolved?
3. What action could the student affairs administrators have taken to change the outcome?
4. What can be done to increase the awareness of cultural similarities and differences?
5. What guidelines for student organizations can be developed to ensure more unity within the student body? Include consequences for violations.
6. How can members of the majority culture develop an understanding of the discrimination experienced by minority student groups?

Research Activities for Further Exploration

1. Conduct research on your campus by interviewing four or five Muslim students. Ask them to describe what it is like to be a Muslim on a predominately Christian campus in the U.S.
2. Write a research paper comparing the policy of diversity and race relations of several colleges and universities. Provide recommendations for your university.
3. Visit a mosque in your community. Write a reflection paper on your experience.

ISLAM MEANS PEACE

Dafina Lazarus Stewart

Description of the Institutional Environment

Thomas College is a predominantly white, private four-year institution. Thomas College has approximately 2,600 students, of whom 3.7 percent are African American, 2.8 percent are Asian American, and 2.7 percent are Hispanic or Latino; no American Indian students currently are enrolled. Due to the strength of its international education program, Thomas College also is host to a relatively large number of international students, primarily from the Middle East and Africa. Thomas College is a moderately selective institution and is considered one of the best-kept secrets in the nation.

Description of the Surrounding Community

Thomas College occupies approximately 800 acres of land in a rural community in the Midwest. The college has cordial relations with the neighboring town but has no formal association with it. The campus is very impressive and many of the academic buildings boast Gothic architecture. Contrary to the diversity reflected in the campus population, the neighboring town is mostly white.

Primary Persons Involved in the Case

- Dr. Mary O'Boyle is the Vice President for Student Affairs and the Dean of Students at Thomas College. Dr. O'Boyle has been at Thomas College for five years.
- Anne Tims is the Director of Student Activities. She has been at Thomas College for three years.
- Franklin Chambers is the Director of the Office of International Education. He has been at Thomas College for nearly 20 years and is credited with launching the international education programs, which have become quite popular.
- Zaha Fadhi, is a third-year Saudi Arabian student who came to Thomas College to earn a bachelor's degree in education, in order to return home to teach in one of the public schools for girls. As an adherent to traditional Muslim beliefs, including wearing traditional dress, Zaha found her first year at Thomas to be quite challenging. Zaha is serving her second term as President of the International Student Association (ISA), which represents the interests of all international students on campus and endeavors

to educate the larger campus population about the cultures, values, and customs of its international students.

- Michael Smith, a white male from the neighboring town, is a junior majoring in political science. He is the President of the Student Programming Board (SPB).

Information Germane to the Case

- Prior to September 11, 2001, Thomas College seemed to be doing a very good job of actively seeking to engage all students on campus regardless of their race, ethnicity, nationality, or religion. Although many of the domestic minority and international students were quick to point out how far Thomas had to go, they were largely satisfied with their experience, and the retention rate for these students was high when compared to similar institutions.

The Case

At Zaha Fadhi's urging, and with Franklin Chambers' support, the ISA has presented a proposal for a week-long series of events aimed at dispelling the myths surrounding Arabs and Islam and educating students, faculty, and staff about the beliefs, customs, and political interests of Arab nations. The events would include airing a popular movie like "The Siege" and discussing portrayals of Arabs and Arab Americans in the film, inviting a guest speaker from the Arab American Institute, holding town meetings for students to gather together to express their hopes and fears about the future, and hosting debates about the efficacy of "regime changes" brought about by external military forces. The ISA also wants to cosponsor an interfaith memorial service with the Campus Christian Fellowship (CCF), which already has indicated that they would be very interested in this event.

However, because the budget required to fund the proposal exceeds ISA's allotment, Zaha has written a proposal to the SPB requesting that they underwrite a large portion of the expense. Information about the ISA proposal found its way into the student newspaper and the SPB meeting at which Zaha was scheduled to defend the proposal was unusually crowded. Several students brought signs protesting the use of student fees (which make up the majority of the SPB discretionary funds) for programs that support terrorists and people friendly to terrorists. Several residents of the neighboring town also were in attendance, threatening to see to it that the college loses its federal funding if these events are allowed to take place.

In the midst of all this commotion, Zaha made her appeal. Following Zaha's comments, the Commission on Black Student Interests (of which

Zaha's roommate is the secretary) spoke in support of the proposal. Several members of the SPB asked Zaha questions about what would be said at the various forums and what views their speaker would espouse. Michael Smith finally asked why the SPB should support these events when the mere suggestion had caused so much disruption on campus and the majority of the campus population obviously did not support the proposal. However, the tumult in the room had grown so loud that Michael had to table the discussion and adjourn the meeting. He stated that the SPB would reconvene in secret later in the week to discuss the proposal and vote on whether they would support it.

The following day, while Michael was discussing the meeting with Anne Tims (she also had attended) and seeking her advice, a very distraught and disappointed Zaha met with Franklin Chambers to discuss the possibility of returning to Saudi Arabia at the end of the semester. Right before Zaha arrived, he received a confidential memo from Mary O'Boyle, informing him that if the SPB denied the ISA funding request, she would fund the proposed activities out of her administrative account.

Discussion Questions

1. In what ways can the current development of Zaha Fadhi and Michael Smith be explained by Phinney's model of Ethnic Identity Development and Helm's White Racial Identity Development model, respectively?
2. If you were Anne Tims, what would you say to Michael when he came to your office? How do the principles of multicultural competence inform your comments?
3. If you were Franklin Chambers, what would you say to Zaha when she came to your office? How do the principles of multicultural competence inform your comments?
4. Should Dr. Mary. O'Boyle fund the ISA activities if the SPB denies the request? Why or why not? What would be the repercussions of her actions in either case?
5. How can Dr. O'Boyle lead in this tenuous situation?
6. How would your strategies change if Thomas College were a public institution? How would they change if Thomas College were a community college?

Research Activities for Further Exploration

1. What is your institution's policy on the use of student fees to fund contro-versial programs sponsored by student organizations?
2. Find out information about the Arab, Arab American, and Islamic popu-lations on the college and university campuses in your state and region.
3. Interview three to five international students on your campus. Discuss with them whether they feel included in the campus community and ask for their perceptions of how the campus climate toward international stu-dents (particularly Middle Eastern students) was affected by the September 11th attacks.

HOW DO WE SUPPORT RELIGION?

COREY ELLIS

Description of the Institutional Environment

Alpha College (AC) is a highly selective private four-year liberal arts col-lege located in the suburb of Velvet Fields. The college was founded with the support of an established, ultraliberal Christian organization, but it currently has no religious affiliation. It enrolls 1,300 students, 94 percent of whom are traditional aged; the 6 percent who are nontraditional students are enrolled in AC's highly renowned accelerated MBA program.

Description of the Surrounding Community

Velvet Fields is a predominantly white (95%) affluent suburb of Hollow, a southern city with 2.5 million residents, which is supported heavily by the tourist industry. The majority of the residents of Velvet Fields are upper-mid-dle-class retirees. Most people of color in Velvet Fields are blue-collar work-ers employed in service industries. Several of the highly influential families in Velvet Fields are very politically active and have vested interests in AC as alumni or as parents whose children attend Alpha.

Primary Persons Involved in the Case

- Ryan O'Neil, a first-generation college student, is a senior majoring in political science. He is the President of Rho Iota Theta (RIT), the largest fraternity at AC.

- Jimmy Smith is a sophomore and a new member of RIT. He is a very introverted student who was pressured into joining a fraternity by his father, who was a fraternity man himself.
- Deanna Smith is Jimmy's mother. She is very involved in Jimmy's life. She is the CEO of a family-owned and -operated hardware chain in Hollow.
- Dr. Trishelle Davis is the Dean of Students and Vice Chancellor at AC. She is in her ninth year in this position after a 12-year stint as the Dean at the University of Gloucester in England. She oversees Residential Life, Student Involvement, Judicial Affairs, Student Leadership Programs, Greek Life, and the Counseling Center. She reports to the Chancellor.
- Dr. Donald Reznick is AC's Chancellor. He tends to shy away from sensitive issues, attempting to be everyone's friend and not making decisions that would divide the campus.
- Thomas Harris, Sr., is a retired businessman. He has close ties to many of the wealthy private-sector residents of Velvet Fields and Hollow. His father was very influential in the opening of AC in Velvet Fields and also was the spiritual leader of the founding Christian organization.
- Thomas Harris, Jr., Esquire, CPA, is a member of the AC Board of Trustees.

Information Germane to the Case

- The Trustees are very involved in the everyday activities of the college.

The Case

During his second year at AC, Jimmy Smith began to investigate ideas of religion and spirituality. He found camaraderie in a group of students who seemed to be undergoing the same exploration. As Jimmy became more involved with this group, he began to form an opinion about what was right and what was wrong at AC. Jimmy and the other students in this group felt that the college was suffering financial problems because it had become estranged from its religious underpinnings. As they became more organized, they began to call themselves "Outreach Citizens" (OC) and they wanted to share their message with the entire campus community. Their message is that college students have become immoral sinners and they need to repent immediately. The group also feels that AC supports this behavior by allowing drinking at parties, encouraging students to explore "alternative lifestyles," and so forth. Jimmy began to organize flyer and poster campaigns. The group placed paraphernalia throughout the campus asking students to repent, atone for their misdeeds, and give their lives back to God.

This "outreach" has begun to consume Jimmy's life and he has become the visible leader of OC. He decided that it was time to organize meetings for other people who may support OC's views. After he was elected social chair for RIT, he organized a Bible study group under the auspices of the fraternity. When fraternity members arrived at the first meeting they found nonmembers who were there to advocate the ideals of OC. The meeting began as a conversation about the basic tenets of the Bible, but quickly became inflammatory, with several OC members accusing fraternity members in general of blasphemy. Several members of the chapter were extremely uncomfortable at the end of this meeting.

With Jimmy's leadership, the members of OC continue to promote their events through the guise of RIT. Meetings are advertised as social events, but actually are Bible studies at which OC members preach to those who attend. Even the Christian fraternity brothers are very disturbed about OC's tactics. They finally bring this to Ryan O'Neil's attention. Ryan has always been good friends with Jimmy and is unsure how to approach the situation so he arranges to meet with Dr. Trishelle Davis for advice.

In the meantime, Jimmy decides to pursue getting Outreach Citizens recognized as an official campus organization. AC never had a clear policy about denying recognition to student organizations and administrators have paid little attention to the process. The only requirements have been to find an advisor and complete the paperwork. Based on that history, OC is given organizational status.

By the time Ryan finally met with Dr. Davis, he was at a loss. He is a Christian and believes in some of the ideals that OC is putting forward. However, because Jimmy has held many OC meetings at the RIT house, the fraternity is now being associated with OC and some members are extremely upset and uncomfortable. Four members of the chapter who are atheists are considering leaving the fraternity.

Ryan was even more confused after confronting Jimmy about the members' concerns. Jimmy responded with specific references to the chapter's ritual that can be interpreted as being in line with OC's position. Ryan did not know how to make Jimmy understand that RIT does not want to be associated with OC activities. He also is concerned about Jimmy's emotional and mental health. Jimmy is now living every moment for OC. Dr. Davis asked Ryan if the actions of this organization are infringing on the rights of others. He said, "No," but he thinks they are extremists and push too hard. When she asked Ryan what he would like done about the situation, he suggested removing the organization's recognition status. He feels that this will make the organization pull back on some of its tactics. He also wants Dr. Davis to bring Jimmy in for a conversation.

Trishelle scheduled a meeting with Jimmy for the following week under the guise of talking to him about his mother. During this conversation, she also asked questions about OC. Jimmy became fidgety and defensive, stating that OC members are carrying out their "God-given right"; they are tired of the lack of values at AC and they intend to convert every member of the college by any means necessary.

After her conversation with Jimmy, Trishelle decided that the best course of action was to remove the organization's recognition status because of "cultist activities." She is concerned that the tactics of this organization are infringing on the civil rights of others.

Jimmy was extremely upset when he learned that OC's organizational status had been revoked. His immediate response was to continue planning events without mentioning a sponsoring organization on the publicity, but he noticed that attendance at OC meetings has decreased. Eventually, Jimmy and called his mother. She called her good friend, Thomas Harris, Sr., to express her frustration with AC's administration. He then called his son to ask him to rectify the situation. Harris, Sr. does not believe that a college founded on Christian values should prevent students from performing Christian activities, such as proselytizing and converting nonbelievers. His son called Donald Reznick to express his irritation and threatened to withdraw his generous support of six endowed faculty chair positions.

Discussion Questions

1. What issues of diversity exist in this case? What are the pertinent facts needed to design an intervention?
2. The Chancellor referred Thomas Harris, Jr.'s call to you as the Dean of Students. How would you construct conversations with the following people: (a) Ryan O'Neil; (b) Thomas Harris, Jr.; (c) Thomas Harris, Sr.; (d) Deanna Smith; and (e) Donald Reznick?
3. Was Dr. Davis's decision to revoke the organization's status justified? Why or why not?
4. When you meet with Jimmy, he appears to be in a state of depression and is in danger of failing all of his classes and dropping out of college. Based upon your knowledge of student development and counseling theories, design a personal action plan to help Jimmy stay in college.
5. How would you compose strategies and policies that would prevent this situation from occurring again at AC?
6. How does one reconcile the founders' religious values with the college's current unaffiliated status?

Research Activities for Further Exploration

1. Using archival research techniques, research cases dealing with religious issues that have occurred on your campus. What is the institution's stance about recognizing student organizations, especially those that advocate religious and/or political positions?
2. Conduct a historical research project on the personal lives of your institution's first ten trustees or board members. Were there any views that would appear contrary to the institution's mission and vision today?
3. Conduct a content analysis of the policies of six religiously affiliated institutions for handling student expression that may be contrary to the views of the sponsoring religion.

A THIN LINE BETWEEN PREFERENTIAL TREATMENT AND ACCOMMODATION

LISA A. GUION

Description of the Institutional Environment

Rigor University is a public four-year institution located in a small town. With a student body fast approaching 15,000, it is one of the fastest-growing universities in the region. A large endowment and subsequent grants funded the creation of a campus extension that holds a state-of-the-art agricultural and natural resources research center with technologically superior classrooms and residence halls. Currently, the racial demographic breakdown is as follows: 1 percent American Indian, 1 percent African American, 2 percent Hispanic/Latino, 4 percent Asian/Pacific Islander, and 92 percent white.

Description of the Surrounding Community

Rigor University is located in a remote town that is a three-hour drive to the nearest major city. The town is less diverse than the university, and there is a clear separation between those who have roots in the town and those who relocate. Agricultural industries and the university provide the economic base for the town.

Primary Persons Involved in the Case

- Rashid Mohammad, a Muslim who was born in Syria, is entering his final semester in the undergraduate agricultural engineering program. He is a U.S. citizen and plans to live and work in the U.S. after graduation.
- Dr. Margaret Washington, Rashid's academic advisor, is an Assistant Professor (and the only woman) in the Department of Agricultural Engineering. She has been with the department for four years and she plans to submit her tenure packet next year.
- Dr. Edward Thomas is a distinguished professor who teaches the practicum/internship course in agricultural engineering. He is a widely published academic who is well respected by agricultural industry leaders, which, in large part, is why he is so successful with student placement.
- Dr. John Davis is the Chair of the Department of Agricultural Engineering.
- Dr. Paul Wainwright is the Associate Dean of International Student Services (ISS).

Information Germane to the Case

- The Islamic religion requires Muslim men, beginning at the age of puberty, to attend Jum'uah congregational prayers that are held every Friday after midday. The only mosque in town, which also serves the surrounding communities, has been holding the Jum'uah prayers at the same time every Friday afternoon since it opened its doors five years ago.
- After the September 11, 2001, terrorist attacks in New York and Washington, D.C., derogatory graffiti and racial slurs directed at Muslim students and their religion began to appear on campus. As a result, Rashid Mohammad and other Muslim students founded the Islamic Student Organization (ISO) to provide a support system for Muslim students and a forum to unite them to address issues on campus.
- The ISS has a reputation as being a strong advocate for international students.

The Case

As Rashid Muhammad registered for spring semester courses, he noticed that the required practicum course is offered only on Friday afternoons. Rashid attends Jum'uah congregational prayers at the mosque every Friday afternoon at that time.

When he discussed this conflict with Margaret Washington, she encouraged him to speak with Edward Thomas to see if they could work something out. When he met with Dr. Thomas to explain his situation, Dr. Thomas stated that he would have to attend the practicum course sessions just like every other student in the class. Rashid then rushed back to Dr. Washington's office to ask for more advice, but she told him that there was nothing she could do. Still not satisfied, Rashid called John Davis to explain the situation. Dr. Davis said that he would investigate the matter.

Dr. Davis met with Dr. Thomas to discuss the situation. Dr. Thomas was firm in his view that he could not give preferential treatment to Rashid. He insisted that attending the class was critical because organizational theory and strategies for effectively working in the agricultural engineering industry are discussed. Also, the course serves as a forum for discussing workplace problems, issues, and solutions that the students encounter during the practicum experience. Likewise, there is no way to do make-up work or substitute this course. Dr. Thomas indicated that the course is scheduled during the summer on a different day. He further stated that Rashid could take the course then and Dr. Davis agreed with him.

ISO members suggested that Rashid contact the ISS office. When he met with Paul Wainwright, Rashid explained how attending the scheduled practicum course would prevent him from participating in religious prayer sessions that are held each Friday. However, taking the course in the summer would postpone his planned May graduation until July. Rashid confided that he did not want to take this issue to a higher level in the university or pursue any further action because Dr. Thomas has connections and a solid reputation in the relatively small agricultural engineering industry. Rashid thanked Dr. Wainwright for empathetically listening to him and offering much needed emotional support. Ultimately, Rashid knew that this was a difficult decision, but one that he must face.

Discussion Questions

1. Should the department make an accommodation for Rashid? If so, what could they do? If not, why not?
2. Do you feel that Dr. Washington appropriately carried out her advising role? If so, discuss why. If not, what could she have done differently or additionally?
3. What would you do if you were Dr. Thomas? Why? What would you do if you were Dr. Davis? Why?
4. Is it important for the faculty and leadership involved in this issue to understand the Islamic religion? If so, what should they know? How should they use this information in their decision making?
5. Given your knowledge of student development theory, are there any other strategies or techniques that Rashid could try with Dr. Thomas? If so, discuss.

6. Does your institution have or do you know of an institution that has a method for educating faculty and administration about different religious practices, customs, beliefs, and observances? If so, what method is used? Discuss. Evaluate those methods to determine if they are effective. Why or why not? Do you feel that the ISS office could have aided Rashid more? If so, how?

Research Activities for Further Exploration

1. Using information from the library, research the norms, practices, and beliefs of the Islam religion.
2. Conduct focus group research on your campus with eight to 12 Muslim students to determine if they feel that there are barriers to them exercising their religion and if there have been conflicts that have arisen similar to Rashid's situation.
3. Using research databases, analyze descriptive studies of Muslim students on U.S. college and university campuses prior to September 11, 2001, and compare key issues and outcomes with reports published after that date. Write a paper summarizing your findings.

RELIGIOUS DISCOURSE AT A SMALL PRIVATE COLLEGE

SHARON L. HOLMES & CHERYL M. ANDERSON

Description of the Institutional Environment

Braxton College (BC) is a small, private, four-year liberal arts college for women, which was founded by the Methodist Church. Average SAT and ACT scores for incoming students exceed 1100 and 25, respectively. BC serves primarily a white population, but approximately 450 of the 3,300 students are African American women and 375 are international students (e.g., from China, Africa, and Latin America). The student-faculty ratio is 12 to 1, the campus environment is collegial, and many programs and services are designed to bring students, faculty, and administrators together for community service and social activities.

Description of the Surrounding Community

Braxton is located in a predominantly white affluent community of 46,000 on the East Coast. The surrounding community enjoys having the college located in their town and a significant number of local residents attend the annual campus lyceum series, which includes special lectures and performing arts presentations. Local residents support the college's decision to provide a multiethnic learning environment, and many open their homes to international and other students, particularly during the holidays when they are unable to return home.

Primary Persons Involved in the Case

- Rebecca Tyler is the Director of Enrollment Services and coordinates the weekly chapel services at Braxton College.
- Ming Young, Kim Sue, and Chung Lee are new incoming first-year students from China.
- Dr. Sarah Mavery is the Dean of Students. She is Rebecca Tyler's supervisor.

Information Germane to the Case

- All students are required to attend a weekly service in the college chapel.

The Case

Although Braxton College has a strong religious foundation, the campus environment is liberal and students are not confined by an excessive amount of rules and regulations that restrict their movements or behaviors. The administrators believe that this type of institutional setting encourages the development of civic responsibility, moral character, and critical thought. However, one rule that is rigidly enforced is that all students are required to attend a 90-minute chapel service every Friday afternoon. Students must wear a dress to chapel and they must sign in and out to verify their attendance. At the weekly chapel services, the students sing songs from a Christian hymnbook, listen to lectures on topics selected to enhance the students' spiritual and moral development, and participate in the closing prayer. Rebecca Tyler, who coordinates the services, also schedules the visiting alumnae, lecturers, and college professors who lead the discussions. For the most part, students enjoy the weekly services because the topics often are thought provoking and the presenters usually are animated in their presentation. However, Ming Young, Kim Sue, and Chung Lee are practicing Buddhists and are uncomfortable attending the mandatory services. They are offended by the constant references to Jesus and they do not feel it is appropriate to require them to pray using his name.

Following the chapel service during the second week of classes, Ming

Young and Kim Sue went to Chung Lee's residence hall to discuss their thoughts and share their feelings about the "American" chapel service. In the tradition of Chinese culture, the students feel that they must follow the rules regarding chapel attendance, so that they will not appear to be disrespectful to authority. However, they are discouraged and wonder if Rebecca Tyler would exempt them from chapel because the services conflict with religion in Chinese culture. They decide that Chung Lee will draft a letter of appeal on their behalf to Ms. Tyler and copy it to Dr. Sarah Mavery.

Discussion Questions

1. What are the key issues in the case?
2. Are the experiences of these three students similar to those that other international students new to U.S. higher education might have? How could the college have prepared them better for the cultural differences they encountered?
3. Is it important for Rebecca Tyler to have information regarding religion in Chinese culture before responding to the women's request? If so, what should she know? Should Ming Young, Kim Sue, and Chung Lee have just simply complied with the "American" chapel service along with everyone else, and practiced their religious customs in private?
4. How might the concerns raised in the case differ if Braxton College were a public institution?
5. What factors should govern any decision to exempt the women from chapel services?
6. How would one go about changing policies at a private institution? How would the process differ at a public institution?

Research Activities for Further Exploration

1. Interview a student affairs professional responsible for planning orientation activities for prospective students to ascertain how religious diversity is considered when various programs and services are developed.
2. What is your institution's policy related to religious diversity, and what steps have been taken to incorporate the religious differences of all students on campus? Be specific.
3. Investigate Buddhism. Then write a short paper to describe how the religion is practiced. Incorporate into your paper the number of students that currently attend your college or university who have identified themselves as Buddhists.

WHY ARE YOU WEARING THAT "THING"?

Barbara J. Johnson & Lynne Guillot-Miller

Description of the Institutional Environment

Martin University is a predominantly white public four-year institution with approximately 5,000 students. The average SAT score for the first-year class is 1125. The racial and ethnic composition of the student body is 72 percent white, 13 percent African American, 6 percent Asian American, 4 percent Mexican American or Puerto Rican, and 5 percent international (primarily representing Africa, Pakistan, India). Martin's student-faculty ratio is 22 to 1.

Description of the Surrounding Community

Martin University is located in Leake, a small northern town of 28,000 residents. Leake is conveniently situated between two larger cities that are each about 45 minutes away. The university estimates that it employs 5 percent of the town's residents. Approximately 78 percent of Leake's residents have a high school diploma, 16 percent hold an associate's degree, and 15 percent have a bachelor's degree. Most of the town's residents work in one of Leake's three manufacturing plants. The town is predominantly Protestant and 70 percent of the churches are affiliated with Baptist or Methodist denominations.

Primary Persons Involved in the Case

- Zainab Suleman, a native of Pakistan, is a sophomore. She selected Martin because of the high percentage of graduates who gain entrance to medical school. Zainab plans to return to Pakistan and serve as a role model for Pakistani women.
- Mahereen Baksh, a native of Pakistan, is a sophomore who is also a pre-medicine major. Zainab and Mahereen are roommates and have been best friends since they were 10 years old.
- Caleb Pinoche, Coordinator for Student Activities, is in his first professional position. He is from a rural southern town and is actively involved in a Baptist church adjacent to campus.
- Kaleigh Johnson is a Graduate Assistant in the Office of Student Activities; she reports to Caleb Pinoche.
- Adrienne Lewis, a Catholic, is a white female from the Midwest.
- Ta'Shawn Foster, an African American female, is a Baptist from a nearby town.

- Selena Baez, a Latina, is a Catholic from a northern metropolitan area.
- Sybil Tillman, a Presbyterian, is a white female from the Southeast.
- Yolanda Brown, a Methodist, is an African American female from the Northeast.
- Amy Chang, an Asian American female, is an atheist from a metropolitan city.

Information Germane to the Case

- Zainab and Mahereen are Muslims and wear the Hijab as part of their adherence to the teachings of the Koran. Hijab is a commonly used term that refers to the headscarf used to cover the hair and neck but not the face of Muslim women. Always controversial within and outside the Islamic world, the Hijab has been everything from a highly political statement against the West to a deeply personal religious act to a requirement in such countries as Iran and Saudia Arabia.

The Case

As part of a class assignment, Zainab Suleman, Mahereen Baksh, and their classmates must keep updated on daily events by watching televised news broadcasts. Before class, several class members gathered in the common area of the student union. The area has tables so students can watch the mounted televisions, eat, study, and gather between classes. Offices for Student Life, Student Health Services, Student Government, and others surround this area. About 15 minutes into the program, six female students (Adrienne Lewis, Ta'Shawn Foster, Selena Baez, Sybil Tillman, Yolanda Brown, and Amy Chang) entered the common room and began to play cards at a nearby table. As they played, they were so noisy that the students attempting to hear the news had to move closer to the television. When the noise became too distracting everyone except Zainab and Mahereen gave up and left. When the group got too rowdy and loud for Zainab and Mahereen to hear, they turned up the volume but it seemed as though each time they increased the volume, the card players got louder too. Finally, Zainab walked over to the group and quietly informed them that she was watching the news for a class assignment and couldn't hear the TV set. The card players stared blankly at Zainab and then began to talk among themselves. Adrienne told her to go watch the news in her residence hall. Zainab stated that she didn't have time to walk across campus to do that and she repeated the importance of watching the news for her class. She also suggested that they could just as easily go to their own residence hall to play cards, but perhaps they should be studying instead of playing cards.

They were not happy with Zainab's last remark and began talking about people from other countries who came to the U.S. and tried to run everything. Selena turned to Zainab and stated, "If you would take that thing off your head you probably could hear better."

"Why are you wearing that thing on your head over here anyway? You aren't in Iraq you know," Amy said, adding, "Aren't you hot in that thing?" The group then burst into laughter and began talking about those "foreigners" as though Zainab was not standing there. She glanced over at Mahereen who was motioning for her to return to the TV set. However, Zainab told the group that she was from Pakistan and that what she wore was her own business.

"Do you hear someone talking?" Yolanda asked the others, and the chorus of wild laughter began again as Mahereen joined Zainab and whispered that they should go. Just as Mahereen and Zainab turned to leave, Sybil got up from the table stating that she needed something to drink. As she passed between Mahereen and Zainab she brushed against an unsuspecting Mahereen so forcefully that Mahereen fell to the floor. While Zainab bent over to help Mahereen get up, Ta'Shawn walked by and awkwardly lost her balance in a staged manner. As she fell, she thrust her hands out wildly and ended up grasping the back of Zainab's Hijab, pulling it tightly around her throat and causing her to fall backward to the floor. The laughter erupted again as Adrienne interjected, "See, that's why you shouldn't wear that thing over here." Mahereen bent down beside Zainab to help her stand up but Zainab was not moving. Mahereen began to shake Zainab vigorously and tried to call for help but her voice was barely audible through her tears. The jubilant laughter stopped as the group ran from the common room. Finally, Mahereen ran into the Student Activities Office and called campus security. While listening to Mahereen's conversation with the police dispatcher, Caleb Pinoche and Kaleigh Johnson went into the common area to check on Zainab, who was starting to regain consciousness. Campus security officers arrived and informed Kaleigh and Caleb that it would be helpful to have someone from the university accompany Zainab to the hospital. Because Zainab and Mahereen were so upset, both Kaleigh and Caleb escorted them to the emergency room.

Discussion Questions

1. What are the issues or problems presented in this case?
2. What are some of the typical issues that international students encounter when they attend college in the U.S.? Is this case typical or atypical? Explain your answer. Finally, discuss what may have precipitated this event if it had occurred before and after September 11, 2001, and how this

may impact the outcome.

3. How could Zainab and Mahereen's situation affect current and prospective Martin students who are from different religious, ethnic, and cultural backgrounds?
4. What should student affairs administrators at Martin do about this incident? Does Martin University have an obligation to ensure that the religious beliefs of its students are not infringed upon?
5. Design programming that addresses religious, ethnic, and cultural diversity. Cite specific theories that support the interventions or strategies suggested. How might the type of programming offered vary for faculty, staff, and students?
6. How would you evaluate the campus culture for religious and ethnic diversity? Discuss evaluation methods that can be utilized to assess the effectiveness of diversity programming.

Research Activities for Further Exploration

1. Interview the Director of the Multicultural Center, Director of International Students, and Director of Residence Life on your campus to gain a broad perspective of programming offered to students related to diversity issues (e.g., religion, sexual orientation, race, ethnicity, gender).
2. Using your institution's student code of conduct, investigate the difference between a hate crime and discrimination, the judicial process, and when criminal assault charges should be filed.
3. Conduct interviews with six to eight international students at your institution about their experience of discrimination in the U.S. (e.g., discomfort because of their religious beliefs or status as international students). Report your findings and discuss steps the institution can take to be more inclusive.

HONORING NONTRADITIONAL MULTIPLE CULTURAL IDENTITIES

Linda G. Castillo

Description of the Institutional Environment

State University (SU) is a major public teaching and research university that was founded in 1850 and is considered the flagship institution of the state of Utah. It has approximately 27,000 predominantly white students, the majority of whom are members of the Church of Jesus Christ of Latter-day Saints (LDS). The average age of undergraduates is 24. Many LDS students leave SU after their first year to complete an 18- to 24-month religious mission.

Description of the Surrounding Community

SU is located in River City, which is the largest city in the state of Utah with over 800,000 people. Approximately 51 percent of the population in River City identify as LDS members.

Primary Persons Involved in the Case

- Jose Gomez, a 30-year-old Latino student from Puerto Rico, is a junior majoring in mathematics at SU. He plans to be a middle school teacher upon completion of his bachelor's degree. He was born and raised as a Catholic in New York City. His mother is Puerto Rican and his father is Cuban American. He moved to Utah to attend SU, where he met his wife Jillian. When they got engaged, he became an LDS member.
- Jillian Smith Gomez, a white LDS member, is Jose's wife.
- Nathan Smith is Jillian's father. He is a white LDS member.
- Linda Gonzales, a Chicana counseling psychologist, works in SU's Student Counseling Center.

Information Germane to the Case

- Hispanics make up 3 percent of the student population at SU.
- The Church of Jesus Christ of Latter-day Saints is the primary religion in River City and a dominant force, particularly on the social, political, and cultural levels, with a strong belief in traditional family roles. There is a deep division between LDS members and nonmembers.
- While Jillian works full time outside the home, Jose takes care of their five children (ranging in age from two to eight years old) and completes household chores. He also works part time in addition to attending classes.

The Case

Two weeks ago, Jose went to the Center for Ethnic Student Affairs (CESA) to get tutoring assistance. There he met Linda Gonzales, who volunteers at CESA as an advisor. When Jose learned that she was a psychologist, he told her that he was upset and depressed because his wife recently had left him, taking their children with her. Jose and Linda agreed to meet for counseling the following day.

During the counseling session, Jose shared with Linda his distress over losing his children. He talked about how he missed seeing them every day and worried that his wife wouldn't know how to take care of them properly. He stated that during a recent visit with his children, he found the home in disarray. He also talked about his concern about being able to pay for food, rent, and tuition. He stated that his wife was the primary income earner and his part-time job did not cover his expenses.

In subsequent counseling sessions, Jose discussed his past treatment by his father-in-law, who called him names. He also talked about his struggle with the court system to gain visitation rights with his children while he fought for custody. He stated that the judge told him that he had no rights to his children if he couldn't support them "like a man should." During these sessions, Jose displayed depressed mood, insomnia, and self-deprecating thoughts. He also stated how he missed going to Mass and felt the need to go to confession.

Discussion Questions

1. What are Jose's nontraditional cultural identities?
2. The LDS and Latino cultures both value traditional gender roles. What are potential issues with which Jose may struggle due to his nontraditional role in his family?
3. Jose and Linda both come from Latino backgrounds. What are the benefits and disadvantages of having a counselor of a similar cultural background?
4. Although Jose was distressed, he did not go to the counseling center until after he met a counselor who happened to be at CESA. What could university counseling center staff do to help students of color feel more comfortable about going to the counseling center?
5. What are Jose's current concerns? What can counseling center staff do to help him with these concerns?
6. Two religions play a significant role in Jose's life. What should Linda know about these different religions in order to help Jose? How could she apply this knowledge to help Jose?

Research Activities for Further Exploration

1. Research the term "cultural identity." Explain what this term means and why it is important to be aware of a person's cultural identity.
2. Conduct a focus group with four to six couples who are married or in committed relationships in which each partner comes from a different religious background. How do their families and religious groups view interfaith

relationships? What interfaith conflicts have they addressed as a couple? How do they resolve these issues?

3. Interview higher education and student affairs professionals at your institution's counseling center and/or student affairs offices about their preparation for religious diversity, the influence of their own religious or spiritual background and belief system, religious or spiritual issues that arise most often in their work, and unmet needs regarding religious diversity on campus.

Chapter 5

STUDENTS WITH DISABILITIES CASE STUDIES

TO WITHDRAW OR NOT TO WITHDRAW

CATHERINE CHOI-PEARSON

Description of the Institutional Environment

Western Mountain University (WMU) is a public four-year university that was established in 1885. The university is part of the state's university and community college system, which is governed by a Board of Regents. WMU offers over 75 majors in its 10 academic colleges and schools. Each year, enrollment has grown steadily: last year approximately 15,000 students were enrolled.

Description of the Surrounding Community

WMU is nestled in the foothills of the Western Mountains and is a short drive away from several major metropolitan cities. The university is located four blocks north of Western City. The population of Western City is approximately 500,000.

Primary Persons Involved in the Case

- Shawn O'Connor is a fourth-year undergraduate student at WMU. He has a 3.8 grade point average and plans to graduate at the end of this academic year.
- Monica Lebaz is the Director of WMU's Disability Resource Center (DRC). She is responsible for the administrative functions of the office and she also works with students individually in a counselor role.

- Cassidy Parks is the Director of Student Life at WMU. The Department of Student Life is primarily responsible for student withdrawals and exit interviews. Students who wish to withdraw from courses but have failed to meet university deadlines (e.g., dropping a course by the eighth week of school), must meet with Cassidy to determine if an appeal to policy is warranted. In all cases, appeals are granted only if the student is able to document extenuating circumstances that explain why university policy was not followed. Although students meet with Cassidy regarding appeals, the appeal is granted or denied by the Student Affairs Appeals Board.

Information Germane to the Case

- WMU has experienced significant growth in the number of students who come to campus with documented disabilities. From 1996 to 1997, the number of students with disabilities at WMU doubled (from 130 to 260 students); currently, approximately 600 students are registered with the DRC.
- While 12 credits are considered a full-time load, for students registered with the DRC, a full-time credit load consists of 9 credits.
- Although the number of students with disabilities at WMU has increased, the number of resources available for these students in Western City has not increased. Similarly, mental health services in the area are not well funded; only one state mental health hospital services the entire Western City area. WMU's counseling center operates with a brief therapy model, which generally consists of 10 to 12 sessions per student. Long-term cases often are referred to therapists or agencies in the community.

The Case

In the ninth week of the semester, Monica Lebaz referred Shawn O'Connor to Student Life. Monica has been Shawn's counselor since he entered the university four years ago as a first-year student with a documented learning disability. Monica has described Shawn as a responsible student who is serious about completing his education at WMU and moving on to graduate school. She referred him to Student Life to discuss the possibility of withdrawing from half of his current course load due to the exacerbation of psychological symptoms.

When Shawn met with Cassidy Parks he indicated that he was experiencing significant stress in his life and a reduced course load would allow him to concentrate on his remaining classes and maintain his high GPA. Although hesitant to share at first, Shawn reported a history of drug abuse and chronic mental illness. He stated that he has been in treatment with both a therapist and a psychiatrist in the community for several years. He reported that two weekends ago his girlfriend had to call his psychiatrist to help him "stabilize his condition." Shawn indicated that lately he has been feeling paranoid and has experienced auditory hallucinations in class during which he hears voices in his head that make it difficult for him to concentrate on what the professor is saying. He denied suicidal or homicidal ideation and indicated that he has been clean and sober from all substances for the past five years. Shawn reported feeling much better since changing his medication, but his doctor also recommended a decrease in his course load as a way to reduce his stress level. Shawn's therapist also supports the recommended course reduction.

Cassidy Parks informed Shawn that WMU's policy clearly states that under no circumstances will partial withdrawals be processed after the eighth week of school. That is, students may be permitted to withdraw from all courses but are not allowed to drop single courses after the eighth week of school. Although Shawn provided documentation from several sources (i.e., Monica Lebaz, his psychiatrist, and his therapist) to support his request, Cassidy cannot help process the withdrawal because it would violate university policy. She then explained his remaining courses of action:

1. Shawn can totally withdraw from the fall semester. If he does so, he will not be able to graduate in the spring because he will be deficient in the 12 credits he needs to graduate.
2. Shawn can remain in all of his classes against his doctor's, therapist's, and Monica's recommendations.
3. Shawn can attempt to negotiate with his professors for "Incomplete" grades in two of his courses.

Discussion Questions

1. Should the term "diversity" apply to individuals with disabilities? Explain your answer.
2. How would you advise Shawn to proceed? Which course of action seems most appropriate to pursue? Discuss the effectiveness, feasibility, and possible outcome of each course of action recommended by Cassidy Parks.
3. What are the major differences between psychological and physical disabilities? Should individuals with psychological disabilities be treated differently than individuals with physical disabilities?
4. Shawn was hesitant to share his story with Cassidy because he was embarrassed. Discuss aspects of the university, community, and national culture that could have contributed to his feelings of shame.
5. Explain what is meant by the term "invisible disability."
6. WMU policy applies to all undergraduate students. Give two reasons why

you believe the policy was created in the first place.

Research Activities for Further Exploration

1. The Americans with Disabilities Act (ADA) calls for reasonable accommodations for individuals with documented disabilities. Define "reasonable" according to the ADA. Provide an example of a reasonable accommodation in a classroom setting for a student who suffers from Attention Deficit Hyperactivity Disorder.
2. If an individual suffers from a psychological disability but is currently taking medication that treats the primary symptoms, should this person still qualify for disability services? Discuss the factors (e.g., functional limitations) that you would consider to make your decision. Find out how the United States Supreme Court defines disability and incorporate this definition into your response.
3. The ADA differentiates between drug addiction and alcohol addiction. If you are currently using drugs, are you considered disabled? If you are currently using alcohol, are you considered disabled? Discuss the two interpretations of the ADA and reasons why disabilities for drugs and alcohol may be different.

RESIDENCE LIFE

Norbert W. Dunkel

Description of the Institutional Environment

Valley State College (VSC) is a public four-year institution with 11,500 students (including 2,000 graduate students). VSC offers 4,500 spaces for students to live in campus housing, but there is no residency requirement for campus housing. This institution recently celebrated its 75th anniversary and is proud of its rural heritage.

Description of the Surrounding Community

Valley State College is located in a rural area of the Midwest. The local community is very supportive of the institution and cosponsors a number of annual events and activities with the institution including July 4th, Labor Day parade, homecoming activities, and a spring carnival. The community has very little commercial involvement with heavy industry or technology but rather supports the farm economy with farm equipment dealers, grain companies, and cooperative extension services. Several clubs in town encourage students as patrons.

Primary Persons Involved in the Case

- Sally Thompson is the Director of Housing. She has been at VSC for 10 years. Her responsibilities include maintenance services, custodial services, and residence life. Over the years, personnel from several campus offices have complained about her apparent inattention to much-needed renovations in the 60-year-old residence halls.
- Paul White is the Associate Director of Residence Life. He has been at VSC for three years. He coordinates the selection and training of residence hall staff, residence hall programming and judicial programs, and safety and security of residence life staff. He reports to Sally Thompson.
- Greg Black is a Graduate Hall Director (HD) in one of the residence halls. Greg supervises four Resident Assistants (RAs) in a coeducational hall of 200 residents. He also coordinates the campus-wide RA selection process. Greg reports directly to Paul White.
- Sara Kennedy is a sophomore at VSC. She is legally blind and has a guide dog. She lives on the ground floor of her residence hall. Sara has been very active in the residence hall government and programs. Additionally, she is the President of the Valley State College Students with Disabilities Club.

Information Germane to the Case

- VSC has only 15 students with declared disabilities. Working with students with disabilities has not been an institutional priority. Only two VSC students use a wheelchair; most mobility-impaired students choose to attend other institutions due to the winter weather.
- The six-story, 60-year-old residence halls do not have passenger elevators and were constructed with many internal corridors and stairwells. Only one residence hall has a ramp at the main entrance.
- For the past three years the housing operation has struggled to find good RAs. The candidate pool has dwindled in part because the pay has not increased and students can make more money working at other student jobs on campus.

The Case

Every November the housing operation at VSC advertises its openings for students to become RAs. The application deadline is January 15th. The selection process takes place over two months and consists of a series of interviews and small-group exercises observed by the housing staff. The process concludes prior to spring break with job offers to successful applicants. The future RAs participate in early training for the balance of the spring semester and return early the following fall for additional training prior to fall residence hall opening.

Greg Black has actively publicized the RA application process. He visited with a number of student organizations on campus and explained the position responsibilities, expectations, length of contract, and compensation. Sara Kennedy invited him to speak at the next meeting of the Students with Disabilities Club. Greg was a little hesitant about speaking with this club so he consulted with Paul White, who recommended that he visit with the club and share the same information he has shared in his other presentations.

After the January 15th application deadline, Greg reviewed the stack of applications and he noticed that Sara Kennedy has applied. He notified Paul White that she is blind with a guide dog. Paul White then spoke to Sally Thompson, who told him to pull her application because blind students cannot apply. Paul reminded Sally that there were no statements in the application materials or position description that prevent a blind student from applying. She responded that it did not matter whether or not it was not stated; the student would not be allowed to proceed in the selection process. Paul White and Greg Black ask Sara Kennedy to meet with them. Paul announced that her application has been withdrawn due to the fact that she is blind. Sara was very upset and left the office stating that she was going to write a letter to the editor of the institution's newspaper.

Discussion Questions

1. Were any of the housing staff proper in they're conversations regarding Sara Kennedy?
2. Should Sara have been offered the opportunity to continue in the staff selection process? Why or why not? Does the housing operation need to provide Sara with reasonable accommodations to fulfill the responsibilities of the RA position? Explain.
3. What factors should have been considered before withdrawing Sara's RA application due to her blindness?
4. How should the housing staff have identified essential functions of the RA position? What are some typical essential functions of an RA?
5. With whom should the housing staff have consulted before withdrawing Sara's RA application from the candidate pool? When? Why?
6. Who else is affected by the decision to withdraw Sara's RA application? How should those parties be handled?

Research Activities for Further Exploration

1. Research the term "essential functions" as it relates to position descriptions and individuals with a disability.
2. What is your institution's policy regarding the employment of individuals with disabilities?
3. Acquire copies of position descriptions for a single type of position (e.g., Director of Housing, RA, etc.) from several institutions and compare and contrast responsibilities and essential functions.

ACCOMMODATING ALICE

DEBORAH CASEY & ALFRED SOUMA

Description of the Institutional Environment

Catalina Community College (CCC) is a two-year public institution offering Associate of Arts (AA) and vocational degrees in areas from culinary arts to sign language interpreting. Approximately 12,000 students attend this racially diverse institution. The racial demographics of the school are as follows: 34 percent African American, 20 percent Asian American, 1 percent American Indian, 45 percent white. There are 422 students who have self-identified as having a disability and are receiving services from the Disability Support Service (DSS) office.

Description of the Surrounding Community

Catalina Community College is an urban college located in a northwestern city of 250,000 residents. The city of Catalina offers all the modern amenities of a large contemporary city and is considered a leader in outdoor recreational opportunities due to the proximity of the Olympic and Cascade mountain ranges. The college is situated in a neighborhood that is known for its acceptance and encouragement of alternative lifestyles. CCC has large English as a Second Language (ESL) and Adult Basic Education (ABE) programs. Many of the students are first in their families to attend college and are economically disadvantaged.

Primary Persons Involved in the Case

- Alice Whitaker, a 30-year-old white female, is a first quarter student at CCC working on her Associate of Arts degree.

- Robert England is the DSS coordinator. He is responsible for maintaining documentation on students who request accommodations and consulting with faculty and staff on academic modifications and adjustments. Robert's area of specialization is psychiatric disabilities. He reports to the Vice President of Student Affairs.
- Renalta Quintaba is the Vice President of Student Affairs and reports directly to the President of CCC.
- Elizabeth Montague is a prealgebra faculty member. Alice Whitaker is in her developmental math class.
- Jennifer Hall is a CCC counselor assigned to the math department to assist students with transfer degree issues, faculty concerns, and short-term general counseling when appropriate. She is one of 10 full-time faculty/counselors in a decentralized system assigned to a specific academic department.

Information Germane to the Case

- Catalina Community College (CCC) is known for its diverse student self-expression, the liberal political philosophies of faculty and students, and creative classroom academic programs.
- Many Catalina students have been unsuccessful in previous higher education environments yet are determined to complete a college degree. The institution is noted for its academic support services for diverse student populations including students with a variety of physical and mental health disabilities. A recent article in a national magazine specifically recognized CCC as an institution working creatively to meet the needs of a diverse inner-city community.

The Case

Elizabeth Montague first noticed Alice Whitaker when she would talk incessantly in class and seemed to see herself taking on the instructor's role. At one point, the instructor, Ms. Montague, reported to Jennifer Hall, that Alice approaches the blackboard while students are individually working out math problems and begins to instruct them on how to solve the problems. The instructor disclosed to Jennifer that during the quarter she asked Alice to leave the classroom for this disruptive behavior. However, after several weeks of these repeated actions, the disruption escalated to the point of unacceptable behavior in the classroom. The counselor met with Alice after being notified by Ms. Montague of the repeated behavior and assessed Alice as having serious mental health issues. Jennifer talked to Alice about the seriousness of her disruptive behavior and offered to continue counseling her on an individual basis. However, Alice's disruptions continued in class unabated. At this point, Jennifer consulted with the DSS office. This consultation resulted in a consensual meeting between Robert England, Jennifer, and Alice.

During the meeting it quickly became apparent that Alice was in a manic state. Alice's self-reported symptoms included feelings of grandeur, constant talking without paying attention to the words of others, a heightened sense of urgency to finish community college in order to go on to more "glorious heights," and a sleep pattern that indicated she functioned on one or two hours of sleep per night. Robert and Jennifer conferred and made a referral and appointment on behalf of Alice for a mental health evaluation with a psychiatrist at the local community mental health center. Alice kept her appointment and reported to the DSS office that the physician diagnosed her with bipolar disorder and gave her a prescription for two medications. Expecting immediate results from her medications, Alice came back to school after missing only one day and was eager to continue her class work. The DSS office did not receive complete documentation of Alice's disability and did not see Alice again until Ms. Montague filed a code of conduct incident report to Renalta Quintaba within a week of Alice's doctor's visit. The incident report indicated that Alice continued her disruptive behavior in class despite previous warnings and "something needed to be done" since the rest of the class also was being affected. Vice President Quintaba met with Jennifer and Robert for consultation regarding the student's behavior, actions that were taken, and how to best address the code of conduct violation.

Discussion Questions

1. Is a student with a disability exhibiting disruptive behavior protected under the American with Disability Act? Does the Act and related regulations mean that a college or university must excuse behavioral manifestations resulting from such disorders?
2. What options are available to Renalta Quintaba regarding this student?
3. What should the instructor, counselor, disability officer, and Vice President of Student Affairs know about bipolar disorders and how they impact students?
4. What are some of the typical issues and barriers encountered by students with mental health issues? Did Alice face any of these issues or barriers?
5. Does Elizabeth Montague have a right to know that Alice has a disability? If so, why?
6. What would be reasonable academic adjustments for Alice? Describe some of the accommodations or resources you would recommend to the

faculty and student affairs staff.

Research Activities for Further Exploration

1. Conduct a focus group with six to eight students with disabilities. Repeat the focus group with faculty and administrators. Determine if each group understands the legal aspects of the Americans with Disabilities Act, student code of conduct, and policies for disruptive behavior in the classroom. Report the findings and develop a training program to educate students, faculty, and administrators on these areas.
2. What is your campus policy on disruptive behavior in the classroom? Survey your faculty and administrators to evaluate how they would handle disruptive behavior of a student with a disability.
3. Trend studies reveal that the number of students on campuses with psychiatric disorders is increasing. Research and evaluate national trends regarding students with psychiatric disabilities and compare them to your campus population. How can you advocate for this underrepresented group on your campus?

SUPPORTING THE LEARNING DISABLED STUDENT

LaRonta M. Upson

Description of the Institutional Environment

Southern State University (SSU) is a large public institution with an enrollment of approximately 33,000 students. This predominantly white university offers 105 baccalaureate degree programs and over 200 postbaccalaureate degree programs. SSU is nationally recognized for its contribution to research in the areas of science, technology, and mathematics, and consistently has been identified as one of the most competitive and academically demanding universities in the nation.

Description of the Surrounding Community

SSU is located in Montclair, a small city in the south central region of the United States. The campus spans 28 acres of downtown Montclair. The city is diverse, fast paced, and serves as the location of many state governmental agencies, professional associations, and historical landmarks.

Primary Persons Involved in the Case

- Dr. Ron Reardon is an Associate Professor of Sociology. He teaches Sociology 101, a large class consisting of approximately 300 students. This is a required course for all first-year students. Dr. Reardon is known for his fast-paced lecture style and exhaustive list of readings.
- Michelle Anderson is a first-semester student at SSU. She is originally from a small city in northern Indiana.
- Laura Powell is the Coordinator of the Disability Services Office (DSO) at SSU. She is responsible for protecting the rights of students with disabilities in accordance with the Americans with Disabilities Act (ADA) and Section 504 of the Rehabilitation Act of 1973.
- Donna Sullivan is an academic advisor for undergraduate students in the College of Arts and Sciences.

Information Germane to the Case

- SSU recently has been accused of discriminatory practices against students with disabilities. However, an investigation by the Office of Civil Rights, the agency within the U.S. Department of Education that is responsible for investigating noncompliance with disability legislation, found no such evidence of discrimination. In order to prevent future allegations, SSU recruited Laura Powell to oversee, implement, and enforce laws designed to protect students with disabilities.
- Although a few complaints remain, Ms. Powell has been quite successful in securing services and resources for disabled students. She also holds monthly seminars to inform university faculty and administrators of the unique needs of students with disabilities and the responsibilities of the university in accommodating those students. Unfortunately, the seminars are not mandatory and very few faculty members attend.

The Case

After being accepted at three other top schools, Michelle ultimately decided to attend SSU. Although it is five hours away from her friends and family, SSU has an excellent reputation and has offered her a partial scholarship for the remainder of her time there. Initially, Michelle had a difficult time adjusting to the large school environment and the long distance from home. However, she maintained a positive attitude and has since made lots of friends.

Michelle now is midway through her first semester and, with a full course load, finds it increasingly difficult to keep up with reading assignments because long book chapters do not readily lend themselves to rereading for comprehension as she did in high school. In Dr. Reardon's sociology course, in particular, she received a grade of "F" on the first two exams because she was never able to complete all the items. The exams consisted of 75 multiple-choice and essay items that had to be completed within the 50-minute class period. This seemed almost impossible to Michelle since she forgets most of what she reads and has to reread it. Now she is frustrated and fears losing her scholarship. She wants desperately to pull up her grades before the end of the semester.

Michelle decided to speak with Donna Sullivan about getting a tutor. She explained the difficulty she was having in Dr. Reardon's course and admitted to feeling overwhelmed by all of the readings and examinations required in the class. Ms. Sullivan learned that Michelle's problems were specific to sociology and she was doing quite well in her math and computer classes. She now suspects that Michelle may have a learning disability and referred her to Laura Powell for additional help.

Ms. Powell discussed the nature of learning disabilities with Michelle and directed her to the appropriate services for evaluation. After being tested at the Learning and Evaluation Center on campus, Michelle learned that she did, in fact, have a learning disability in the area of reading. Ms. Powell provided Michelle with helpful learning strategies and classroom accommodations that could help her to be more successful in class, including more time to take tests and audiotaping lectures.

Although relieved to have a name for what she was experiencing, Michelle began to doubt her ability to overcome her difficulties and often loses confidence in her ability. She has started to question if she belongs in college and believes that most students at SSU are just smarter than she is. To add to her concerns, when Michelle requested accommodations from Dr. Reardon, he refused, stating that he holds every student to the same standard and could not lower expectations for one student.

Discussion Questions

1. Define learning disability. What problems or characteristics might a student with a specific learning disability in reading, math, or writing exhibit?
2. How important was it that Donna Sullivan immediately recognized that Michelle might need an evaluation for a learning disability rather than tutoring or some other service?
3. Identify and describe two federal legislative mandates that protect the rights of students with disabilities. Does Dr. Reardon's refusal to allow Michelle additional testing time violate these laws? Explain your answer.

4. Given the information in the case, design an individual education plan for Michelle. Include specific intervention strategies for academic, personal, and social-emotional improvements. What reasonable accommodations would you recommend for Dr. Reardon to help Michelle be more successful in his class while maintaining the highest standards?

5. What personal issues surfaced when Michelle learned of her disability? Discuss supportive services on campus that might be beneficial for her. How might poor resolution of these personal issues impact educational performance?

6. Based on your knowledge of laws protecting students with disabilities, design a plan to evaluate SSU's current practices in meeting the needs of these students. What actions should be taken to ensure that all university employees are in compliance with the federal laws? Cite relevant legislation.

Research Activities for Further Exploration

1. Research your institution's policies on accommodating the needs of students with disabilities. What special provisions are made regarding admissions, transportation, classroom adaptations, and waiver of course requirements?

2. Contact the coordinator or director of disability services at your college or university. What resources are available? What are the eligibility requirements for receiving services? Is this information consistent with other colleges and universities in your state?

3. Create a list of local and national support organizations for college students with learning disabilities.

HOW ARE REASONABLE ACCOMMODATIONS DEFINED?

John Schuh

Description of the Institutional Environment

Central Metropolitan University (CMU) is a doctoral-intensive university with a mission to serve the Central City area and the surrounding five counties. CMU is a commuter institution with fewer than 500 residential students out of an enrollment of 12,000. Many students are returning adults who see their enrollment at CMU as their last, best, and only chance to complete a college degree.

Description of the Surrounding Community

CMU is located in a metropolitan area with a population of nearly 500,000. The economic base is built on a combination of manufacturing and service industries, with fewer college graduates in the population than in other metropolitan areas of the state. Nevertheless, as the economic base of the community has begun to evolve from manufacturing to information technology, CMU's importance to the community has grown.

Primary Persons Involved in the Case

- Sally Johnson, a returning adult student, is a junior majoring in general studies at CMU. She is married, has three adult children, and has a degenerative spinal problem as well as other significant health problems (circulatory and heart problems). She uses a wheelchair on campus.
- Nancy Higgins became the director of services for students with disabilities six months ago. She reports to the Dean of Students.
- James Jackson is the Dean of Students. In addition to services for students with disabilities, he provides oversight for student conduct, student activities, residence life, orientation, and Greek letter organizations.

Information Germane to the Case

- CMU attracts a number of students with disabilities to the campus each year. Because the campus has no hills, is compact, and is located geographically in a moderate climate, on average, more than 45 students who use wheelchairs enroll each semester.
- The cost of providing services to students with disabilities has escalated each year for the past five years. CMU's senior fiscal officers have placed pressure on James Jackson and Nancy Higgins to cut expenditures.
- Faculty generally have cooperated in providing academic accommodations for students, but in a few situations, they have been uncooperative such as not providing class materials in large-type font for students with vision impairments.

The Case

Sally Johnson's health has deteriorated since she became a student at CMU. While she is classified academically as a junior, it has taken her nine semesters of academic work to get to this point in her academic career. Usually, she begins each semester with a full academic load (15 credits or more) against the advice of her academic advisor. Unfortunately, as a consequence of her physical condition, she drops courses, takes incompletes, or barely passes her courses. As a consequence of her heavy academic loads, she suffers from stress and fatigue. More than once she has had to seek medical treatment for exhaustion at the end of a semester.

CMU provides a notetaker for her in class or a transcription service to transcribe tape recordings of lectures to help alleviate stress and fatigue. In addition, CMU has invested substantial resources to help Sally with her course work. This has included sophisticated equipment to help her with laboratory science courses, tutoring help when she has fallen behind in her classes, and other support to help her navigate the campus physically. Some would view these expenditures as a waste of money, since equipment was purchased for three science courses to assist Ms. Johnson, but she dropped each of the courses a few weeks into the semester. In spite of what CMU has done for her, she is quite unhappy with the university. Rightly or wrongly, she blames CMU when she has problems with her coursework. She has threatened to file complaints with the appropriate federal authorities so that a "full and complete investigation" of CMU is undertaken to determine if the university is in compliance with Section 504 of the Rehabilitation Act as well as with the Americans with Disabilities Act.

Sally was publicly opposed to the appointment of Nancy Higgins as director of services for students with disabilities. Her concern was that Nancy did not have any experience in leadership positions, and that her academic background was in history. Nancy had worked as a volunteer in the office for 10 hours a week for three years prior to her appointment, but that was the extent of her experience on a college campus. Additionally, although Sally never said so, some observers have the impression that she and a few other students would have preferred to have a person with a disability lead the office.

Sally's situation went from bad to worse last week. Her back problem caused her nearly continuous pain all week. The parking space provided for her as a disabled student was taken by another car and calls to the police department did not resolve the problem quickly. The usually reliable automatic door that she had to pass through to enter the classroom building did not work and she had trouble getting into the building. These problems have led to academic difficulties. When she was late to a class as a consequence of having to hunt for a parking space, her notetaker left the classroom thinking she was not going to attend class, and the professor forgot to tape record the lecture. She did poorly on an exam, mostly due to her inability to concentrate because of the back pain. When she asked her professor for some additional time, the professor indicated that the time could not be provided because he had a meeting with a visiting candidate for a faculty position.

Alternative proctoring in his view could not be arranged on such short notice.

Nancy Higgins had been out of town for most of the week, attending a national conference. When Sally complained about her various problems to James Jackson, he was unable to address them immediately because he had to complete a report that the president assigned to him at the last moment. In exasperation, Sally decided to file a complaint with the regional office charged with enforcing compliance with Section 504. She also decided to rally other students with disabilities to support her cause and encouraged them to file complaints. As part of this process, she contacted the local newspaper and television stations and informed the media about how badly she had been treated. Essentially her complaints were that CMU had not provided her the kind of specific support she needed, that buildings were inaccessible, and that accommodations such as additional time to complete assignments were not provided.

Discussion Questions

1. What are the major issues of this case?
2. Has CMU failed to provide reasonable accommodations for Sally Johnson? Explain.
3. Are Sally's complaints related to issues that CMU can address?
4. What steps should CMU take to determine if the issues identified in the case require accommodations? What resources should be consulted in this process?
5. If tremendous costs are associated with accommodations needed for students with disabilities, must the institution provide the accommodations? Why or why not?
6. With its emphasis on information technology, how might CMU use adaptive technology to assist Sally?

Research Activities for Further Exploration

1. Construct a model institutional policy related to accommodations for students for disabilities. Explain why the various elements are included.
2. How does the Americans with Disabilities Act apply to faculty and staff? What are the key elements of this legislation?
3. If a student's disability interferes with his or her ability to complete a curriculum satisfactorily, must an accommodation be made? For example, must an accommodation be made for a quadriplegic who desires to become a dental hygienist?

OBSTACLES IN THE SCIENCE LAB

RANDY MOORE

Description of the Institutional Environment

The University of the River is a large land-grant university with about 45,000 students enrolled in more than 300 fields of study. Within the university is University College, whose mission includes preparing selected students for transfer to degree programs within the university and developing models for teaching and advising underprepared students. University College enrolls disproportionately high percentages of disabled students and ethnic minorities. The racial demographics of the college are 15 percent African American, 3 percent American Indian, 18 percent Asian American/Pacific Islander, 5 percent Chicano/Latino, and 59 percent Caucasian. These students have an average ACT composite score of 20.5. In 2001, the University of the River ranked among the top three public research universities in the nation.

Description of the Surrounding Community

The University of the River is a world-class metropolitan campus nestled among the bluffs of the Mississippi River, just minutes east of downtown Riverville. The university, a classic Big Ten campus, is strongly supported by the community and state. A few miles to the east is Rivertown, whose more rural campus is connected to the Riverville campus by a shuttle system. The Rivertown-Riverville area includes something for everyone, including a nationally renowned arts and theatre community, several Fortune 500 companies, and several professional sports franchises. More than 90 percent of University College students are from the Midwest; most of these students are from the Rivertown-Riverville area. University College has numerous student-support programs and links with the community, including programs for recent immigrants and students with families (e.g., through the Student Parent Help Center).

Primary Persons Involved in the Case

- Casey Evans is a 20-year-old first-year student in University College at the University of the River. She is majoring in biology, and is therefore required to take introductory biology, which includes a hands-on laboratory experience. She comes from a low-income family and has been visually impaired since birth.

- Daniel Shelly is an academic advisor in the Academic Advising Center in University College. He has never advised a visually impaired student enrolled in a science course.
- Jonathan Morris is a biology teaching assistant in University College. He has never taught a visually impaired student.

Information Germane to the Case

- Like many other universities, the University of the River is "supportive" of issues related to disabilities, but there has not been a strong desire to progress beyond the position that there are disabled students on campus, and that these students should be respected and, when possible, accommodated. Within University College there is an oft-stated commitment to serving disabled students. Several faculty and staff in University College have disabilities, and there are several accommodations for disabled students. In general, University College faculty and staff try to help disabled students with as many projects, programs, and advising issues as possible.

The Case

Casey Evans has enrolled in Introduction to Biological Science, a rigorous course comprised of three hours of lectures and two hours of laboratory per week. She likes the course and gleans much information from her taped recordings of lectures. However, she soon encounters difficulties in lab, where she has trouble because of its emphasis on visual imagery. Specifically, she cannot see with microscopes, and also has trouble grasping information presented with visual aids, such as biological models, videos, slide presentations, and blackboard diagrams. Her lab partners often become frustrated with her slow progress in lab and, fearing that her slow progress will affect their grades, they provide little or no help. Jonathan Morris, who is Casey's lab instructor, acknowledges her disability but cannot provide all of the help that she needs. At mid-semester, she is making a D in the course, largely because of her poor performance in lab. She seeks help by meeting with Jonathan, who becomes increasingly frustrated and tells her, "You've got to do the lab exercises yourself. No one gets a helper. I'm doing all I can to help you in this course, but maybe you should major in something else."

Casey becomes discouraged but she does not want to abandon her goal of becoming a biologist so she schedules an appointment with Daniel Shelly. Like others in University College, he is empathetic to Casey's disability but tells her, "There's nothing I can do. I don't give out the grades in the course;

grades are up to you and your lab instructor." He then encourages Casey to drop the course and seek a new major, adding, "science just isn't for you." Casey becomes increasingly despondent. She likes science and wants to be a biologist, but feels that she is not being given a fair chance to pursue her goals. Knowing that she needs high grades to pursue a career in science, she becomes depressed, feels increasingly isolated and inadequate, and begins considering dropping out of school.

Discussion Questions

1. What are the issues or problems presented in this case? Be specific.
2. Disabled students have long been steered away from science-related careers. Does an institution have an obligation to ensure the success of disabled students? Why or why not?
3. Were the comments made by Jonathan Morris and Daniel Shelly appropriate? What could each have done differently? Explain your answer.
4. How would you design a science lab that would best accommodate visually impaired students?
5. According to the U.S. Census Bureau, about 20 percent of all Americans have some form of disability. What are some typical barriers that visually impaired students encounter in science labs? How could these barriers be minimized or eliminated? When answering these questions, be sure to consider physical facilities (e.g., the design of labs and lab benches), technology (e.g., computers, microscopes, and large-screen monitors), and pedagogy (e.g., alternative assignments for disabled students).
6. Why do so few disabled students pursue careers in science? Explain your answer.

Research Activities for Further Exploration

1. Interview three to five visually impaired students on campus to determine if they've felt pressure from parents, classmates, or advisors to avoid science and science-related careers. Report your findings and discuss their importance.
2. What does your institution do to accommodate visually impaired students? What about your institution's science departments? Be specific.
3. Write a research paper describing the history of disabled students in higher education in general, and in science in particular. Be sure to discuss historical information, the contributions of visually impaired students to science and society, and current statistics and research.

THE AT-RISK STUDENT

Mary Lee Vance

Description of the Institutional Environment

Genoa State is a small public four-year liberal arts institution located in the Midwest. Only 100 of the 7,000 students are domestic students of color, including 30 African Americans, 25 Chicanos, 25 American Indians, and 20 Asian Americans.

Description of the Surrounding Community

Genoa State is located in a city of 50,000 residents and is the only four-year institution within a one-hour driving distance. The city also houses a community college and a technical school. A midsized airport in the city connects residents to larger airports, so there is a constant flow of travelers entering and exiting the area. Overall, the residents of the community seem to be generally receptive to the college students.

Primary Persons Involved in the Case

- Mildred Smith is a first-year student.
- Cal Johnson is a general academic advisor in the Academic Advising Office.
- Dr. George Mullen is the Director of the Multicultural Center. Now in his third year at Genoa State, he is looking to be more proactive to help all students succeed on campus.
- Dr. David Schmidt is the institution's Chancellor. He has been at Genoa State for four years.

Information Germane to the Case

- Prior to Mildred Smith's arrival at Genoa State, the administration and faculty had long realized that most of their university-wide committees lacked racial diversity. They were determined to turn things around, and began to look for every opportunity to increase student involvement, especially students of color.
- Having been adopted from Korea as an infant by a white midwestern couple, Mildred had little experience with people of color. Everyone in her tiny community of 3,000 knew she was Henry Smith's daughter, and tend-

ed to overlook her skin color. On occasion, they would even tell her that they didn't consider her a minority, which she took as a compliment. Once in a while, she would be reminded of the fact that she was not white, such as when a friend told her she could not go to Mildred's house for a visit because her grandfather had fought in WWII and hated "Japanese people."

- Although Mildred enjoyed literature, she did not do well in mathematics. All through her elementary and secondary education, Mildred struggled to keep up with her classmates in the math courses. She was not strong in the natural sciences either, and ended up dropping high school chemistry because she was in danger of failing. When she took the ACT exam for college, Mildred was chagrined to learn she had the lowest score in her class. Despite her shaky academic background, she had been accepted to Genoa State, and had declared art as her area of interest. Her father made it clear to Mildred that if she did not earn at least a 2.00 GPA each semester, he would immediately discontinue support for her education.

The Case

Upon her arrival at Genoa State, Mildred Smith discovered many interesting extracurricular activities and found herself volunteering more and more each week as the semester progressed. She eventually became a common sight at concerts where she sold tickets, at festivals where she helped organize vendors, and other events where she found herself in leadership roles. Soon, the administration and faculty began to notice her, and began requesting her presence at events they were coordinating. Mildred dutifully attended every meeting Chancellor David Schmidt asked her to attend. He was so appreciative that he added her to even more committees. According to her schedule book, there were some weeks when she spent more time in meetings than she did in her classes!

At first, George Mullen ignored Mildred. He was predominantly concerned with the retention of students of color, primarily African American students and secondarily Chicano and American Indian students. He did not focus on issues related to Asian American students because he thought they were not at academic risk. One day Mildred went to see him because she wanted to learn more about the issues concerning students of color. His respect for her grew as he saw how she tried to understand their concerns about the campus climate, and he encouraged her to continue with her committee work.

Eventually, Mildred began to realize that academically she was drowning. Her grades were suffering, especially in math. She decided to see an advisor, and chose Cal Johnson because he also advised a student group she had joined earlier in the semester. She told him that she was afraid she might have to drop out if her GPA slipped below 2.00 because her father would not provide further financial support. She also told Cal that she couldn't cut down on her committee work because everyone was depending on her to be a representative for students of color, especially those who weren't as comfortable as she was in speaking up about the issues. Finally, Mildred noted that she thinks she has a learning disability.

Discussion Questions

1. What are the issues in this case from Mildred's perspective?
2. What stereotypes and presumptions about Asian American students come to mind as you consider Mildred Smith's current situation at Genoa State?
3. Mildred learned that she was adopted as a young child. How would this affect your assessment of the current situation?
4. At this point, what is the institution's responsibility regarding Mildred's situation? What should be done by David Schmidt and/or George Mullen, if anything? What could have been done differently and why?
5. You are Cal Johnson. What does Mildred need from you?
6. As Cal Johnson, what would you advise Mildred to do? How would you approach the situation? Why?

Research Activities for Further Exploration

1. Review scholarly research and personal accounts (fiction and/or nonfiction) written by and about Korean-born individuals who grew up in the United States after being adopted by U.S. citizens. Consider how physical features don't necessarily reflect internal identity and discuss complications that might arise from external misidentifications or assumptions.
2. Research literature concerned with Asian American students. As a professional in higher education, what would you need to and/or want to know in order to better serve these students? Do you believe they need anything more than what currently is provided on your campus? Why or why not? Are these reasons based on fact or on assumptions?
3. Meet with the student affairs professional on your campus who coordinates programs and services for Asian American students. Ask about current issues on your campus, and then volunteer to assist with an upcoming event (or at least observe). Write a position paper that discusses your findings related to student concerns at your campus. Support your findings and make suggestions for changing the current climate. Outline a plan of action for addressing a top need.

WHAT IS THE VALUE OF A COLLEGE EDUCATION?

SUSAN WEIR

Description of the Institutional Environment

Southwest University (SU) is a medium-sized comprehensive institution in the southwestern United States. Undergraduate enrollment is approximately 20,000. The majority of the students are state residents and 81 percent of the student body is white.

Description of the Surrounding Community

Southwest University is located in Plains City, a small community of about 39,000. Larger urban centers are located within a day's drive. The local economy depends largely on the university, as well as farming, manufacturing, and health care. Most of the residents are white.

Primary Persons Involved in the Case

- Ashley Coleman is a 24-year-old senior majoring in sociology. She has attended SU for six years and is within one semester of completing her bachelor's degree. Her academic progress has been hindered by her physical condition, a form of muscular dystrophy for which there is no known cure. Ashley was first diagnosed in junior high school, when she began to have difficulty walking and the disease has been progressing steadily since then. She began to depend on a wheelchair at age 17. Complications from the disease, often requiring surgery, have forced Ashley to temporarily withdraw from college on several occasions. She grew up in a small farming community about three hours away from SU. Her parents and extended family still live in the same town.
- Janet Davis is an academic advisor for sociology majors. She is 45 years old, earned a master's degree in English, and has been advising at SU for 15 years.
- Dr. Richard Beacher, a sociology professor, has worked at SU for 20 years. He is tenured, widely published in his field, and well respected on campus.
- Dr. James Whitaker, 35, has worked at SU for seven years. He has been the Coordinator for the Office of Student Disability Services (SDS) for the last three years.

Information Germane to the Case

- The SDS office offers academic support services for students who provide proper documentation of a physical or learning disability. Services include instructor notification, specialized testing, classroom accommodations, recorded textbooks, and assistive technology.
- In general, the SDS office has been successful in meeting the academic needs of disabled students on campus. Ashley Coleman registered with the office prior to her enrollment at SU. Her condition was properly documented and she consistently utilized all recommended accommodations each semester.
- Persons living with Ashley's form of muscular dystrophy rarely survive beyond their early twenties.

The Case

Despite her condition, Ashley enjoys college and is very determined to complete her degree. Ashley's family also has done everything possible to help her achieve this goal. Ashley tries to lead a typical college student life. She lives in a campus residence hall and regularly socializes with friends. She is generally well liked by her peers and her professors. During her junior year, the campus newspaper published an inspirational article about Ashley's courage and persistence to complete her degree. However, by Ashley's senior year, she has become very severely disabled, with virtually no use of her limbs and limited ability to speak. She refuses to accept the prognosis of an early death and insists on planning for the future. She has been visiting with her academic advisor, Janet Davis, to explore career options.

Janet feels very uncomfortable discussing career options with Ashley because she cannot imagine any type of employment for her. Janet consults with James Whitaker in the SDS office regarding options and resources for Ashley. Dr. Whitaker states that it is not the disability services office's duty to find or suggest employment options for disabled students.

Ashley tells Janet that she is very interested in criminology and wants to work for the FBI. Janet is very surprised by this announcement and does not quite know what to do or say. She briefly discusses this occupational choice with Ashley and then hesitantly gives Ashley the telephone number of the local FBI recruiting office so that Ashley can seek further information on her own. Although she feels that she should treat Ashley like any other student, Janet also feels guilty for allowing Ashley to believe that she could find employment with the FBI. Yet she does not feel that confronting Ashley would be appropriate, even though she cannot imagine very many opportunities, given Ashley's very limited motor skills.

Meanwhile, as Ashley's physical condition worsens, her ability to attend class regularly and complete assignments diminishes. Two months prior to graduation, Ashley's family contacts Janet to inform her that Ashley's physician now believes that Ashley has less than six months to live. Richard Beacher, one of Ashley's sociology professors, becomes very frustrated with Ashley's poor attendance and poor academic performance and meets with Janet to express his concerns. He explains that in order to be consistent with all students, he cannot excuse Ashley from assignments or excuse her absences. He feels that if she cannot attend class regularly, she should withdraw. His course is required for the sociology degree, so Ashley must successfully complete it in order to graduate. Janet explains how important the degree will be for Ashley and her family, and begs him to be lenient with her because Ashley is now so close to graduation.

Discussion Questions

1. What are the issues or problems presented in this case?
2. Based on your knowledge of student development theory or counseling theory, how would you respond to Ashley's interest in a career with the FBI? What developmental and emotional issues are pertinent for Ashley?
3. Based on your knowledge of moral development theory, what would you recommend to Dr. Beacher about handling the situation with Ashley?
4. Many students choose to attend college primarily to expand their employment options, which are limited for Ashley because of her illness and related physical disabilities. In this case, what is the value of a college education for Ashley? How might the value of a college education differ for other groups of minority students?
5. Does SU or the SDS office have an obligation to help students with disabilities find employment? Why or why not?
6. Based on Ashley's interactions with Janet Davis and Richard Beacher, as well as James Whitaker's comments, how would you evaluate the campus culture relative to students with disabilities?

Research Activities for Further Exploration

1. Visit the student disability services office on your campus. Find out what accommodations are available for students with physical and/or learning disabilities, and how current legislation applies to students with disabilities on your campus.
2. Interview students with physical and/or learning disabilities. What challenges have they faced as students on your campus? What changes in policy or campus culture would they like to see?

3. Spend a day attending classes in a wheelchair, either by yourself or with a group. Find out first hand what improvements are necessary or might be helpful for students with physical disabilities on your campus.

SLIPPING THROUGH THE CRACKS

CARL CHUNG

Description of the Institutional Environment

Axell College is one of eight colleges admitting first-year students at the University of Middleton (UM), a major research university enrolling 46,000 students. The college's primary mission is to provide access to the university's programs and resources for at-risk students who do not meet the increasingly competitive admission requirements of the other colleges. The college enrolls a total of 1,900 students, with an annual incoming class of 875.

Description of the Surrounding Community

UM is the flagship institution of the state. It is located in a large urban center with a population of 400,000. With a minority population of 15 percent, the metropolitan area is much more diverse than the surrounding communities. A variety of outreach programs link UM with the urban community.

Primary Persons Involved in the Case

- Sara Wheaton is a first-year student at Axell College. She is deaf and communicates using American Sign Language (ASL).
- Dr. James Varley is an assistant professor at Axell College.
- Jonathon Provine is Director of the Academic Success Center at Axell College.
- Alex Brandon is an instructor who teaches in the writing program at Axell College.
- Mary Jane Hobart is a disability specialist helping Sara adjust to life at UM.

Information Germane to the Case

- UM's Disability Service Office (DSO) offers a variety of services: screening for students who might have learning or behavioral disabilities; counseling; test-taking services; translation services for blind students; interpreting services for deaf and hard-of-hearing students; and information for faculty and staff working with students with disabilities. The office also writes letters to faculty outlining concrete suggestions for reasonable accommodations for each student.

• Axell College requires students to complete first-year composition and four additional courses that qualify as "writing intensive." Writing-intensive courses must (a) include 15 pages of formal writing in addition to informal writing assignments and written examinations, (b) include instruction on the writing aspect of assignments, and (c) include at least one assignment in which students must rewrite a draft in light of instructor comments.

The Case

James Varley sits in his office with a stack of notebooks on his lap. Students in his Introduction to Film course have just turned in their viewing journals and he is anxious to read them. In class, he stressed that students write in their own voices and not worry so much about correct grammar, punctuation, or paragraph development. Instead he wanted them to capture their feelings and reactions to the films as authentically as possible.

However, when he reads through Sara Wheaton's journal entries, he pauses and shakes his head. Sara clearly is a determined and capable student, but he has trouble understanding her writing. The verb tense and perspective shift in a way that seems almost random to him, and individual sentences often are fragments without verbs, or verb phrases without subjects. In addition, sentences often begin with a description but then jump to evaluation, analysis, or commentary and then back to description. But from what he can gather, Sara carefully viewed the films, thought about them, and has some interesting ideas.

Several weeks later, he begins grading the first formal essay for the film class. Students were required to analyze a particular scene using the vocabulary and concepts they had discussed in class. The assignment was very specific and regimented, asking the students to accomplish a series of tasks in a definite order. Sara Wheaton's essay borders on incomprehensible to Dr. Varley, who cannot make out what she is communicating. In addition to the sudden shifts in tense and perspective he encountered in the journal entries, he also is puzzled by numerous slang expressions.

During a meeting with Sara to discuss her draft, Dr. Varley has no trouble understanding her when she communicates using ASL and an interpreter. In fact, she is funny, articulate, and insightful. When he brings up the difficulty he has understanding her writing, Sara says that she has never been a strong writer, mostly because her primary mode of communication is ASL, but that she really wants to improve and will work hard. After the meeting, he is convinced that Sara is capable of doing the writing for his course but just needs some specialized tutoring. He calls Sara's advisor in Axell College and explains the situation. The advisor suggests that he contact Mary Jane Hobart and Alex Brandon.

Mary Jane agrees that, ideally, Sara needs someone who specializes in teaching writing to deaf students. Unfortunately, the DSO does not have the resources to hire such a tutor. She suggests that Dr. Varley treat Sara as if she were an ESL student, that is, someone who knows a primary "home" language and is learning written English as a second language. Later, Dr. Varley meets with Jonathon Provine, who looks over Sara's work and then shakes his head, saying, "My tutors can't help this student. The problems here are just too severe given what our staff are trained to do."

Then, Dr. Varley finds Alex Brandon in his office. Alex pulls out a file and shows him Sara's most recent essay for his class; there are more comments than text. The two have a long discussion about how to fairly grade Sara's work. Should they grade her based on overall improvement and not against some fixed standard? Is it right to give her passing marks, given the fundamental difficulties they continue to see in her writing? From Alex's point of view, Sara's writing has improved over the semester, but only marginally so, and he confesses that he's not sure how to grade her work. Dr. Varley agrees. Then he smiles wryly and points out that according to UM's writing-intensive course requirements, he can't pass Sara because she has not demonstrated a "basic competency" in writing.

Discussion Questions

1. Why is James Varley unsure about how to grade Sara Wheaton's written work?
2. Summarize and briefly explain the major issues raised by the case.
3. List three examples from your own experience or institutional context in which students "slip through the cracks" and do not get the support they need.
4. Would it be a "reasonable accommodation" if Dr. Varley changed the standard of grading for Sara's written work? Why or why not?
5. As written, the case sets up a tension between a deaf student, support services available to that student, and university requirements. How else might we make sense of the main points of the case? For example, interpret the case in terms of a clash between the dominant "normal" hearing culture and the subculture of deaf or hard-of-hearing people. What issues become important?

6. How should Dr. Varley grade Sara's written work? According to what standard? Justify your answer as best you can.

Research Activities for Further Exploration

1. Learn more about the culture and worldview of deaf and hard-of-hearing people by conducting interviews or studying the National Association of Deaf People's web site.
2. Imagine that you are in charge of a Task Force writing a new policy on students with disabilities and meeting University requirements. Explain how you would go about gathering more data to inform your policy and who you would want on your task force.
3. Find out what changes have occurred at your home institution in light of the Americans with Disabilities Act and determine whether those changes accomplish the original goals set forth in the legislation.

IT'S ALL IN YOUR MIND

JOSEPH BAGGOT & JERLANDO F. L. JACKSON

Description of the Institutional Environment

Heartland State University (HSU) is a public four-year university that awards bachelors', masters', and limited doctoral degrees. HSU's total enrollment is 15,000 students. It is primarily a residential college with approximately 70 percent of the students living on-campus or within a five-mile radius of the university. Highlights of the student profile at HSU are as follows: (a) women make up 60 percent of the student population, (b) 94 percent of the students identify their race as white, and (c) approximately 7 percent of the students report having a disability.

Description of the Surrounding Community

Heartland State University is located in Riverton, a Midwestern community of 75,000 residents. Riverton is the educational, cultural, and economic hub for the region. The planned city contains many parks and green spaces that are used for frequent festivals. Riverton is also home to a relatively small but thriving faith-supported liberal arts college. Riverton touts itself as a friendly-community in which citizens live, work, and play. In the last 30 years, the community has successfully transformed from a manufacturing-based, to a technological and service-based economy.

Primary Persons Involved in the Case

- Marie Walinski is a first-semester student at HSU. She resides in one of the residence halls. Marie graduated from high school in the top quartile of her class.
- Dr. Anne McDowell is the Director of the Disability Services Office (DSO) at HSU. After completing law school, she earned a doctorate in special education.
- Dr. Steven Keegan is a tenured history professor who has been released from his teaching duties to serve as Director of HSU's Experiential Learning Center (ELC). He has extremely high expectations of students and has a reputation for being callous and caring at the same time.

Information Germane to the Case

- In the previous year, the HSU administration highly publicized their appointment of Anne McDowell as the first director of the newly created DSO.
- Prior to arriving at HSU, Marie Walinski contacted Anne McDowell to inquire about services for students with disabilities. She assured Marie that students with disabilities are offered equal access to the curricular and cocurricular activities and facilities at HSU. After hearing this, Marie disclosed that she had been diagnosed with a neurologically based disorder (i.e., depression) and that she would like to request reasonable accommodations because of her disability.
- Anne reviewed the information Marie provided and determined that she had sufficient documentation to support her request for reasonable academic accommodations. She recommended that Marie be provided with (a) a notetaker in all of her classes so that if her illness caused planned or unplanned absences she would still have a set of notes to study and (b) time extensions to complete work she will miss while she is away receiving treatment during the semester. Both Marie and Anne were confident that this plan offered equal access at HSU.

The Case

Marie Walinski enrolled in five courses during her first semester at HSU. At the beginning of the semester, she shared a copy of her accommodation plan with each of her professors and with her residence hall director. All of her professors were accommodating to her needs, and Marie proved herself to be a strong student. Feeling secure in the classroom, Marie actively sought out cocurricular activities as well. After attending a variety of introductory and informational meetings, Marie decided to join the Future Leaders Organization (FLO) coordinated by the ELC. FLO is highly respected by the students, faculty, and administration at HSU. Although academic credit is not earned for participating in FLO, a certificate of completion is awarded to students who complete the program. Many HSU graduates credit FLO as one of their most significant undergraduate learning experiences, and potential employers have informed the career services director at HSU that they prefer to hire students who have completed the FLO program.

Steven Keegan expects all FLO students to attend weekly meetings and three weekend programs each semester. He is very up front about these expectations and students who are unable to commit the necessary time are dropped from the program. Initially, he was excited to have Marie participate in FLO, but became concerned when she informed him about her treatment schedule, which will cause her to miss two weekly meetings and one of the scheduled weekend programs. He did not feel it would be fair to allow Marie to continue at this time and decided that she would have to postpone her participation until a future semester.

Marie greatly wanted to participate in the FLO program and appealed to everyone at HSU who would listen. However, Dr. Keegan could not be convinced to change his mind even after many advocated on behalf of Marie. Ultimately, HSU administration determined that while he may in fact be inconsiderate, he was not being discriminatory toward Marie since he was consistent in applying attendance expectations. Marie completed all of her first-semester courses. After the semester ended Marie and her parents met with Anne McDowell to discuss Marie's future at the institution. Of great concern to Marie and her family was the institution's inability and/or unwillingness to compel Steven Keegan to allow Marie to participate in the FLO program. The family stated that given Marie's treatment plan, it was quite possible that she would never be available for all of the meetings and programs during future semesters. Marie was angry, disappointed, and frustrated and she asked Anne to defend her statement that students with disabilities were offered equal access at HSU.

Discussion Questions

1. What are the important issues presented in this case?
2. Why do you think Marie Walinski desired to participate in the FLO program?
3. Create a written transcript of a mock discussion between Anne McDowell and Steven Keegan.

4. Do you agree with HSU's decision that Steven Keegan was not being discriminatory? Why or why not?
5. How should Anne McDowell respond to Marie when asked to defend her
statement about equal access at HSU?
6. Anne McDowell plans to evaluate the accessibility of all cocurricular
activities at HSU. What are your recommendations for this undertaking?

Research Activities for Further Exploration

1. Conduct research on your campus to determine the accommodations and
other services offered to students with disabilities.
2. If possible, interview two or three students with disabilities on your campus. Do they feel they are offered equal access to the curricular and cocurricular activities and facilities on campus? If you are unable to interview
students, substitute appropriate faculty and/or staff.
3. Using national data, determine whether students with disabilities graduate
at the same rate as their nondisabled peers. How does this compare with
the graduation rates of students on your campus?

FACILITATED COMMUNICATION

MARY LEE VANCE

Description of the Institutional Environment

East Coast University (ECU) is a public institution with a prestigious
research reputation. The university grants doctoral degrees in several areas,
including special education. Approximately 5,000 of the 22,000 students at
ECU have self-identified as having some form of disability. Of this group,
over one-third have "invisible" disabilities, including but not limited to learning disabilities, psychological disabilities, and rheumatoid arthritis.

Description of the Surrounding Community

ECU is located within an easy driving distance from the nation's capital.
The metropolitan Washington, D.C. area includes a bustling, highly active
"beltway" with numerous lobbying agencies, political groups, and legal
offices within and near the capital. Two major airports in the metro area constantly introduce a steady stream of diverse travelers. Due to the easy accessibility of the public transportation system, the area is quite popular for peo-

ple with all types of disabilities. A nearby university provides a curriculum in American Sign Language.

Primary Persons Involved in the Case

- Tommy Duluth is a first-year student with autism who requires facilitated communication.
- Dr. Marian Duluth, a 45-year-old career woman, is Tommy's mother. She insists on being called Dr. Duluth, since she has a doctorate in special education, and wants to make sure everyone knows that she has had special education training.
- Rhoda McLeod is the coordinator for students with disabilities.

Information Germane to the Case

- The Office of Programs for Students with Disabilities (OPSD) is housed in the Academic Advising Department. The Director for Academic Advising reports to the Provost, and has obvious connections and linkages to the academic deans, department chairs and faculty. Except for the rare faculty member who is unable to understand or accept the need to reasonably accommodate a legally eligible student with a disability, the OPSD has been quite successful in meeting students' needs. As a special initiative, the OPSD implemented a focused orientation program for incoming students with disabilities and their family members. During the first summer, over 60 students and family members participated.
- A Facilitative Communicator (FC) assists another person in the communication process by verbally communicating what that person might be trying to spell out on a talking board or other device with words or letters on it. In terms of reasonable accommodation, the FC would be employed for interactions with instructors or with classmates during class periods.

The Case

Tommy Duluth was admitted to ECU for the fall semester. On paper, Tommy looked brilliant with excellent test scores, a high GPA, and a well-written essay. Since Tommy did not participate in either the personal interview or OPSD orientation, the OPSD was not made aware of his disability until his mother phoned with a request for special services to accommodate Tommy's autism. She insisted that ECU had admitted Tommy and therefore was obligated to immediately provide the services he needed.

Rhoda McLeod was more than willing to provide Tommy the usual reasonable accommodations but was taken aback when his mother insisted on a Facilitative Communicator for periods outside the classroom (including study times) and a personal assistant (PA) to keep an eye on Tommy between classes. Rhoda had never received such a request before and she expressed concern that disclosing these needs during the first week of classes and expecting immediate services was hardly reasonable.

As an initiator and promoter of facilitated communication, Dr. Duluth insisted that Tommy had a right to have an FC with him the entire time he was on campus as well as when he was studying at home. She explained that the FC needed to be with her son while he did his homework in order to record what he wanted communicated on his assignments. Apparently the PA was needed to monitor Tommy in the bathroom; otherwise he would stuff rolls of toilet paper down the toilet and perform other random, illogical acts. The PA also was needed to hold Tommy's hand while walking between classes to prevent him from wandering away. Tommy was not able to be alone.

Rhoda tried to clarify the distinction between the FC and PA roles, and explain what the institution could reasonably cover, but Dr. Duluth was resistant to anything other than her own ideas. In addition, Dr. Duluth copied everything said by university officials to her electronic list so that hundreds of people advocating facilitated communication were updated on Tommy's struggles.

Dr. Duluth was particularly incensed to learn that at least one faculty member was questioning whether Tommy was capable of being a university student. The faculty member stated that he doubted Tommy was even doing any work because the FC was actually doing the work for him. Dr. Duluth demanded that sensitivity training on facilitated communication be made mandatory across campus. She also complained to the university president about Rhoda's resistance to PA support, with a copy of the letter going to her electronic list. The president's office sent the matter to you (the director of academic advising and Rhoda's direct supervisor) to resolve.

Discussion Questions

1. What is autism?
2. What are the issues in this case? Are Dr. Duluth's requests reasonable? Why or why not?
3. How do reasonable accommodations and parent involvement in higher education differ from the elementary and secondary levels? What constitutes reasonable accommodation in higher education?
4. Could this case have been handled more appropriately? How? What else could Rhoda McLeod suggest and/or provide?
5. How do you believe Tommy has been handled by the university officials?

Has the process been appropriate? Would it have made a difference if ECU had been informed sooner about Tommy's situation?

6. As the director of academic advising, what would you recommend to Rhoda McLeod, the university, and Marian Duluth?

Research Activities for Further Exploration

1. Research the difference in accommodations provided for students with disabilities while they are at the elementary and secondary levels and while completing their postsecondary education.
2. Develop an informational presentation about facilitated communication for a student affairs office of your choice.
3. Conduct library research to learn more about autism in general and facilitated communication in particular. Identify key support groups, issues, and concerns related to this population.

A STIFLED START FOR LAURA

KELLY A. NORTON

Description of the Institutional Environment

The University of Big Rock (UBR) is a private four-year institution with an enrollment of 5,000 students, approximately 3,000 of whom are enrolled in the undergraduate day program, 800 in the undergraduate evening program, and 1,200 in one of seven graduate programs. The predominantly white university attracts a number of students of color. African American and international students make up the largest nonwhite student groups. African American students hold four of eight class officer seats, and the International Club is among the most active student organizations on campus. At UBR, 61 percent of the students, including three-fourths of evening school students, are female.

Description of the Surrounding Community

UBR is located in Hollis Lake, a small Southeastern town 50 miles from Midville, the state's capital and largest city. The institution is Hollis Lake's only provider of higher education. Residents who do not attend UBR must relocate or drive more than an hour each way to attend classes at one of Midville's 12 colleges and universities.

Primary Persons Involved in the Case

- Laura Bishop is a 19-year-old high school senior awaiting graduation. She plans to attend the FreshStart program at UBR. When she was 12 years old, a fall left her paralyzed below the waist. She uses a motorized wheelchair for mobility. Her vision has been deteriorating since the accident, and she now is legally blind but she has not learned to read Braille. She still is able to recognize some shapes and colors.
- Marilyn Tapley is the Assistant Dean of Academic Affairs and founder and coordinator of the FreshStart program.
- John Richmond, the Director of the Learning Assistance Center (LAC), supervises the tutoring program, approves accommodations for students with disabilities, and assists each summer with FreshStart.
- Reginald Tucker is the Director of Residence Life. He operates the 12 residence communities on campus, including the hall that houses FreshStart students.

Information Germane to the Case

- Laura's parents have played a central role in attending to her hygiene, medical needs, transportation, and academic progress. To help Laura compensate for her low vision, her parents read her textbooks aloud and assisted with homework.
- Students with disabilities make up 5 percent of the student population, or approximately 250 students. Three years ago, university officials centralized all disability-related services in the LAC, a three-person office that provides tutoring, computer training, and other workshops. Since that time, there has been a sharp increase in the number of students who have declared a disability but very little improvement in services, funding, or administrative support.
- The FreshStart program was established to combat low retention rates of conditionally admitted students by providing students with an opportunity to begin postsecondary work in a structured academic environment, with a reduced course load and individual interaction with faculty and administrators. During the four-week program, students also participate in athletic competitions, overnight trips, and service-learning activities.

The Case

Laura Bishop was admitted to UBR unconditionally so the FreshStart program is not required, but she hopes that attending FreshStart will allow her to become familiar with the campus while she is taking a part-time course load. Having fewer students on campus during the summer also is encouraging since she will be learning her way around a strange, new environment. Laura currently lives with her parents in Tarpon Springs, a small community 15 miles from the University, but she has decided the social benefit of living in a residence hall will be rewarding.

Early in the spring, after receiving her acceptance letter from the University, Laura emailed Marilyn Tapley for more information about FreshStart. In a letter, Dr. Tapley expressed her excitement to have Laura in the program. She mentioned Laura's National Merit Scholarship with congratulations and applauded Laura's enthusiasm to participate in FreshStart. Dr. Tapley explained that Laura will learn strategies for studying course material, identify her personal learning styles, and learn to manage her time and her health. In the program, Laura will enroll in three courses: a reading-intensive academic skills course, an activity-based wellness course, and a first-year course of her choice. The program will incorporate an extensive activity schedule, including a volleyball tournament, an overnight hiking trip, and a home construction service-learning project. In closing, Dr. Tapley recommended that Laura contact Reginald Tucker, Director of Residence Life, to reserve a space in the FreshStart housing unit.

Laura telephoned Reginald the same day to request a housing application for FreshStart. He was polite and helpful, answering all of her questions about residence hall and dining area locations, roommate matching, and bathroom arrangements. However, when Laura mentioned her use of a wheelchair and low vision, he audibly stumbled, a common reaction when she discloses her disabilities. His answers became short, and Laura felt he ended the call abruptly.

The next day, Laura received a call from Marilyn Tapley, who stated that she had discussed Laura's condition with John Richmond at the LAC. They agreed that Laura will encounter great difficulties living on campus without supervision and assistance, participating in the program's mandatory athletic activities, and assisting in the building project. Essentially, Laura was told that the benefit of attending FreshStart will be minimized because of her disabilities. Dr. Tapley strongly suggested that Laura reconsider attending FreshStart.

Discussion Questions

1. What aspects of transition to college life will be especially challenging for Laura?
2. For which items in Question 1 is the institution responsible? Which are Laura's responsibilities?
3. Do you support Marilyn Tapley's suggestion to Laura? Why or why not?

As Dr. Tapley, how would you have handled the situation?

4. What accommodations need to be in place for Laura to fully participate in FreshStart? Consider her needs as they relate to academic, residential, social, and student life.

5. How can the FreshStart program be altered to take advantage of Laura's abilities?

6. As Laura, how would you react to Dr. Tapley's phone call? Would you attend FreshStart? Would you still attend UBR? Why or why not?

Research Activities for Further Exploration

1. Conduct research on your campus to identify the types of accommodations provided in student programming. Determine what changes are required to ensure equal access for students with various types of disabilities. Investigate the financial impact of implementing the accommodations.

2. Using information from the library or the World Wide Web, investigate the struggle for equal access for persons with disabilities. Develop a timeline of significant events, legal decisions, and compliance deadlines. Report your findings in terms of progress for students with disabilities.

3. Conduct research on your campus to determine the inclusion of disability in the diversity policy. Look for evidence of disability-related themes in diversity programming and admissions recruiting materials. Compare your findings to comparable institutions in your state/region.

ADDRESSING HARASSMENT OF STUDENTS WITH DISABILITIES

JUDITH C. DURHAM & PATRICIA MCKENNA

Description of the Institutional Environment

New Gate University (NGU) is a private, liberal arts institution with a student body of approximately 10,000 students. Of those, 4,000 live on campus in a residential community (traditional dorm and suite-style residences). In addition to a racially and ethnically diverse student population, NGU prides itself on a large population (approximately 3%) of students with disabilities (learning, social, physical, and developmental).

Description of the Surrounding Community

NGU is located in a mid-sized New England town of about 50,000 residents. It provides the comforts of a small school atmosphere, as the campus is located in a residential area just outside a larger metropolitan area. The community offers a variety of outlets for the student body ranging from cultural events, and theaters to restaurants, and other commercial establishments. Students also have numerous opportunities for civic involvement in the community.

Primary Persons Involved in the Case

- John Stevens is a first-semester student who is diagnosed with Asperger's syndrome (a form of autism). John comes from a small-town high school where he had a high level of interaction with faculty and other administrators. He and his mother researched many colleges and universities in the country and NGU seemed to provide the most conducive environment to meet his developmental, educational, and social needs.
- Mary Stevens, John's mother, is a single parent who works as an elementary school teacher. She has worked very hard with various clinicians and other professionals to assist John in an "independent" style of learning. As John grew up, she went to great lengths to work with the school system to provide the best education for her son. She wanted John to have the same opportunities as everyone else his age, regardless of his limitations.
- John's suitemates also are incoming first-year students, none of whom have disabilities:
  - Mark Jacobs is an athlete attending NGU on an athletic scholarship.
  - Allen Levitz, a chemistry major, comes from an affluent town and a wealthy family.
  - James McKewon, a business major, comes from a blue-collar family residing in a typical small town.
- Scott Ferguson, a psychology major, is a second-year RA on John's floor.
- Lindsay Turner, Scott Ferguson's supervisor, is the Area Coordinator (AC) for the area in which John and his suitemates live. She has been a full-time student affairs professional for several years.
- Michael Lane is NGU's new Dean of Students. He has an extensive background in student affairs administration.

Information Germane to the Case

- Asperger's syndrome is a neurobiologic disorder presently described as an autistic spectrum disorder and is sometimes thought of as high-functioning autism. However, in contrast to autism, there are no clinically significant delays in language or cognition. The majority of people diagnosed with Asperger's syndrome have at least an average IQ and many have an IQ in the superior range. While language development seems, on the surface, normal in individuals with Asperger's syndrome, they often have deficits in pragmatics and understanding the nuances of language. Vocabularies may be extraordinarily rich, but persons with Asperger's syndrome can be extremely literal and have difficulty using language in a social context.

- John uses a laptop computer to take notes in class because his writing skills are limited.

The Case

Scott Ferguson, the RA for John's floor, had arranged for a floor meeting to kick off the semester. All of the residents on the floor were required to attend. After the meeting, while Scott talked with other residents, he noticed some rather unusual behaviors from John. These included rapid pacing back and forth, bizarre arm movements (e.g., flapping his hands and pounding his fists into his thighs), and attempts to initiate some form of communication from a distance. Scott approached John and managed to have a conversation with him during which John expressed the feeling that "his roommates did-n't like him." This concerned Scott and prompted him to interact more extensively with John's suite. Over time, John made a connection with Scott.

Scott learned about an incident in which John's suitemates had locked him in his closet and also damaged his laptop computer. Scott told John that his suitemates' treatment of him was wrong, a form of harassment, and informed his supervisor about the incident. Lindsay Turner met with John and determined that substantial harassment against him had been taking place within this suite on a regular basis. Lindsay, in turn, asked Michael Lane to press judicial charges against the suitemates and relocate John to a new suite with new roommates.

John informed his mother of the situation via a phone conversation. She then contacted Michael Lane, demanding that something be done to the students who were harassing her son. She stated that she did not want John to be removed from the suite. However, she did feel strongly about holding the appropriate students accountable. She was very resistant to the idea of moving John to another suite and indicated that she knew what was best for John. As a result of the harassment, the involvement of the administration, and the demands of his mother, John withdrew from academic and social activities and exhibited other behaviors that were indicative of depression.

Discussion Questions

1. What are some typical issues for first-year students with disabilities as compared to other incoming first-year students? Compare and contrast. What specific issues do students with Asperger's syndrome face?
2. How do John's and his mother's desires to have him involved in all aspects of everyday college life create difficulties and conflict for John?
3. How might the campus community establish a climate more conducive to students with disabilities?
4. Does NGU have an obligation to ensure the success of all students with disabilities? Explain.
5. You are a residential life staff member at NGU and one of John's roommates approaches you about his suitemates' treatment of John and some of the other things going on in the suite. Create a dialogue that would demonstrate your understanding of all of the issues associated with the case, as well as a positive outcome.
6. Based on your knowledge of students with disabilities and student development theory, what interventions would you recommend for: John, his mother, his current and future roommates, Scott Ferguson, Lindsay Turner, Michael Lane, and the university administration?

Research Activities for Further Exploration

1. Using information from the library, investigate the research on students with developmental disabilities (e.g., Asperger's syndrome, ADD, and ADHD) in higher education. Compile a paper with this information that includes program descriptions, national statistics, and recent research on retention from various institutions of higher learning that could be used as a fact sheet for prospective students.
2. Through community or Internet organizations, contact parents and/or individuals with Asperger's syndrome. Conduct a qualitative or ethnographic study about their perceptions of the accommodations that would be necessary for a person with Asperger's syndrome to have a successful experience in a college or university setting.
3. Conduct research at other institutions of higher education about the types of accommodations they make for students diagnosed with Asperger's syndrome and also what they do to increase the sensitivity and responsiveness of the other students.

THE PLAGIARIZED PAPER

Lauren Miller

Description of the Institutional Environment

Southern Coastal University (SCU) is a public four-year institution with approximately 17,000 students. The institution has a strong liberal arts tradition and offers 105 undergraduate programs and 60 graduate programs in a variety of different disciplines. Fifteen percent of the student population identify themselves as a member of a minority group. SCU has approximately 400 students who have identified themselves as having a disability and requested accommodations.

Description of the Surrounding Community

SCU is located in a medium-sized city near the Gulf of Mexico. A deaf community is active in the area and a residential school for the deaf is located nearby. Forty-five percent of SCU's alumni live within a 30-mile radius of the institution.

Primary Persons Involved in the Case

- Maggie Johnson is a second-semester student at SCU. She has had a severe to profound hearing loss since birth. She does not use sign language and relies heavily on reading lips.
- Sandra Johnson, Maggie's mother, is an SCU alumna. She owns a successful business in the community and gives a large annual donation to the university.
- Dr. Elizabeth Sandridge is a faculty member in SCU's Psychology Department.
- William Fitzgerald is the Director of the Office for Students with Disabilities at SCU. He is responsible for determining reasonable accommodations and advocating for students with disabilities.
- Dr. Ellen Mathews is the Dean of Students at SCU. She is the student affairs liaison in matters concerning the implementation of the academic honor code.

Information Germane to the Case

- Most SCU faculty members have had a student with a disability in one of their classes. Faculty are informed that a student has a disability when the student gives them a letter from the Office for Students with Disabilities at the beginning of each semester.

- Although SCU has a good reputation for serving students with disabilities, two years ago several students with disabilities publicly expressed their complaints about a professor who refused to provide reasonable accommodations. As a result of this incident, several students with disabilities formed an organization for students interested in disability issues.
- Academic dishonesty is taken very seriously at SCU. Most of the students who have been found responsible for plagiarism have failed the course and been suspended from the university for at least one semester.

The Case

Maggie Johnson submitted a research paper in her social psychology class that contained several required references. When her professor, Dr. Elizabeth Sandridge, read her paper, she recognized some of the passages. When she compared Maggie's paper to a well-known book in social psychology, she realized that the paper contained several direct quotations without citations. Dr. Sandridge approached Maggie after class and Maggie appeared to be surprised by the idea that she was being accused of plagiarism. Maggie's mother called Dr. Sandridge to tell her that Maggie did not understand the instructions for the paper, and that because she has a hearing impairment, Dr. Sandridge should not penalize Maggie. Although Dr. Sandridge does not agree with Sandra Johnson's assertions, she is inclined to excuse Maggie from the assignment because she likes Maggie and does not want to see her do poorly in the course. However, before she makes a decision about whether to pursue academic honor code charges, she wants to consult William Fitzgerald.

Sandra Johnson called Dr. Mathews and William Fitzgerald because she was upset that Maggie had been accused of cheating by Dr. Sandridge. Sandra asked Ellen Mathews to tell Dr. Sandridge that the whole situation was a misunderstanding. She told William Fitzgerald that "as an advocate for students with disabilities, I know you understand how difficult it is for a student with a hearing impairment to get everything that is said in class." Sandra said that she blames herself for what happened because she helped Maggie with the paper, and that Maggie had misunderstood the origin of a resource that her mother sent to her in an e-mail.

William Fitzgerald learns from the alumni relations office that Sandra Johnson plans to file a complaint with the Office of Civil Rights (OCR) and discontinue her donations to the university if the matter is not resolved to her satisfaction. She appears to be using her position in the community to share her displeasure about the way her daughter is being treated.

Discussion Questions

1. What are the main issues presented in this case?
2. Define the term "advocate" from the perspective of the primary persons involved in the case. How do these perspectives differ?
3. What role does confidentiality play in this case? Who has a "need to know" about decisions that are made and why?
4. When Elizabeth Sandridge consults William Fitzgerald, what should they discuss? Dialogue several courses of action for this case and argue the merits of each. Decide which course of action is best and explain the reasons for your choice.
5. Discuss the implications that this case has on the relationship between William Fitzgerald and Maggie Johnson. How can he use student development models and other information to educate Maggie?
6. How can this situation be used to educate faculty and students on disability issues? Discuss the planning and implementation of outreach activities for faculty, staff, and students on disability issues.

Research Activities for Further Exploration

1. Research the history of legislation for persons with disabilities as it pertains to postsecondary education. Define the terms "otherwise qualified" and "reasonable accommodations" as they apply to college students with disabilities. Cite specific cases in which an OCR grievance was filed and summarize the relevant issues in those cases.
2. Ask the director of disability services at your institution to identify several students with disabilities who will allow you to interview them. Choose those with hidden (learning disabilities, psychological disabilities, etc.) and visible (mobility impairment, sensory impairment, etc.) disabilities. Investigate their perceptions of the institutional climate for students with disabilities.
3. Compare and contrast services for students with disabilities at several different types of institutions. Identify the philosophy and/or mission of these institutions and whether they appear to be welcoming for students with disabilities (providing services that go beyond legal obligation) or designed to meet a minimum legal obligation. Identify factors that determine these philosophies and/or missions.

DO YOU HEAR WHAT I HEAR?

Donna S. Davenport

Description of the Institutional Environment

Southwest University (SU) is a very large land-grant university in the southwestern United States. Approximately 46,000 students attend this predominantly white university, including approximately 1,500 international students (almost entirely graduate students). The racial demographics are as follows: 89 percent European American, 5 percent Mexican American, 3 percent African American, and 3 percent international (including Asian, African, South American, and Middle-Eastern). Undergraduate students tend to be politically conservative, Christian, and relatively unfamiliar with diverse cultures.

Description of the Surrounding Community

Southwest University is located in a small city of 100,000 residents. The community is conservative, largely white, and—though supportive of the university—suspicious of "foreigners." Other than those associated with the university and a few physicians, there are almost no Asian Americans in the community.

Primary Persons Involved in the Case

- Misako Kawasaki is a first-year student at SU. She has just relocated from Japan, where her entire family still resides. She has a moderate hearing loss, which is helped somewhat by the use of two hearing aids.
- Kristi Gates, Misako's white roommate, also is a first-year student. She is from a small town in Texas, where she was a student leader in high school.
- Karen Myers is a white Resident Assistant (RA) on the floor in the residence hall where Misako and Kristi live. She is a senior psychology major and active on campus.
- Larry Reynolds is a blind psychologist at the Counseling Center who specializes in diversity issues.

Information Germane to the Case

- SU students tend to be polite toward those perceived as "different" but uncomfortable and socially awkward. There has been a recent attempt to train RAs in ethnic diversity issues. Issues related to disability were covered in a 30-minute lecture, but with no specific information regarding

hearing loss.
- Misako was at the head of her class in a large high school in Japan and accepted a scholarship to attend SU and major in chemistry. Both of her parents are professionals in Japan, and education has been strongly emphasized in the family. Very few Japanese acquaintances knew of her hearing loss because she was adept at reading lips and wore her hair long to cover the hearing aids.

The Case

The move to SU has been unexpectedly difficult for Misako Kawasaki. She is taken aback by what she perceives as an emphasis on social interactions rather than academic achievement. She has trouble understanding the rapid colloquial English spoken by her roommate and others, and she feels very isolated and "different." The other women in her residence hall and in classes are pleasant, but they have made no effort to seek her out or befriend her.

One day, as Misako walked across campus with Karen Myers, she confided that she is thinking about returning home. When questioned, she admits that she is very lonely, and confused, and feels unable to do anything to improve the situation. She is particularly concerned that she and Kristi Gates are not becoming friends, as other roommates seem to be, and that Kristi spends more and more time away from their room. Reluctantly, she discloses that in spite of hearing aids, she sometimes has trouble understanding what others say, but when she asks them to repeat, they tend to become irritable and curt. Accordingly, she has tried to "fake it" by smiling and giving innocuous answers. Later that day, Karen speaks with Kristi, who says she finds Misako inconsistent, weird, and aloof, often not responding to the overtures Kristi makes. She gives the example that the night before after they turned off the lights and went to bed, she tried to talk to Misako, but she received only mumbled comments in response.

Karen contacts her friend Larry Reynolds for advice on how to help Misako. Larry provides some education about the usual adjustment profile for international students, as well as information about hearing loss. Karen learns the rule about "twice the distance/half the hearing," which sums up the fact that sound waves dissipate such that someone eight feet away will hear half as well as they do when they are four feet away. He also explains that most hearing losses are in the high frequency range, which means that consonants often are inaudible. He suggests that Karen encourage Kristi and others to approach Misako differently, and he offers to meet with Misako for counseling to help her become less isolated and more assertive, and to find ways to feel more comfortable on campus.

Discussion Questions

1. What combination of family and cultural factors contribute to Misako Kawasaki's distress? If Misako were male, how might her experience and reactions be different?
2. How similar is Misako's experience to that of other new international students? How much does her hearing loss accentuate her difficulties?
3. What do Kristi Gates and other students need to know to feel more comfortable and motivated in reaching out?
4. In your opinion, are persons who do not have a disability more willing to accommodate individuals without sight than they are individuals with hearing loss? Explain your answer.
5. Create a role play that Karen Myers could use to sensitize her fellow RAs to diversity, particularly the difficulties experienced by students with a moderate hearing impairment.
6. Would an offer from Karen to accompany Misako to her first appointment with Larry Reynolds be appropriate or not? How appropriate might it be for the psychologist to self-disclose some of his own embarrassment regarding blindness? How important is it to help Misako meet other Asian students?

Research Activities for Further Exploration

1. Conduct research on your campus to learn how international undergraduate students meet each other. What services do the various student affairs offices provide to facilitate such interactions?
2. Read about the gender socialization of Japanese girls and women. Discuss how such socialization might complicate the learning of assertiveness appropriate to U.S. college campuses.
3. Videotape a television show that depicts two women friends interacting for about five minutes. Write out the transcript of the dialogue, omitting each "s," "sh," "t," and "f." After practice, read the dialogue aloud as quickly as possible to see if a friend can understand you.

INDEX

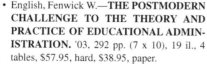